# New Handbook
### *of*
# British Pottery &
# Porcelain Marks

### Geoffrey A. Godden

## BARRIE & JENKINS
### LONDON

*Every effort has been made to verify the information contained in this book. However, the author and publishers are not liable for any loss incurred as a consequence of reliance upon it.*

Barrie & Jenkins Ltd
Random House
20 Vauxhall Bridge Road
London SW1V 2SA
www.randomhouse.co.uk

Copyright © 1968, 1999 by Geoffrey A. Godden
First published 1968 by Herbert Jenkins Ltd
Reprinted 1968, 1969, 1972 (with revisions), 1975, 1977,
1978, 1981, 1982, 1985, 1986, 1987, 1988, 1989, 1990
(with revisions), 1992, 1993, 1994, 1995

Second edition, revised and enlarged, 1999

7 9 10 8

A CIP catalogue record for this book is available from the
British Library.

The Random House Group Limited Reg. No. 954009

ISBN 0 09 186580 8

Designed and typeset by Behram Kapadia
Printed and bound in Great Britain
by Bookmarque Ltd, Croydon, Surrey

# Contents

# Preface

For this revised, new edition, dates and details of the major manufacturers have been rechecked and may well differ from those given in earlier non-Godden works! In the case of the more important manufacturers the reader is informed of specialist books which can offer fuller information or a range of illustrations. A most helpful feature is the warning offered in the cases where reproductions can be expected and the original marks copied. Guidance is also offered on the rarity or the commercial desirability of certain makes or types – although this, like value, can vary with time and be dependent on quality and condition.

The key, identifying, initials of nearly a thousand British ceramic manufacturers from the end of the 18th century onwards are listed, together with the name of the firm and its working period.

A new valuable feature is the chronological listing of the registration entries for new British ceramic shapes or designs, as entered in the official Design Registry files between 1839 and 1883. A list of collectors' clubs and societies has also been added.

Whilst this Handbook cannot compete for comprehensive cover with the large Godden 'bible', the *Encyclopaedia of British Pottery and Porcelain Marks* (first published in 1964) or with the *Encyclopaedia of British Porcelain Manufacturers* (Barrie & Jenkins, 1988), it does provide a convenient, inexpensive, and helpful guide to the markings to be found on collectable British pottery and porcelains, and will lead the reader on to more detailed works of reference.

Every effort has been made to verify the information contained in this book. However, the author and publishers are not liable for any loss incurred as a consequence of reliance upon it.

GEOFFREY GODDEN
*The Square, Findon, West Sussex*

# Introduction

The object of a ceramic trade mark is to enable at least the retailer to know the name of the manufacturer of the object, so that re-orders, etc. can be correctly addressed. In the case of the larger firms the mark also has publicity value and shows the buyer that the object was made by a long-established firm with a reputation to uphold; such clear name-marks as Minton, Wedgwood, Royal Crown Derby and Royal Worcester are typical examples.

To collectors the mark has greater importance, for not only can they trace the manufacturer of any marked object, but they can also ascertain the approximate date of manufacture and in several cases the exact year of production, particularly in the case of 19th- and 20th-century wares from the leading firms which employed private dating systems.

With the increasing use of ceramic marks in the 19th century, a large proportion of British pottery and porcelain can be accurately identified and often dated. With the many hundreds of different manufacturers' marks it is quite impossible to remember all the various devices, sets of initials, or the working periods of the firms concerned. Hence the need for a concise pocket-book such as this, to give the collector basic facts and to lead on to works giving detailed information and illustrations of typical examples. In the few cases where popular marks are known to have been reproduced on forgeries, the reader is warned of this fact.

Ceramic marks are applied in four basic ways:

(a) *Incised* into the still soft clay during manufacture, in which case the mark will show a slight ploughed-up effect and have a free spontaneous appearance.

(b) *Impressed* into the soft clay during manufacture; many name-marks such as Wedgwood are produced in this way from metal or clay stamps or seals. These have a neat mechanical appearance.

(c) *Painted* marks, usually name or initial marks, added over the glaze at the time of ornamentation, as were some stencilled marks.

(d) *Printed* marks transferred from engraved copper plates at the time of decoration. Most 19th-century marks are printed, often in blue under the glaze when the main design is also in underglaze blue.

Information on the method of applying each mark is given in this book, and the information can be of vital importance. For instance the early Chelsea triangle mark must be *incised* not impressed, as it can be on 19th-century fakes. Photographs of typical incised and other basic mark forms are given in my *Encyclopaedia of British Pottery and Porcelain Marks* (1964), Plates 1–8.

There are several general 'Godden' rules for dating ceramic marks, attention to which will avoid several common errors:

(1) Printed marks incorporating the Royal Arms supported by the lion and the unicorn are of 19th- or 20th-century date. The Royal Arms with the inescutcheon, or extra central small shield, are the pre-1837 version. It should be noted that copies of this device can occur on non-British wares!

(2) Marks incorporating the name of a pattern will be post-1830, and are often very much later.

(3) Marks incorporating the diamond-shape design registration device will be between 1842 and 1883. See pp. 168–9 for a full explanation of this device.

(4) Printed, garter-type marks, incorporating the maker's name or initials etc., were popular from about 1840.

(5) Marks incorporating the word 'Royal' tend to postdate about 1850.

(6) Marks incorporating the word or various abbreviations for 'Limited' must postdate the 1861 Limited Liability Act.

(7) Marks incorporating the words 'Trade Mark' must postdate the 1862 Trade Mark Act.

(8) The addition of the word 'England' in a mark indicates a date after 1880 and in general after 1891 when the American Tariff Act came into force. However, the absence of such a designation does not necessarily show that the piece is of an earlier date! Whilst 'England' was the usual description, as it included all the Staffordshire wares, alternative country-names were sometimes used. Scottish firms used 'Scotland' or the earlier name 'North Britain' or simply 'Britain'.

(9) The abbreviation 'UK' or 'United Kingdom' is usually only found on recent productions.

(10) Marks incorporating a registration number, which is usually prefixed

'R$^D$ N$^o$', will postdate 1883. The key to these numbers is given on p. 245.

(11) The wording 'Made in England' (etc.) tends to occur on marks after about 1910. However, this is far from being an inflexible rule and many post-1945 marks do not include it.

(12) Marks incorporating the word 'Copyright' will postdate c.1920.

(13) Marks bearing the description 'Bone China' tend to postdate the 1920s and can be very recent.

(14) Marks incorporating the letter 'R' (usually within a small circle) postdate 1955.

(15) Marks incorporating wording relating to dish-washers, detergents etc. are obviously of a relatively recent period.

(16) Marks incorporating the initials 'PLC' postdate the mid-1970s.

(17) Marks or pattern descriptions incorporating the word 'old' or 'olde' are generally reasonable modern reissues of 19th-century designs or are based on such former patterns. They are nostalgic essays in salesmanship!

(18) Marks incorporating the initials 'BS' followed by a number denote a British Standard quality or performance showing that the object or the body has passed tests. A BS number again denotes a recent date for that mark or product.

These 'Godden' rules relate to the age of a piece, but remember that age in itself is not a virtue! Do not worship age alone.

A high proportion of English pottery and porcelain was made in the district known as the Staffordshire Potteries centred on the present city of Stoke-on-Trent. The Potteries are basically made up of seven separate towns – Burslem, Cobridge, Fenton, Hanley (incorporating Shelton), Longton (also Lane End), Stoke and Tunstall. These towns will be found in the addresses of many firms listed in this book. The initial letters of these towns may be incorporated in several 19th-century initial marks, e.g.

H & G
   B      (Heath & Greatbatch of Burslem)

J & G
   L      (Jackson & Gosling of Longton) etc.

It may be useful at this point to advise readers that the Stoke-on-Trent City Museum at Hanley recently changed its name to The Potteries Museum while this book was in press, and the text has only been altered when convenient.

Remember that many marks relate to the retailer, wholesaler or agent, not to the manufacturer. Such name or initial marks that include the name of a non-pottery-producing city or town will fall into this category. Typical non-ceramic place-names include London, Birmingham, Manchester and Dublin, although most towns had their own retailers, who might specify in their orders the requirement to include their own name rather than that of the maker.

As I have included under each entry in the mark section details of the standard or latest specialist books, it will be helpful to make some general comments on such works. First, one should obtain the most recent work on any factory or subjects, as it may be expected to contain the latest information. This is particularly important if you wish to resort to Price Guides. Secondly, a reference book is not prime source material: it will only include the author's interpretation of available source material or gleanings from other works. It is always worth checking so-called facts. Errors once made tend to be copied by a succession of authors.

Specialist reference books are often published in short runs, so they may well become unavailable within a few years. Of course, we enjoy a splendid Library Service whereby out-of-print books may be obtained, on loan, for a small charge. Various book dealers also specialize in new and out-of-print books on ceramics or on other collecting subjects. Although I cannot mention any one such firm, they tend to advertise from time to time in collectors' magazines such as *Collectors' Guide*, or they may have a stand at a specialist Antiques Fair. Certainly a good, well researched and illustrated reference book should be of lasting value and prove a good investment for the serious collector. On the other hand, general books on a wide variety of subjects cannot be very detailed on any one facet of collecting. Apart from the specialist books listed in the mark section I have also included a general bibliography at the end.

# Pictorial Glossary

This helpful feature shows and gives a brief outline of the various basic types of British ceramics produced from the 17th century onwards. It is arranged in alphabetical order. It is, however, essential to bear in mind the approximate periods within which these differing bodies or styles were popular. One should also note that certain types were very seldom marked. These generally unmarked types include 17th-century and early 18th-century Delft-type tin-glazed earthenwares, the glossy, black-glazed Jackfield type wares, early slip-decorated earthenwares, salt-glazed stonewares and 19th-century lustred wares. Also British ceramics produced before about 1770 will rarely bear a maker's name. This is to be expected and the lack of a mark will hardly affect the commercial value of these types, although in general the presence of a mark will enhance the desirability of a piece.

*British ceramic types featured in the Pictorial Glossary*

DELFT-TYPE TIN-GLAZED EARTHENWARES
17th and 18th centuries

SLIP-DECORATED EARTHENWARE 17th century onwards

STONEWARES 17th century onwards

SALT-GLAZED STONEWARES c.1720 onwards

JACKFIELD c.1720–1770

BLUE AND WHITE (PORCELAIN) c.1748 onwards

CREAMWARE c.1760 onwards

BASALT c.1770 onwards

BISQUE PORCELAINS c.1770 onwards

JASPER WARES c.1770 onwards

PEARLWARE c.1780 onwards

CASTLEFORD c.1800–1820

BONE CHINA c.1800 onwards

LUSTRED WARES c.1805 onwards

IRONSTONE BODIES c.1813 onwards

STONE CHINA BODIES c.1813 onwards

GRANITE CHINA c.1830 onwards

TERRA-COTTA c.1840–1900

PARIAN PORCELAIN c.1842 onwards

REGISTERED DESIGNS c.1842–1883

MAJOLICA c.1850 onwards

PÂTE-SUR-PÂTE c.1870–1939

ART POTTERY c.1870–1920s

ART DECO c.1925–1930s

## ART DECO

The British 'Art Deco' styled wares of the mid-1920s and 1930s are typified by the well-known Clarice Cliff designs and the angular forms made to suit the jazz age, broad, colourful patterns. Like jazz and Odeon cinemas the new style spread rapidly and soon most middle-market potters were following the fashion.

In post-war years these once inexpensive wares, usually earthenwares, have returned to fashion and have become highly collectable. Collectors of such wares have taken the subject seriously and a mini-library is growing to fund the increasing interest in these fashionable and so typically 1930s designs. So-called 'Antique Fairs' now abound with these smart designs and the style is in some cases being revived in current replicas.

Specialist works include *Art Deco Source Book*, by P. Bayer (Phaidon, 1988); *Lyle Price Guide Art Deco Ceramics* (Ebury Press, 1999); *Art Deco & Modernist Ceramics*, by K. McCready (Thames & Hudson, revised edition 1997); *Art Deco China*, by J. Hay (Little Brown, 1996); *Collecting Art Deco Ceramics*, by H. & P. Watson (Francis Joseph, 2nd edition 1997) and *Clarice Cliff and her Contemporaries* by Helen C. Cunningham (Schiffer Publishing, 1999).

*Art Deco*

## ART POTTERY

It is very difficult to precisely define 'Art Pottery' which can differ from Art Potteries! In essence we are concerned with wares (usually earthenwares) made within the approximate period 1870–1920. These ideally should be individually made and hand-decorated, as the William De Morgan earthenware vases shown here. Art Pottery is usually of a decorative type, not table services. Again, usually but not invariably, the wares would be made by individuals or by small groups or firms. There are obvious exceptions, such as the individual signed stonewares made at the Art Pottery Studio, within the large Doulton works at Lambeth.

Because of their decorative and individual qualities, or because the Victorian Art Potteries are typical of their period and can be produced by leading artists or designers, much Art Pottery is highly collectable. Important examples by fashionable artists, craftsmen or designers can be expected to be commercially desirable.

Several of the new entries in this Handbook relate to Art Pottery, and reference books on the different types are listed in the individual sections. General works on Art Pottery and the Art Pottery movement in general

*Art Pottery*

include *Victorian Art Pottery* by E. Lloyd Thomas (Guildart, 1974), and *Encyclopaedia of British Art Pottery* by Victoria Bergesen (Barrie & Jenkins, 1991).

## BASALT

The basalt body was also known as 'Egyptian black'. The black body has a matt (unglazed) exterior and was popular for both useful and ornamental ware from the 1760s into the 19th century. Josiah Wedgwood improved the original body and termed it 'basalt' (c.1773). Wedgwood also adapted it for the manufacture of classical formed vases, relief moulded plaques, etc. Very many 18th and early 19th-century manufacturers produced 'basalt' or 'Egyptian black'. Except for the major makers such as Wedgwood, basalt wares are seldom marked.

The modern standard book on these wares is *Black Basalt, Wedgwood and Contemporary Manufacturers*, by Diana Edwards (Antique Collectors' Club, 1994).

*Basalt*

*Bisque*

## BISQUE

'Bisque' or 'biscuit' porcelain is simply the once-fired body without the addition of glaze. Bisque figures and groups were popular on the Continent in the 18th century, and in England the Derby factory produced tasteful examples from c.1770. It is noteworthy that such pieces were more expensive than the same model which had been glazed and coloured, because the bisque examples had to be perfect in every respect. Several early 19th-century factories produced charming biscuit figures, groups and animals, until the new, creamy-coloured, Parian body became fashionable in the 1840s. Later Continental biscuit porcelains (often coloured) were popular and generally inexpensive. English bisque porcelain is seldom marked, except for Derby examples.

## BLUE AND WHITE

This term relates to a very large class of pottery and porcelain decorated in cobalt blue applied to the bisque body before glazing, giving rise to the description 'underglaze blue'. Much imported Chinese porcelain was of this type and most, if not all of our early porcelain manufacturers produced Oriental-style blue and white. The teapot here shown is Worcester c.1760, painted by hand with a very popular Oriental-taste design.

18th-century British blue and white porcelains are very collectable and can be costly, especially for rare patterns or unusual objects. Specialist books on our main porcelain factories – Bow, Bristol, Caughley, Derby, Limehouse, Liverpool, Longton Hall, Lowestoft and Worcester – will feature a good range of blue and white specimens, as will modern general works.

Apart from the standard book, Dr Bernard Watney's *English Blue & White Porcelain of the 18th Century* (Faber & Faber, revised edition 1973), the reader could consult my *Eighteenth-Century English Porcelain* (Granada Publishing, 1985).

*Blue and white*

*Blue and white (printed)*

## BLUE AND WHITE (PRINTED)

Apart from the hand-painted underglaze blue porcelain (and some earthenwares) much blue and white from about 1760 onwards was transfer-printed. In these cases the cobalt pigment was applied to the once-fired but still unglazed body, by means of transfer paper charged from engraved copper-plates.

This obviously speeded up the decorating process and gave a uniformity where large runs of, say, plates were required. The pair of openwork baskets here shown are Worcester c.1770. The reversed example shows the blue-printed shaded or hatched crescent mark. Most of our 18th-century porcelain (and earthenware) factories produced printed designs. In general these are not as highly regarded as the often earlier and more individual hand-painted examples.

Underglaze blue prints on 18th-century porcelains were made at most British factories, notably at Caughley, Worcester, the Liverpool factories, Isleworth, Derby, Lowestoft and New Hall. Although in general hand-painted designs are more highly regarded some printed designs are scarce and are highly desirable.

General books on early underglaze blue printed porcelains include Dr Bernard Watney's *English Blue & White Porcelain of the 18th Century* (Faber & Faber, revised edition 1973) and specialist works on the individual factories. It is impossible to cover the vast subject of blue-printed earthenwares in this brief glossary.

## BONE CHINA

English bone china is a superbly strong and pleasing ceramic body. It is basically similar to hard-paste porcelain (containing China Stone and China Clay) plus up to 50 per cent of calcined animal bones. Various manufacturers favoured different receipts and within a factory different mixes would be employed to produce different sized articles. A different mix would be required for hand-turned objects, to that needed for the slip-casting process.

It is generally conceded that the body was perfected at the Spode factory at Stoke, in about 1800, although bone-ash had been used in other porcelain mixes from the 1740s. By about 1820 all British porcelain manufacturers were using bone china, of various qualities. The name Bone China was not however, generally used before the mid-1840s. Printed marks incorporating this term will usually be of 20th-century date.

The reader is referred to the late Reginald G. Haggar's chapter 'Bone China, a general survey', in *Staffordshire Porcelain*, edited by Geoffrey Godden (Granada Publishing, 1983). This book illustrates a varied feast of Staffordshire bone china objects.

*Bone China*

*Castleford*

## CASTLEFORD

'Castleford' is a generic term, covering a large class of early 19th-century white (or slightly creamy) semi-porcelainous stoneware, displaying some translucency. It usually has a slight smear-glaze and various designs are moulded in relief. Sets of teapots, covered sugar basins and cream or milk jugs were popular in this body – as they were in the black basalt. Teapots often have hinged or sliding covers and such (usually unmarked) wares were certainly not confined to the Castleford factory or to other Yorkshire potteries. Many seem to have been produced in the Staffordshire Potteries. Most seem to relate to the 1800–20 period. Examples are attractive and not unduly expensive.

## CREAMWARE

Creamware is a light cream-coloured earthenware, introduced, tentatively, in about 1740. After perfection by Josiah Wedgwood it had become by the 1760s the standard refined British earthenware body, largely replacing the earlier tin-glazed (delft-type) earthenwares and salt-glazed white stonewares.

*Creamware*

The potter's term 'cream colour' (abbreviated to C.C.) was replaced for sales purposes by Wedgwood's apt name 'Queens Ware'. It is light in weight, pleasant to use, neatly potted and lends itself to various forms of decoration. Much, however, was sold in an undecorated state, as the 'W(xxx)' marked, pierced-edged plate here shown. The body and glaze was often whitened after about 1785 giving rise to 'Pearlware', better suited to underglaze blue decoration.

The standard specialist book is Donald Towner's *Creamware* (Faber & Faber, 1978), although the 1986 Northern Ceramic Society exhibition catalogue, *Creamware and Pearlware* (Stoke-on-Trent City Museum, 1986) is an invaluable well-illustrated guide and gives details of specialist books on individual types and cites some factory pattern books.

Creamware can be highly interesting and collectable although comparatively few pieces bear a maker's mark. Commercial prices are very variable. The reader is warned of recent creamwares produced in old styles and shapes, underlining the lasting decorative appeal of even undecorated creamware.

# DELFT

Delft-type, or tin-glazed, earthenwares have a clay-coloured rather low-fired body which has been coated with an opaque, whitish glaze, usually incorporating oxide of tin. This glaze was intended to give the general appearance of porcelain and to serve as a base for any added decoration. It is, however, prone to chipping at the edges, so exposing the underlying body. Delft-type wares (a small 'd' when referring to British 'delft') are liable to cracking or other damage and were, in general, superseded by the creamware body.

The Delft technique was widely used on the Continent but the British essays were made at several centres including London, Bristol, Glasgow, Liverpool and Wincanton, from the 17th century into the middle of the 18th century.

Examples can be charming, interesting and highly collectable. Commercial value depends on the object, its decoration, its condition and other factors. A simply decorated, chipped plate can be purchased for a modest outlay but a special article such as the dated 1732 Royal subject large bowl here featured would command several thousand pounds. Most old British delft ware is unmarked.

Specialist books on tin-glazed earthenwares include *Tin-Glazed Pottery*

*English delft*

*in Europe and the Islamic World*, by A. Caiger-Smith (Faber & Faber, 1973); *English Delftware in the Bristol Collection*, by F. Britton (Sotheby, 1982); *Dated English Delftware*, by L. Lipski & M. Archer (Sotheby, 1984); *London Delftware*, by F. Britton (Jonathan Horne, 1987); *British Delft in Williamsburg*, by J. C. Austin (USA, 1994); *Tin-Glazed Earthenwares – from Maiolica, Faience and Delftware to the Contemporary*, by D. Carnegy (A. & C. Black, 1995); and *Delftware. The Tin-Glazed Earthenware of the British Isles*, by M. Archer (HMSO, 1997).

## IRONSTONE-TYPE BODIES

The ironstone body was patented by Charles James Mason (the son of Miles Mason) in 1813. The strong, durable, body quickly established itself, firstly for tablewares, dinner services etc., usually decorated with colourful Oriental-styled designs. It was cheaper than porcelain, but stronger in use and colourful. Ornamental as well as tablewares were soon

*Ironstone*

made ranging from toy or miniature pieces to huge vases or even fire surrounds! Jugs in various sizes and decorated like the example here shown are amongst the best-known examples but ironstone-type wares have been made up to the present time.

Many firms apart from Masons produced ironstone or the similar 'Stone China' or 'Granite China' wares. Various factory marks can occur. Desirability varies according to quality, age, condition, the type of object, the standing of the maker, etc., but in general colourful old ironstone is very collectable.

Various specialist reference books include *Godden's Guide to Mason's China and the Ironstone Wares* (Antique Collectors' Club, 1980) and the general guide to ironstone wares, *Godden's Guide to Ironstone, Stone and Granite Wares* (Antique Collectors' Club, 1999).

## JACKFIELD

'Jackfield' is largely a generic name for a class of British earthenware of a reddish-brick body, which has been coated with a glossy black glaze – giving the opposite effect to white coated delft wares.

Many of the pieces were originally decorated with low-fired enamel decoration or non-permanent gilding. Some examples, like those here

*Jackfield*

shown, are of good form with relief motifs. Such Jackfield type black-glazed wares were produced at various centres, not only in Shropshire. Indeed, most examples certainly have a Staffordshire origin. No marked examples seem to be recorded.

Most examples will have been produced in the approximate period 1720–70. Such 18th-century examples are collectable but seldom very costly unless dated or of extreme importance. As yet no specialist book is devoted to these attractive pieces, which in the main comprise tea or coffee wares and jugs.

## JASPER

Jasper is a decorative fine-grained hard earthenware (really a porcelain as it can be translucent) which can be stained to various tints – usually blue. This serves as a wonderful ground for added white motifs.

Josiah Wedgwood experimented with and perfected the jasper body in the 1770s and his name is rightly always associated with it. It was, however, so successful that various other 18th-century potters sought to emulate

*Jasper*

Wedgwood's success. Some non-Wedgwood jasper wares reached very high standards. Marked examples by Adams, Neale, and Turner are particularly noteworthy and were often decorated with sprigged white-relief motifs, in the well-known Wedgwood manner. Similar wares were made throughout the 19th century but with a falling-off in quality. Messrs Josiah Wedgwood & Sons Ltd still produce their traditional jasper wares.

All jasper has decorative merits. Commercial considerations include the importance, attractiveness or rarity of the object, the quality of potting, the desirability of the maker and the age of the piece.

All books on Wedgwood will give a good account of the jasper wares, as will specialist books on the main makers mentioned above. There is a section on jasper wares in my *British Pottery. An Illustrated Guide* (Barrie & Jenkins, 1974).

## LUSTRE
British lustre ware basically comprises earthenwares covered with an extremely thin metallic based wash, to emulate silver (or silver-plated)

*Lustre*

wares or copper articles. Such metallic decoration can also be applied to porcelains but usually as a border or edge trim, or as pink-lustre decoration, rather than as a total covering as was often applied to earthenwares. The so-called silver-lustre has a platinum coating, not silver which would oxidise. Copper lustre is based on gold.

Most lustre was made in the 1805–80 period but some can be present-century – often made to old shapes or styles. All lustre has a decorative charm but prices vary greatly, depending on the form, condition, age or general desirability of the piece. The copper-lustre jug here shown is a good quality Staffordshire example with printed panels datable to c.1835. Very few 19th-century pieces bear a maker's mark. The splash-lustre style is traditionally associated with Sunderland, but was also made in Staffordshire.

The standard book on this vast subject is *Collecting Lustreware* by Geoffrey Godden & Michael Gibson (Barrie & Jenkins, 1991).

## MAJOLICA
Victorian majolica (as opposed to earlier Italian Maiolica) was introduced to this country by Minton's French Art Director, Leon Arnoux, just prior to the 1851 Exhibition. In essence it is a fine earthenware body normally moulded into intricate decorative forms. The coloured and glazed deco-

*Majolica*

ration gives the effect of pleasing semi-translucent tinted glazes. The leading manufacturers such as Mintons, Wedgwood and George Jones employed talented and often well-known modellers to supply the initial master-models. Good examples by the leading English firms are very desirable and are highly valued today.

Several specialist books feature these earthenwares, including *Majolica – British, Continental and American Wares, 1851–1915* by V. Bergesen (Barrie & Jenkins, 1989); *Majolica. A Complete History and Illustrated Survey*, by M. Karmason & J. Stacke (Harry N. Abrahams, NY, 1989); *Majolica*, by N. M. Dawes (Crown Publishers, NY, 1990); *Majolica: European & American Wares*, by J. B. Snyder & L. Bockol (Schiffer, USA, 1994); and *European Majolica, with Values* by D. M. Murrey (Schiffer, USA, 1997). This is not a complete listing but most of the books on majolica are published in the USA – where, it should be stated, the very keen and seemingly wealthy collectors are based.

## PARIAN

Parian is a typically Victorian ceramic body. It was introduced by Copeland & Garrett and by Mintons almost simultaneously in the early 1840s. It largely replaced the earlier whiter biscuit porcelain for figures, groups and busts. The new body could be readily slip-moulded, had a pleasing slightly creamy tint and a very slight surface sheen.

The original idea was to mass-produce at low cost reduced copies of famous marble statuary, indeed Copeland & Garrett's original name for the new body was 'Statuary Porcelain'. Within a short period, however, it was employed to produce all manner of objects, from small trinkets to large objects, such as fireplaces. Moulded jugs by the tens of thousands were produced.

Generally the body was left undecorated to show its marble-like quality but it could be glazed, tinted or slightly gilt. The leading firms, such as Copelands, Mintons, Wedgwood marked their wares but a host of small firms issued unmarked examples. Some firms specialized in parian producing no other types.

Specialist reference books include *The Illustrated Guide to Victorian Parian China*, by C. & D. Shinn (Barrie & Jenkins, 1971) and the multi-authored work *The Parian Phenomenon*, edited by Paul Atterbury (Richard Dennis, 1989). *The Encyclopaedia of British Porcelain Manufacturers*, by G. Godden (Barrie & Jenkins, 1988) gives details of the various manufacturers, large and small, as parian is a class of porcelain.

*Parian*

# PÂTE-SUR-PÂTE

Pâte-sur-Pâte is the most expensive 19th-century form of ceramic decoration. Leading specialist artists slowly built up the white porcelain or parian relief-decoration in individual designs over a contrasting ground. Such designs were in effect sculptures. It was a slow, painstaking process and the best work was always expensive. The master in this technique was the Frenchman M. L. Solon (1835–1913), who worked for Mintons in the 1870–1904 period. Some plaques were produced in his own time up to his death in 1913. Solon trained various apprentices who worked for Mintons into the 1900s. Their work is not so valued as Solon's figure compositions, a modest example of which is here shown.

Various firms, other than Mintons, also produced decorative articles in the same style – Royal Worcester, Grainger of Worcester, George Jones of

*Pâte-sur-Pâte*

Stoke being the most familiar. Some of these designs can be duplicated as they were worked up from a moulded base work. Such pieces are very decorative but are not valued so highly as the unique designs of the leading (mainly Minton) artists. Some Continental firms also produced very good examples.

The specialist reference book is *Pâte-sur-Pâte. The Art of Ceramic Relief Decoration, 1849–1992*, by Bernard Bumpus (Barrie & Jenkins, 1992).

## PEARLWARE

Pearlware was developed in the latter part of the 18th century as a new basic earthenware body, nearer in appearance to porcelain than to the then standard creamware. It was termed 'Pearl White' by Josiah Wedgwood who mentioned this name in 1779. In essence it was the old creamware mix with the addition of china clay but further whitened by the addition of a small amount of cobalt added to the glaze. An alternative term much used by the potters was 'China Glaze'.

The new whiter body retained the benefits of creamware, it was light in weight, reasonably easy and inexpensive to produce and fire. But most

*Pearlware*

importantly the colour approached that of porcelain and underglaze decoration looked far more attractive on pearlware than on the former creamware.

Underglaze blue printing was applied to pearlware from the 1780s onwards. The early examples in a dark blue usually comprised Oriental-styled designs and in dinner services especially vied with the Chinese porcelain imports. Most of the leading British potters produced pearlwares of various types, enhanced in different styles. It was by the 1790s the standard British earthenware body. Consequently specimens are plentiful and standard patterns on plates need not be costly.

Many modern books illustrate pearlwares, particularly those relating to blue-printed earthenwares. Of special interest is the Northern Ceramic Society 1986 exhibition catalogue *Creamware and Pearlware* published by the City Museum & Art Gallery, Stoke-on-Trent.

## PORCELAIN

Porcelain, as can here be seen, is or should be translucent, as opposed to earthenware or pottery which is usually opaque. However, the translucency of porcelain can be variable. It depends on the thickness of the object and the firing temperature, as underfired porcelain will not show much translucency.

*Porcelain*

18th-century British porcelains are of the soft-paste type, with the exception of Plymouth and Bristol. Various other types (New Hall, Coalport, Chamberlain-Worcester, Miles Mason, etc.) of the approximate period 1780–1810 are of intermediate type, termed hybrid hard-paste porcelain.

Bone china is a type of porcelain, as is the marble-like parian body. The general term china is normally used to indicate porcelain but it is not an exact term!

In contrast, pottery and earthenwares are opaque (unless very thinly potted and fired to a vitrifying temperature). These general terms cover basic British types of ceramic body, such as creamware, pearlware, delft-type tin-glazed wares or terra-cotta. Terms such as 'Semi China', 'Opaque Porcelain' as used in several marks are fanciful marketing terms for earthenware bodies.

Ironstone wares and the related stone china or granite wares are considered to be pottery rather than porcelain although they can display some translucency.

## REGISTERED DESIGNS

This otherwise unmarked plate (overleaf) can be accurately identified and dated to narrow limits by means of the diamond-shaped registration

*Registered designs*

device it bears. This device appears on tens of thousands of articles introduced between 1842 and 1883. In this case the plate shape with its moulded and pierced edging was registered by John Rose & Co. of the Coalport Porcelain Works, on November 30th, 1849.

The key to thousands of these British registered devices, with a brief description of the subjects, is uniquely given in this Handbook. This long listing is arranged in chronological order from p. 171, after the important introduction to that section.

## SALT-GLAZED STONEWARE

British salt-glazed stoneware is one of the basic 18th-century types produced at our main ceramic centres. It is, however, not marked, although very rare examples may be inscribed and dated. Much was sold in the white as a porcelain look-alike. Other examples, as the teapot here shown, were originally decorated with low-fired gilding which has worn away in use.

Other types may be decorated with raised motifs or with incised decoration. This scratched decoration was sometimes accentuated with

*Salt-glazed stoneware*

pigment, usually cobalt blue. Other more costly examples were enamelled with floral, landscape or figure subjects.

All 18th-century (c.1720–70) salt-glaze is collectable and can be delightful in its simplicity. Prices vary greatly; undecorated plates are inexpensive, whilst an important enamelled example can run into thousands of pounds. This fact has led to a few white pieces being decorated at a later period!

Some clay-coloured salt-glaze stoneware was produced in later periods by firms such as Doultons and some is produced by studio potters today. These later wares can be highly interesting and of value but references to salt-glaze stoneware normally relate to 18th-century whitish-bodied articles.

The standard book is the late A. R. Mountford's *Illustrated Guide to Staffordshire Salt-glazed Stoneware* (Barrie & Jenkins, 1971).

## SLIP-DECORATED WARES

Slip wares, or earthenwares decorated by trailing diluted, perhaps coloured, clay (called 'slip') form an old and traditional mode of ceramic

*Slip-decorated wares*

decoration. Certainly, not one confined to Great Britain.

The technique is similar to that of decorating an iced cake. The design may be broad or rudimentary but it has a spontaneous charm and simplicity. Some now rare and costly examples were especially made and bear names or dates.

17th and early 18th-century examples are highly desirable and some damage can be overlooked, for the pieces were in the main of a useful nature. Old examples will not bear an impressed mark but some rare pieces bear a slip-trailed name, such as Thomas Toft, indeed the whole class could almost be called Toft ware! A group of potters working at Wrotham in Kent often added their name or initials to the face of the pot.

General books on early British pottery will include illustrations of typical (if rather special) slip wares. It should be noted, however, that not all examples are old. Reproductions, which may be antique in their own right, occur and some modern potters still practise their traditional skills with the slip-trailer.

Specialist books on British slip-decorated earthenwares include *English Slip-Ware Dishes 1650–1850*, by R. G. Cooper (Tiranti, 1968) and *Mary Wondrausch on Slipware*, by M. Wondrausch (A. & C. Black, 1986).

# STONEWARE

Stonewares comprise several types of normally salt-glazed high-fired clay-bodied useful wares, of which mugs and jugs were the most popular and successful products.

The surface colour can vary, depending on the firing or on any dip added to the surface. Traditional British stonewares were made at many centres including Nottingham and London. 18th-century examples seldom bear a maker's mark, although an inscription may indicate the locality of production.

Utilitarian stonewares depend on their appeal on the turned shape, its surface sheen or colour. Added decoration may be incised or applied in relief – a very popular form of decoration continued into the present century. Some Nottingham stoneware was attractively carved or pierced.

Apart from very important early examples, or documentary inscribed and dated pieces, most stoneware is modestly priced. Doultons in particular continued the tradition into the twentieth century. This firm did not close its Lambeth stoneware factory until 1956.

The standard specialist reference book is *English Brown Stoneware 1670–1900*, by A. Oswald, R. Hildyard & R. Hughes (Faber & Faber, 1982).

*Stoneware*

*Terra-cotta*

## TERRA-COTTA

Terra-cotta is a very ancient form of pottery – basically a fired clay left in its unglazed state. In the Victorian era, however, it was perfected and used to produce in commercial quantities moulded figures or busts and a large array of jugs, pots and other ceramic objects.

Some of these were hand-fired to give a good body appearance and shapes could be turned to give a polished look. F. & R. Pratt of Fenton produced notable terra-cotta type objects usually enhanced with printed decoration. Other firms, not necessarily in Staffordshire, produced graceful terra-cotta forms but relatively few examples bear a maker's mark.

Terra-cotta is rather neglected by collectors, perhaps because of the sameness of texture and colour and consequently unmarked examples are not costly.

# THE MARKS

I t will be appreciated that a convenient Handbook such as this cannot include all the thousands of recorded British marks found on pottery and porcelain. The selection does, however, include the main, collectable, markings which the dealer or collector may come across. It does not include very rare or obscure marks which will be found included in the comprehensive encyclopaedias, such as my *Encyclopaedia of British Pottery and Porcelain Marks* or the specialist *Encyclopaedia of British Porcelain Manufacturers*, both published by Barrie & Jenkins.

The selected entries will, however, where appropriate give details of specialist works, give reliable dates and suggest if the products are currently desirable from the collector's viewpoint.

The arrangement is in alphabetical order of the main factory or personal name from Adams to Worcester.

## WILLIAM ADAMS (& Co.) or (& SONS)

A leading manufacturer of good quality earthenwares, basalt, jasper, porcelains and ironstone-type wares. There were at different times several Adams potteries, mainly situated at Tunstall and Stoke in the Staffordshire Potteries. Production ranges from c.1769 to the present day (within the Wedgwood group). Early wares made before about 1780 are unlikely to be marked.

**ADAMS**

Early impressed mark, c.1785–1819.

Various fancy marks occur impressed or printed from c.1800 onwards, incorporating the simple name – Adams.

**W. ADAMS & SONS**

Various impressed or printed marks incorporating the new '& Sons' or '& S' style, sometimes using 'Stoke-upon-Trent', c.1819–64. Rare Adams parian bears this impressed name.

**ADAMS**
**W. ADAMS**

Various mid-19th-century wares can bear these simple marks in various forms.

**W. ADAMS & Co.**    Various impressed or printed marks incorporating the new style or the initials W. A. & Co, can usually be dated c.1893–1917.

Standard mark found on Wedgwood-type jasper wares, c.1896+.

Standard mark on Adams stonewares and 'ivory' bodied wares, c.1890s+.

Standard printed mark widely used with slight variations from c.1914 onwards.

Early Adams earthenwares and the 19th-century porcelains are certainly rare and collectable. The later pieces are more plentiful but are always of good quality and have decorative merit.

A standard specialist book is *William Adams, an Old English Potter*, by W. Turner (Chapman & Hall, 1904). Standard works on blue-printed wares will feature this important aspect of the Adams production. The reader should note that there were several other potters of this name active in the 19th century, see G. Godden's *Encyclopaedia of British Pottery and Porcelain Marks*.

## SAMUEL ALCOCK & CO.

Manufacturers of porcelain, parian and earthenware at Cobridge and Burslem, Staffordshire, c.1828–59. Much Alcock porcelain is unmarked. It is generally of good quality and of a decorative nature. As a grouping it is not rare but pieces are collectable and decorative. Prices are generally rather less than those for better-known contemporary firms such as Rockingham, Minton or Derby.

**SAML. ALCOCK & CO.**
**COBRIDGE**

Various name-marks with place-name 'Cobridge' employed during the 1828–53 period.

**PUBLISHED BY**
**S. ALCOCK & CO.**
**BURSLEM**

**ALCOCK & CO.**
**HILL POTTERY**
**BURSLEM**

Numerous name-marks with place-name 'Burslem' were employed during the 1830–59 period. Other marks incorporate, or consist of, the initials 'S. A. & Co.'

**ALCOCK'S**
**INDIAN IRONSTONE**

Impressed marks on ironstone earthenwares, recently found on the factory site; one piece is dated 1839.

For further information see 'The Samuel Alcock Porcelains', ch. 21, *Staffordshire Porcelain* (Granada, 1983).

## CHARLES ALLERTON & SONS

Manufacturers of earthenwares and china, at Longton, lustre decoration a speciality, c.1859–1942. Many marks occur with the name or initials of this firm. The printed marks reproduced here cause confusion on account of the date incorporated in the marks; they were not used until the 20th century. Most marked examples are not antique. Prices and demand rests on the decorative merit of the piece.

### G. L. ASHWORTH & BROS (LTD)
Manufacturers of earthenwares at Hanley, c.1861 to 1968 when retitled Mason's Ironstone China Ltd.

ASHWORTH

A. BROS

G. L. A. BROS

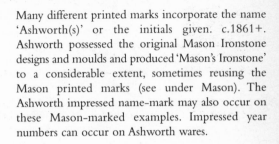

Many different printed marks incorporate the name 'Ashworth(s)' or the initials given. c.1861+. Ashworth possessed the original Mason Ironstone designs and moulds and produced 'Mason's Ironstone' to a considerable extent, sometimes reusing the Mason printed marks (see under Mason). The Ashworth impressed name-mark may also occur on these Mason-marked examples. Impressed year numbers can occur on Ashworth wares.

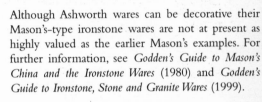

Although Ashworth wares can be decorative their Mason's-type ironstone wares are not at present as highly valued as the earlier Mason's examples. For further information, see *Godden's Guide to Mason's China and the Ironstone Wares* (1980) and *Godden's Guide to Ironstone, Stone and Granite Wares* (1999).

### J. AYNSLEY & SONS
John Aynsley established a porcelain works at Longton in c.1856, trading firstly as Aynsley & Co. This prospered and in about 1879 the style was changed to Aynsley & Sons. The Aynsley porcelains are of good quality and typical of their period. They are respectable collectable wares that are not costly. The firm has traded since 1971 as Aynsley China Ltd.

AYNSLEY

Various, mainly printed, marks incorporate this trade-name. Such porcelains are usually of 20th-century date, often post-1920.

# B

## WILLIAM BADDELEY

EASTWOOD

Manufacturer of earthenwares, often in Wedgwood style, at Eastwood, Hanley, c.1802–22. Impressed mark, the place-name 'Eastwood'. Examples are now rarely found but are not as desirable as those of the better-known makers such as Adams, Davenport or Spode.

## BAKER, BEVANS & IRWIN

Manufacturers of earthenwares at the Glamorgan Pottery, Swansea, Wales, c.1813–38. Although these Glamorgan earthenwares are of a routine type, mainly restricted to blue-printed tablewares, they are in demand by collectors of Welsh ceramics. Marked examples will command a premium over most Staffordshire examples.

Standard impressed name-mark, c.1813–38.

Several different printed marks incorporate the initials B. B. & I, B. B. & Co. or G. P. Co. (for Glamorgan Pottery Co.), c.1813–38.

B. B. & I.

B. B. & Co.

G. P. Co.

As with all aspects of Welsh pottery and porcelain the standard work is still E. Morton Nance's now costly book *The Pottery & Porcelain of Swansea & Nantgarw* (B. T. Batsford, 1942). Robert Pugh's slim guide *Welsh Pottery* (Towy Publishing, 1995) is also of interest.

## FRANK BEARDMORE & CO.

This firm produced a large range of useful and decorative wares at their Sutherland Pottery, Fenton, between 1903 and 1914.

F. B. & Co.
F. B. & Co.
F

Various initial marks, c.1903–14.

Standard printed mark, found with or without the trade name Sutherland Art Ware.

Victoria Bergesen's *Encyclopaedia of British Art Pottery* (Barrie & Jenkins, 1991) gives further information.

## BELLEEK

This famous pottery in County Fermanagh, Northern Ireland was established c.1863 by David McBirney & Co. and has continued to the present day under various changing ownerships. Earthenwares, parian and porcelains have been produced but Belleek is best associated with delicately potted glazed parian, often in marine-based forms.

BELLEEK

BELLEEK
CO. FERMANAGH

BELLEEK
POTTERY

Various impressed or printed name marks have been employed.

An impressed or printed harp device is a rare early mark. This can be crowned or uncrowned, c.1863–90.

The wolf-hound, tower and harp printed mark is the standard basic mark. The first version, c.1863–90, is normally printed in black.

Second, black-printed version, c.1891–1926, with additional wording 'Co Fermanagh Ireland'.

The third, black-printed, version has the words 'Deanta in Eirinn' (Made in Ireland) with the registered number of the new trade-mark device, c.1926–46. The fourth mark was printed in green, not black, c.1946–55. The fifth mark has the addition of ® signifying that the mark was registered, c.1955–65. Later versions were smaller in size and 'Co Fermanagh' was deleted from the scroll leaving only the word 'Ireland', c.1965–81. The colour of the basic printed mark became gold, c.1981–92. From 1993 the earlier black mark (with ®) has been used but printed in blue.

Delicate woven baskets normally have an applied pad-mark; the country of origin IRELAND should appear on post-1890 examples.

Early Belleek and rare or imposing shapes and designs are highly collectable. There is a Belleek Collectors' Society with an international membership. Specialist reference books include *Belleek*, by Richard K. Degenhardt (revised edition, Batsford, 1994); *Belleek Porcelain & Pottery*, by G. M. Smith (Toucan Press, 1979); and *Belleek Irish Porcelain*, by M. Langham (privately published, 1992).

NB. Some American potters used the name Belleek on Irish-styled wares.

## J. BESWICK (LTD)

John Beswick company was established at Gold Street, Longton in 1936, in succession to J. W. Beswick. The firm was taken over by Doulton & Co. and an extended range of porcelains have been produced.

**BESWICK
ENGLAND**

Various printed Beswick name marks have been used from 1936 onwards and an interesting range of decorative models have been produced.

The Beswick models have become very collectable and numerous price guides feature these non-antique wares. Such often non-British books include the Charlton *Standard Catalogue of Beswick Pottery*, by D. & J. Callow (Charlton Publishers, Canada, 1997).

## JOHN BEVINGTON
Manufacturer of decorative (Dresden-style) porcelain at Hanley, c.1872–92.

Blue painted mark, often on floral-encrusted porcelains or figures, c.1872–92. Examples are illustrated in my *Staffordshire Porcelain*.

The Bevington porcelains can be very decorative and consequently examples can be costly. It should be noted that several other Bevington firms produced porcelains in the second half of the 19th century.

## EDWARD BINGHAM
Manufacturer of pottery (in early style) at Castle Hedingham, Essex, c.1864–1901.

E.B.

Moulded relief mark on early-looking pottery (sometimes with incorrect dates). The signature mark also occurs incised, as do the initials 'E. B.'

A typical specimen with a photograph of Bingham, is included in Godden's *Illustrated Encyclopaedia of British Pottery and Porcelain*. Although these pieces look very old, their appeal is very limited and current values are rather low.

## BISHOP & STONIER (LTD)

Manufacturers of porcelain and earthenwares at Hanley, c.1891–1939.

**B. & S.**

Several different printed marks incorporate the initials B. & S.

Printed trade marks, often with trade-name, 'BISTO', 'ENGLAND' added to these basic marks on most examples.

Other marks of this firm included the name in full, c.1891+.

The desirability of such wares depends on the decorative value of the example, with most prices of a modest nature.

## BLAKENEY POTTERY LTD

This firm was founded as the Blakeney Art Pottery, in Stoke-on-Trent, in 1969. Apart from standard products and commemorative earthenwares the company produces a range of decorative articles in the style of collectable 19th-century ceramics such as ironstone or blue-printed wares. Such objects normally bear prominent but perhaps misleading old-style marks, often incorporating versions of the Royal Arms or crowned-garter devices.

Additional Blakeney wording includes: 'VICTORIA', 'VICTORIAN', 'IRONSTONE STAFFORDSHIRE' and 'ENGLAND'. The initials 'M. J. B.' or 'T. M.' can also occur with the Royal Arms or garter devices.

Blakeney pieces are decorative but not antique – although they are sometimes represented as such when sold in the smaller Antique Fairs or markets.

## BOOTH(S) (LTD)

Manufacturers of earthenwares at Tunstall, c.1891–1948, producing a good range of mainly useful earthenwares using various name-marks – as the post-1900 samples shown.

'England' or 'Made in England' can appear with these and similar marks. Month and year of potting numbers can also occur impressed into the body, i.e. 7.36, for July 1936.

However, the firm also produced a range of fine quality earthenware copies of mainly 18th-century scale-blue ground Worcester porcelains. Such earthenwares usually bear this crescent-like 'CB' mark. Although such articles are earthenware copies of much earlier porcelains they are decorative and can be quite highly valued.

For further inform..tion see *The Earthenwares of Booths*, by W. M. Parkin (Keeling Collection, Matlock, 1997).

## CHARLES BOURNE

Manufacturer of porcelain, Fenton, c.1817–30. These porcelains are attractive and collectable, the price range being approximately equal to the rather more plentiful Minton or Spode wares.

His good quality, well-decorated pieces often bear a painted initial mark 'CB'. On repetitive designs these initials are shown over the pattern number in fractional form.

For further information see *Staffordshire Porcelain*, Chapter 16, or the *Encyclopaedia of British Porcelain Manufacturers*.

## J. BOURNE (& SON LTD)

Manufacturer of stoneware and earthenwares at Belper and Denby, Derbyshire, c.1812–present day.

Early wares are seldom marked but some mainly utilitarian stonewares bear impressed 'Belper & Denby' or 'Bournes Potteries Derbyshire' marks. Later, mainly 20th-century marks comprise or include the trade-name 'Denby'.

c.1910+

c.1930+

c.1948+

The trade name 'Danesby Ware' also occurs mainly on wares of the 1930s.

The Denby wares can be quite extensive in range, they are not confined to the well-known tablewares. Denby wares, in particular the more unusual items, are collectable but at relatively modest price levels.

For further information see *Denby Stonewares, A Collector's Guide*, by G. & A. Key (Ems & Ens, 1995); *Denby Pottery*, by I. & G. Hopwood (Richard Dennis Publications, 1997); and *Bourne at Denby*, by G. & A. Key (Ems & Ens, 1998).

## BOW PORCELAIN FACTORY

This factory, also known as 'New Canton' (a name which occurs on very rare simple inkwells), was established in the 1740s and with the Chelsea and

Limehouse works ranks as one of the earliest British manufactories of porcelain. Specimens, especially the early pre-1760 articles, are rare and desirable, but many pieces do not bear a factory mark. The factory closed c.1776.

Examples of several early incised marks, c.1750–60.

**NUMERALS PAINTED IN UNDERGLAZE BLUE**

Specimens decorated in underglaze blue often have workmen's numbers painted on the bottom (not on the inside of the footrim as on the similar Lowestoft porcelains).

Painted anchor and dagger mark normally in red and found on post-1760 figures and groups. The marks also sometimes occur on French 'hard-paste' reproductions.

This impressed 'repairer's' mark is found on Bow (as well as other) porcelains (see 'Tebo' Toulouse).

The Bow porcelain body (like that employed at Lowestoft) contains a high proportion of bone ash. Typical specimens can be seen at the Victoria and Albert Museum and at the British Museum in London but relatively few specimens bear a factory mark. For further details and illustrations, see *Bow Porcelain* by E. Adams & D. Redstone (revised edition, Faber & Faber, 1991); *Bow Porcelain, the collection formed by Geoffrey Freeman*, by Anton Gabszewicz (Lund Humphries, 1982); and *Bow Porcelain Figures, 1748–1774*, by P. Bradshaw (Barrie & Jenkins, 1992). Good specimens of Bow porcelain are highly desirable, particularly early specimens. Condition is important.

### G. F. BOWERS (& CO.)

Manufacturer of porcelain and pottery at Brownhills, Tunstall, c.1841–71.

**G. F. BOWERS
TUNSTALL**

**G. F. B.**

Impressed or printed name-mark. The initials 'G. F. B.' were incorporated in other marks, c.1841–71.

For further information see my *Encyclopaedia of British Porcelain Manufacturers*. The marked Bowers porcelains are usually teawares. Although collectable they are not highly valued.

### E. BRAIN & CO. LTD

Manufacturers of porcelain at Foley Works, Fenton, 1903–63.

Early printed mark, c.1903+.

Printed mark, c.1905. The word 'FOLEY' was extensively used on many different marks to 1963, with the initials 'E. B. & Co.' or the name in full. Sample later marks are given below relating to good quality porcelains. Value depends on the decorative merits of examples.

| 1913+ Later 'Made in England' replaces 'England' | 1930+ | 1936+ |

The 'Foley' trade-name was also used by Wileman & Co. in the 1892–1925 period.

## C. H. BRANNAM LTD

Manufacturers of earthenwares at Barnstaple, Devon, c.1879 to present day.

C. H. BRANNAM
BARUM

Incised signature mark in writing letters; many other impressed marks occur, incorporating the name 'BRANNAM' with the place-name 'BARNSTA-PLE' or 'BARUM', c.1879+.

These often individual pieces are decorative and collectable. For further information see *Art Potters of Barnstaple* by A. Edgeler (Nimrod Press, Alton, 1990) and the *Encyclopaedia of British Art Pottery* by Victoria Bergesen (Barrie & Jenkins, 1991).

## BRETBY, see Tooth & Co.

## BRISTOL

The city of Bristol was one of the earliest centres of the British ceramic industry. Tin-glazed delft-type earthenwares were produced in the first half of the 18th century, but such wares are seldom marked. Various earthenwares were also produced and porcelain as early as c.1749–51. The early porcelains are of a soaprock type porcelain. Very rare examples can be marked BRISTOL or BRISTOLL moulded in relief and are known as 'Lunds Bristol'. Marked specimens are usually decorated in underglaze blue and will be of considerable value.

For further information see my *Encyclopaedia of British Porcelain Manufacturers*, p. 495 and Dr B. Watney's *English Blue & White Porcelain of the 18th Century* (Faber & Faber, revised edition, 1973).

## BRISTOL (HARD-PASTE)

This porcelain factory c.1770–81 is related to the earlier Plymouth venture where English hard-paste porcelain was introduced. The Bristol wares made under Richard Champion's management are rare and usually attractive. Not all examples are marked but the factory marks comprise:

A painted cross or letter B, often with a painter's or gilder's number added. Reproductions occur, mainly in a soft-paste body; these reproductions often have a date below the cross mark.

The crossed-swords mark (of the Dresden factory) occurs in underglaze blue on Bristol porcelain of the 1770–81 period, often with painters' or gilders' numerals added in overglaze enamel or in gold. NB. Not all crossed-swords marks relate to Bristol!

This impressed or moulded 'repairer's' mark also occurs on some Bristol porcelain, see under 'Tebo' Toulouse.

Bristol porcelain is highly collectable and can, rightly, be costly especially for rare forms or figures and unusual decoration. Most tablewares bear floral decoration.

For further information and illustrations, see *Bristol Porcelain*, by F. Hurlbutt (1928); *Champion's Bristol Porcelain* by F. Severne Mackenna (F. Lewis, 1947); and my *Encyclopaedia of British Porcelain Manufacturers* (1988). Good examples can be seen in the Bristol City Art Gallery and Museum, and at the Victoria & Albert Museum in London.

## WILLIAM BROWNFIELD (& SONS)
Manufacturers of earthenwares and porcelain (the latter from 1871) at Cobridge, c.1850–1892.

W. B.

W. B. & S.

W. B. & Son

Various printed, impressed or moulded marks incorporating these initials were used, with '& S.' or '& Son' added from 1871. The name 'Brownfield' was also used.

The concern was continued by a form of cooperative, the Brownfield Guild Pottery Society, 1892–1900.

The standard book on these wares is *William Brownfield & Sons*, by T. H. Peake (privately published, 1995). The porcelains in particular can be of high quality and are in general undervalued.

## BROWN-WESTHEAD, MOORE & CO.
Manufacturers of high-grade earthenwares and porcelain at Cauldon Place, Hanley, c.1862–1904.

Various printed marks incorporating the initials 'BWM' or 'BWM & Co.' used 1862–1904. The name of the firm in full was also used.

The products of this firm are very diverse. The better quality examples are very collectable and important pieces can, rightly, be costly. For further information and illustrations, see my *Staffordshire Porcelain* (1983).

## BURGESS & LEIGH (LTD)
This Burslem partnership produced a wide range of earthenwares from c.1862 up to the present day. Ltd was added to the firm's title c.1889.

The earlier marks usually bore the name Burgess and Leigh or initial marks B & L.

Later wares from the 1930s onwards usually bear one of many marks incorporating the trade-name Burleigh Ware.

Whilst by no means all Burgess & Leigh wares can be regarded as collectable, some pieces, especially the Art Deco styled wares of the 1920s and 1930s, are in demand; see *Collecting Burleigh Jugs*, by E. Coupe (Letterbox Publishing, 1998).

## BURMANTOFTS

Wilcock & Co, at Burmantofts near Leeds in Yorkshire, produced a range of Art Pottery, mainly decorated with pleasing coloured glazes, from c.1882 into the present century.

BURMANTOFTS
or
BURMANTOFTS
FAIENCE

Standard impressed mark, c.1882–1904.

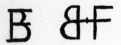

Monogram marks, often with model number added, c.1882–1904.

Burmantofts Art Pottery is collectable and the more important or unusual pieces can be costly. For further information see the *Encyclopaedia of British Art Pottery*, by Victoria Bergesen (Barrie & Jenkins, 1991).

## CARLTON WARE

The decorative earthenwares marketed under the trade-name 'Carlton Ware' have become very collectable and popular in recent years. They originated with Messrs Wiltshaw & Robinson (Ltd) of the Carlton Works at Stoke, a partnership founded c.1890. Early printed marks are reproduced below but the now more fashionable products relate to the post-1910 period, indeed some of the later post-1930 products are now highly regarded for their period charm.

| c.1890+ | c.1894 onwards, variations occur | c.1906 onwards |

Typical marks are here reproduced.

c.1925+        c.1925–57

The old title was changed to Carlton Ware Ltd in January 1958 and this became part of the Arthur Wood & Son group in 1967. After various take-overs production ceased in 1969. Some reproductions of popular Carlton lines exist and can bear misleading marks.

A specialist book *Collecting Carlton Ware* by Francis Salman was published in 1993 (K. Francis Publishing). There is a Carlton Ware Collectors' Club, which publishes an informative magazine *The Carlton Times* (Helen & Keith Martin, PO Box 161, Sevenoaks, Kent, TN15 6GA).

## CAUGHLEY

Porcelain works, situated near Broseley in Shropshire. Good porcelain in the Worcester style was made by Thomas Turner from c.1775 to 1799, when John Rose of the nearby Coalport factory took over the Caughley concern.

SALOPIAN

Impressed 'Salopian' name-mark on porcelains in upper or lower case letters, c.1775–99.

Blue painted or printed 'S' marks often with a small cross or circle after, found on underglaze-blue decorated wares, c.1775–c.1795.

Printed and painted 'C' marks relating to Caughley but this initial mark is sometimes mistaken for a Worcester crescent mark, c.1775–95.

Numerals disguised as Chinese characters occurring on blue printed porcelains were traditionally attributed to Caughley, but research shows that these are Worcester marks of the 1770–83 period.

ROYAL ARMS

A recessed but relief-moulded version of the Royal Arms is very rarely found under late Caughley jugs of the cabbage-leaf type.

The later 1795–99 wares, often decorated with simple floral motifs, do not appear to have been marked. The overglaze enamelled Caughley porcelains are likewise seldom marked.

Caughley porcelain is highly collectable and rare shapes or patterns, plus of course, inscribed and dated examples are highly regarded. Excavations on the factory site have shed much fresh light on the productions, and the reader is referred to *Caughley and Worcester Porcelains*, by G.A. Godden (revised edition, Antique Collectors' Club, 1981). Good selections of Caughley porcelain are to be seen at the Victoria & Albert Museum and at the Coalport factory which is part of the Ironbridge Gorge Museum in Shropshire.

## CHAMBERLAIN (& CO.)

Manufacturers of porcelain at Worcester from c.1788 to 1852.

| | |
|---|---|
| **Chamberlain's** <br> **Chamberlain's Worcester Warranted** | Painted name-mark in writing letters often with place-name 'Worcester' or 'Worcester Warranted' added; the pattern number was sometimes added c.1790–1810. On teapots the mark is inside the cover. Different spellings, even of 'Worcester', occur. |
| **CROWN DEVICE** | A crown and/or the word 'Royal' added to name-marks from c.1811 to c.1840. |
| **REGENT CHINA** | New 'Regent' body introduced c.1811 and description added to marks. The 'Regent' body was expensive and is rather rare. |
| *Chamberlain's Worcester & 63, Piccadilly, London.* | Address of London retail shop added to name-marks from 1814 to mid 1816. |
| **55 NEW BOND STREET** | New London address added to marks from July 1816. |
| **CHAMBERLAIN & CO.** | '& Co.' added to style and marks from c.1840; new address 'No. 1. Coventry Street London' also occurs (c.1840–5). |
| **CHAMBERLAINS WORCESTER** | Impressed mark, c.1846–50. |

Printed mark, c.1850–2. Factory continued by Kerr & Binns.

For further information and illustrations, see G. A. Godden's *Chamberlain-Worcester Porcelain 1788–1852* (Barrie & Jenkins, 1982). Good marked Chamberlain Worcester is very collectable but the value depends on the decorative merits of the piece, on its rarity and condition. Whilst single standard cups and saucers are not highly priced, a superb marked vase will be costly.

## CHELSEA PORCELAIN WORKS

Produced attractive decorative figures, etc., as well as useful wares in porcelain from c.1745 to 1769, when the Chelsea-Derby period commenced. Early Chelsea porcelain is rare and desirable.

Incised (not impressed) triangle mark on early wares, which were sometimes left undecorated. The place-name 'Chelsea' and a date occur on some very rare specimens with an incised triangle mark, c.1745–50. All triangle marked examples are rare.

Very rare underglaze-blue crown and trident mark, c.1748–50.

Rare raised, moulded mark of small size, called the 'raised anchor mark', c.1749–52. Marked examples are rare and desirable. On some examples the anchor is picked out in red.

Photographic reproductions of the above four Chelsea marks are included in the *Illustrated Encyclopaedia of British Pottery and Porcelain*, Plates 115, 116, 122A and 126.

*Small* anchor painted in red – the 'red anchor mark' used c.1752–6. In some cases numerals occur with the anchor device, as on the example reproduced. Red anchor period Chelsea porcelain is desirable.

*Small* anchor painted in gold – the 'gold anchor mark' used c.1756–69. Many reproductions of gold anchor period Chelsea porcelain bear this mark, often painted larger than the original; *any anchor mark over a quarter of an inch in height should be treated with great suspicion.*

Most general reference books give at least a brief history of the factory and illustrate some specimens. Specialist books include F. S. Mackenna's *Chelsea Porcelain, the Triangle and Raised Anchor Wares* (F. Lewis, 1948), *Chelsea Porcelain, the Red Anchor Wares* (F. Lewis, 1951), *Chelsea Porcelain, the Gold Anchor Period* (F. Lewis, 1952), and *Chelsea Porcelain* by Elizabeth Adams (Barrie & Jenkins, 1987); also Arthur Lane's *English Porcelain Figures of the 18th Century* (Faber & Faber, 1961), and *English Porcelain 1745–1850* (Benn, 1965) edited by R. J. Charleston. A good selection of illustrations is included in *Godden's Illustrated Encyclopaedia of British Pottery and Porcelain*, Plates 112–46.

Genuine 18th-century Chelsea porcelain is extremely collectable and is usually costly. However, many reproductions have been produced over more than a hundred years. Gold anchor marks should be treated with extreme caution. Chelsea produced soft-paste porcelains, and examples should show some manufacturing faults. Reproductions are usually of a Continental hard-paste body. Good representative collections can be seen in most large museums, particularly in the Victoria & Albert Museum.

## CHELSEA-DERBY

William Duesbury, the proprietor of the Derby porcelain factory, purchased the Chelsea works in 1769. Porcelain continued to be made or decorated at the Chelsea factory until 1784 under Duesbury's direction.

The former Chelsea gold anchor mark was continued and two new marks were introduced, incorporating the Chelsea anchor and the Derby crown or initial 'D'. These Chelsea-Derby marks are normally painted in gold. The decoration is tasteful and restrained (see Godden's *Illustrated Encyclopaedia of British Pottery and Porcelain*, Plates 147–52).

The Chelsea-Derby porcelains are always of good quality and are tastefully decorated. In general, however, they seem to be underpriced.

## JAMES & RALPH CLEWS

Manufacturers of earthenwares etc. at Cobridge, c.1815–34.

CLEWS
WARRANTED
STAFFORDSHIRE

Several different impressed or printed marks were used by the Clews, each including the name. Good quality blue printed earthenware as well as 'Stone China' was made, much of it for the American market. Porcelain was made in the 1821–5 period, but this does not appear to have been marked.

Clews earthenwares are collectable, especially the rarer or more interesting blue printed designs. For further information on the problematical porcelains see the *Encyclopaedia of British Porcelain Manufacturers*.

## CLARICE CLIFF

Clarice Cliff (1899–1972) was a designer rather than a manufacturer. Her jazz-age colourful designs of the 1920s and 1930s are currently very popular and collectable. Some but by no means all examples are costly.

Several different printed marks feature or include her signature, as the sample marks here reproduced.

Numerous articles and specialist books give a good account of her life and work. This handbook can only refer the reader to these sources of detailed information and importantly repeat that not all pieces bearing her signature, as part of standard factory marks, are valuable and that her work has been copied and reused, long after her death in 1972.

The specialist works include *Collecting Clarice Cliff*, by H. Watson (K. Francis, 1988); *Clarice Cliff The Bizarre Affair*, by L. Griffin & L. & S. Meisel (Thames & Hudson, 1988); *Clarice Cliff Price Guide*, by P. & H. Watson (Francis Joseph, 1995); *Rich Designs of Clarice Cliff* by R. Green & D. Jones (Rich Designs, 1995); and *Clarice Cliff and Her Contemporaries*, by Helen C. Cunningham (Schiffer Publishing, 1999).

## COALPORT

The Coalport porcelain works near Ironbridge, in Shropshire, were established by John Rose and his partners in the 1790s. The very early examples are unmarked. Name-marks were rarely employed before about 1815 when the standard mix was of the hybrid hard-paste type. Bone china or the Feltspar variety can be expected from c.1820.

The above red painted name-marks are very rare.

Name-marks painted in underglaze blue can occur from c.1820 into the 1840s, mainly on floral encrusted porcelains. 'C. Dale' and the 'CD' marks relate to the place-name Coalbrookdale.

This impressed mark will be found on many examples of Coalport plates, dishes, etc., of the 1815–25 period, other numbers 1 or 6 rarely occur.

The printed Society of Arts marks reproduced below were used for a few years from June 1820. Several slight variations were used.

Several different written or printed name-marks occur in the approximate period 1830–50. The alternative place-name 'Coalbrookdale' can also occur.

Neatly painted CBD (Coalbrookdale) initial mark, c.1851–61.

So-called ampersand mark, neatly painted, c.1861–75.

Mock, popular, Continental marks can also occur on Coalport porcelains in the Sèvres or Dresden style, c.1840–70.

Printed crown marks, c.1881–1939+. 'England' added c.1891. 'Made in England' occurs from c.1920.

Printed marks of the post-war period (above). Variations occur, which give details of the pattern or style.

Revised standard mark, 1960+.

Two post-1970 Coalport China Ltd printed marks.

The Coalport company has passed through several hands from the early John Rose days. In 1926 production was moved from Coalport to the Staffordshire Potteries. Today it is part of the Wedgwood Group. Coalport porcelain is in general of good quality and can be highly decorative. Unusual, early or later signed pieces are likely to be costly but standard designs on tablewares are not necessarily expensive.

Specialist books include *Coalport & Coalbrookdale Porcelains*, by Geoffrey Godden (revised edition, Antique Collectors' Club, 1981) and *Coalport 1795–1926*, by Michael Messenger (Antique Collectors' Club, 1995). The old factory, now part of the Ironbridge Gorge Museum, includes a very good representative collection of Coalport porcelains.

## SUSIE COOPER

Susie Cooper OBE (1902–95) was a talented designer who worked under her maiden name and started her ceramic career with A. E. Gray & Co. From c.1930 she traded as Susie Cooper Pottery (Ltd) at Burslem, and later as Susie Cooper China Ltd (1950+) and Susie Cooper Ltd. In 1966 she joined the Wedgwood group. Her design work, renowned for elegant forms and tasteful restrained patterns, won world-wide acclaim. Some later reproductions occur.

Various printed marks occur as the samples here reproduced.

A
SUSIE COOPER
PRODUCTION.
CROWN WORKS,
BURSLEM,
ENGLAND

*Susie Cooper*

CROWN WORKS
BURSLEM
ENGLAND

Whilst most standard productions are not rare or antique they are typical of their period and are collectable. Numerous articles and general books on 20th-century ceramics feature her work. In 1987 the Victoria & Albert Museum published a specialist book by Ann Eatwell, *Susie Cooper Productions*. Later works include *Susie Cooper Ceramics, a Collectors' Guide* by Andrew Casey (Jazz Publications, 1992); *Susie Cooper*, by A. Woodhouse (Trilby Books, 1992); and *Susie Cooper, an Elegant Affair*, by B.Youds (Thames & Hudson, 1996).

## COPELAND & GARRETT

Manufacturers of earthenwares, parian, fine porcelain, etc., at Stoke, 1833–47, succeeding Spode (see under Spode). W. T. Copeland & Sons continued from 1847 (see next entry).

C. & G.

COPELAND & GARRETT

Several printed and impressed marks incorporate the name or initials of this partnership, c.1833–47.

Three typical marks are reproduced.

The Copeland & Garrett wares are usually of high quality and are consequently collectable although they are not as favoured as the earlier Spode pieces. A good selection of pieces are displayed at the Spode factory at Stoke. For further information see my *Encyclopaedia of British Porcelain Manufacturers* or *Staffordshire Porcelain*, Chapter 7.

## W. T. COPELAND & SONS

Manufacturers of earthenwares, parian and fine porcelain at Stoke, 1847–1970, then continued under a new title 'Spode Ltd'. Successors to Copeland & Garrett (see preceding entry).

COPELAND

Standard impressed mark found on earthenware, porcelain and especially the parian figures and groups popularized by this firm, c.1847+.

Rare printed mark, c.1847–51.

Standard printed mark, c.1851–85, a fancy version of the rare earlier mark (see above).

Four standard printed marks found on earthenwares, c.1867–90; c.1875–90; c.1894–1910; c.1891 into 20th century.

Printed mark, sometimes in gold on fine porcelains, c.1891 into 20th century.

Example of several post-war printed marks which incorporate the old name 'Spode'.

Impressed month and year initials and numerals will often show the date of potting of post-1870 examples, e.g. J.01 for January 1901. The fine quality Copeland wares, the porcelains in particular, are very collectable and rightly can be costly. A good selection of examples are included in the Works Museum at Stoke. For further information see *Staffordshire Porcelain*, Chapter 8 or my *Encyclopaedia of British Porcelain Manufacturers*.

**CROWN DEVON**, see S. Fielding & Co. (Ltd)

## CROWN STAFFORDSHIRE PORCE-LAIN

Manufacturers of high-grade porcelain at Fenton, c.1889–1948. In 1948 the firm was retitled Crown Staffordshire China Co. Ltd., and later became a part of the Wedgwood Group. The Crown Staffordshire name has, however, been phased out from the mid 1980s.

Three basic printed marks, c.1889+. The name 'England' often added from 1891, also date of establishment 'A.D. 1801'.

These porcelains can be of very high quality. Some charming figure models and bird groups were produced in the post-1920 period as were floral compositions. In general, I feel, the Crown Staffordshire products are not as highly regarded as they should be. For further information see my *Encyclopaedia of British Porcelain Manufacturers*.

# D

## HENRY & RICHARD DANIEL (DANIEL & SONS)

Manufacturers of high-grade decorative porcelain and earthenwares at Stoke and Shelton, c.1822–46.

**DANIEL & SON**    Very rare form of mark, c.1822–6.

**H. & R. DANIEL**    Rare form of mark, written or printed, c.1826–9.

Rare printed mark, c.1826–9.

**H. DANIEL & SONS**    Rare form of mark, c.1829–41.

All Daniel porcelains are of very fine quality and desirable but are seldom marked. The reader is referred to M. Berthoud's excellent book, *H. & R. Daniel 1822–1846* (Micawber, 1980) and to his *The Daniel Tableware Patterns* (Micawber, 1982) plus the 1997 *Daniel Patterns on Porcelain* (Micawber). Helpful general works illustrating typical Daniel porcelains include *Staffordshire Porcelain*, Chapter 19 and *Encyclopaedia of British Porcelain Manufacturers*.

## DAVENPORT

Manufacturers (under various styles, W. Davenport & Co., etc.) of earthenwares, porcelain and glass at Longport, c.1793–1887.

Davenport

Standard early impressed marks on earthenwares. The earliest 'Davenport' mark is found in upper and lower case letters, c.1793–1820. The last two numerals of the year of manufacture were sometimes added each side of the anchor, '42' for 1842, etc. on examples of the 1840–60 period.

Standard printed mark found on 'Stone China' wares, c.1815–20.

DAVENPORT

Very many printed wares of the 1815–50 period bear different printed marks incorporating the name 'Davenport' and often the name of the pattern.

Overglaze printed mark on porcelains, c.1815–30. Basic mark used later (c.1840+) but then occurs in underglaze blue.

DAVENPORT
LONGPORT

Rare printed mark on early porcelains, prior to 1820; on some early Davenport porcelains only the name 'LONGPORT' occurs.

DAVENPORT
LONGPORT
STAFFORDSHRE

Standard printed mark, c.1870–87.

Whilst by no means all Davenport wares are of great consequence, the earlier examples and especially the quality porcelains are collectable and can be costly. Some good, typical examples are included in the City Museum, Stoke-on-Trent collection. Examples of Davenport wares are shown in Terence Lockett's and Geoffrey Godden's *Davenport China, Earthenware and Glass, 1794–1887* (Barrie & Jenkins, 1989), Godden's *Illustrated Encyclopaedia of British Pottery and Porcelain*, Plates 190, 200. See also *Staffordshire Porcelain*, Chapter 10.

## WILLIAM DE MORGAN

Manufacturer of decorative earthenwares at Chelsea, Fulham, etc., c.1872–1907 (decoration continued to 1911).

**W. DE MORGAN**

Several different marks incorporate the name 'DE MORGAN', sometimes with addresses; 'Merton Abbey', c.1882–8; 'Sands End', c.1888+. '& Co.' added to most marks after 1888.

Merton Abbey address mark, and other marks incorporating this place-name, all relate to the period 1882–8.

Impressed or painted mark, 1882+.

Sands End address mark. Others were used, all may be dated from 1888 onwards.

Impressed initial mark, with the last two numerals of the year.

The initials of various decorators also occur, 'F. P.' for Frederick Passenger, etc.

The decorative and mainly individually painted, and often lustred, De Morgan earthenwares are very collectable. Good examples can be costly. For further information and illustrations, see *Catalogue of Works by William De Morgan* (Victoria & Albert Museum,

1921); *Victorian Pottery*, by H. Wakefield (H. Jenkins, 1962); *British Pottery*, by G. Godden (Barrie & Jenkins, 1974); and *The Designs of William De Morgan* published by Richard Dennis (1989). Victoria Bergesen's *Encyclopaedia of British Art Pottery* (Barrie & Jenkins, 1991) is also helpful and gives details of assistants with good references to magazine articles on the De Morgan wares.

**DENBY**, see J. Bourne (& Son Ltd)

## DERBY PORCELAIN WORKS

William Duesbury commenced the manufacture of porcelain at Derby, c.1750. The original factory closed in 1848 (a small works continued in the same tradition, see King Street, Derby, in this section). A new company was formed in 1878, which now continues the tradition of Derby fine porcelain.

### Duesbury Period

Extremely rare early incised marks, c.1750–5. Most products prior to about 1770 were unmarked.

**PAD MARK**

Three 'pad marks' or dark patches occur on the bases of Derby figures, groups or vases. These were formed by the wads of clay placed under the bases to prevent the object sticking to the base of the saggar. A photograph of a typical pad-marked base is included in Godden's *Encyclopaedia of British Pottery and Porcelain Marks*, Plate 8, and in the *Encyclopaedia of British Porcelain Manufacturers*, p. 293.

Incised initial, rarely found on flatware – plates, dishes, etc. – not to be confused with abbreviation of 'number' placed before the model number on the base of figures, etc., c.1770–80.

Rather rare painted mark, normally in blue, c.1770–82.

Standard post-1782 mark, *incised* under the bases of figures, groups, vases, etc. *Painted* neatly and of small size, in puce, blue or black, c.1782–1800. *Painted* in red, often carelessly, c.1800–25, into Bloor period.

Impressed printer's type capital letters can occur c.1782–1805 as at Pinxton.

Derby porcelains are in general of very high quality and are very collectable. Special examples can be very costly. Fakes of Duesbury period Derby porcelain exist, including figures and groups which bear copies of standard marks. There is a large selection of specialist reference books which illustrate a wide range of types. The most recent books include *Derby Porcelain, the Golden Years*, by D. G. Rice (David & Charles, 1983); *Derby Porcelain Figures 1750–1848*, by P. Bradshaw (Faber & Faber, 1990); *Derby Porcelain 1750–1798*, by G. Bradley (T. Heneage, 1990); and *Derby Modellers, 1786–1796*, by A. Ledger & C. Roth (Derby Porcelain International Society, 1995). One must not, however, forget older classics such as J. Haslem's 1876 book *The Old Derby China Factory*.

There is a flourishing Derby collectors club, 'The Derby Porcelain International Society', which publishes an interesting newsletter and other publications and organizes seminars and lectures. Most large museums display good representative collections of Derby porcelain. There is also the Derby City Museum collection and the Derby works collection.

**Bloor Period**

Robert Bloor managed the Derby porcelain factory in 1811 and continued until c.1848. The products made before c.1825 bore the old cross batons, 'D' and crown mark painted in red. Whilst products made in the Bloor period are not as commercially desirable as the earlier Duesbury examples, they can be of good quality and colourful.

Earliest painted or transferred (by the thumb) Bloor Derby mark, in red, c.1825–40.

Painted or printed Bloor Derby marks, c.1825–48.

### King Street, Derby

After 1848 a group of six former Derby workmen opened a small factory in King Street. This continued under various owners until absorbed by the Royal Crown Derby company in 1935. The King Street works is often referred to as Stevenson & Hancock Derby as the standard post-1860 marks includes the initials 'SH'. It is probable that the early King Street porcelains bore a close copy of the former Duesbury Derby mark but with crossed swords replacing the old crossed batons. Other early marks include the following but these are rarely found.

    1849–59          1859–62          1849–63

Standard so-called 'Stevenson & Hancock' mark (old Derby mark with new initials 'S' and 'H' at the sides), 1862–1935. This was usually painted in red but can occur in puce, c.1915–35. Initials such as W. P. L. also occur from 1917.

The King Street Derby porcelains can be of very good quality and are certainly collectable. Recent specialist books feature these surprisingly varied productions. These include *Derby Porcelain. The Factory at*

*King Street, 1849–1935*, by A. Bambery & R. Blackwood (Derby Museum & Art Gallery, 1993); *In Account with Sampson Hancock, 1860s–1880s*, by J. Twitchett (D. J. C. Books, 1996). There is also a good chapter on the King Street adventure in *Royal Crown Derby*, by J. Twitchett & B. Bailey (Antique Collectors' Club, revised edition, 1988).

## Royal Crown Derby

In 1876 a new company was formed with a large factory in Osmaston Road. This was initially termed the Derby Crown Porcelain Company but in 1890 Queen Victoria granted the Royal Warrant and permission to use the trade-name Royal Crown Derby.

Standard painted mark (no words), c.1876–89.

Standard printed mark, from January 1890, note wording 'Royal Crown Derby' added to former mark; the word 'England' was added to mark from 1891, and was replaced by 'Made in England' in about 1921.

Various devices were added below the last two standard marks; these show the year of decoration for any object from 1882 onwards. The key to this dating system is given in Godden's *Encyclopaedia of British Pottery and Porcelain Marks* (1964) and in the *Encyclopaedia of British Porcelain Manufacturers* (1988).

Royal Crown Derby porcelains are always of good quality and enjoy a high reputation. Important examples, especially signed examples by leading artists, can be costly but repetitive standard patterns will obviously be less desirable. Specialist books on the later Derby wares include *Royal Crown Derby*, by J. Twitchett & B. Bailey (Antique Collectors' Club, revised edition, 1988) and *A Case of Fine China*, by H. Gibson (The Royal Crown Derby Porcelain

Company, 1993). Good typical specimens of the later Derby porcelains can be seen in the City Museum and in the Derby works collection.

## DOULTON & CO. (LTD)

Manufacturers of stonewares and earthenwares at Lambeth, London, c.1854–1956, and at Burslem, Staffordshire (where porcelains were also made), 1882 to present day.

### Lambeth

DOULTON & WATTS
LAMBETH POTTERY
LONDON

Standard impressed mark of Doulton & Watts partnership, c.1820–54.

DOULTON LAMBETH

Standard impressed mark, c.1854+. *Ornamental* wares date from about 1870; about this period an oval impressed mark incorporating these words with the date of production added.

Impressed mark, c.1877–80.

Impressed or printed mark on *earthenware*, c.1872+.

Standard impressed mark, c.1880–1902. The word 'England' added below from 1891.

DOULTON
LAMBETH
ENGLAND

Impressed mark on small pieces, c.1891–1956.

Five marks found on special bodies from c.1881 into the 20th century.

DOULTON
& SLATER'S
PATENT

Sample *incised* decorators' marks found on Doulton stonewares. Monograms of: Arthur B. Barlow, c.1872–9; Hannah Barlow, c.1872–1906; George Tinworth, c.1867–1913. Other decorators' monograms are given in Godden's *Encyclopaedia of British Pottery and Porcelain Marks* and in D. Eyles's *Royal Doulton 1815–1965*.

Standard impressed mark, c.1902–22 and c.1927–36, also used on wares made in Burslem.

Standard impressed mark (without earlier crown), c.1922–56.

The Doulton stonewares made at the Lambeth Pottery are extremely diverse. Different types are collectable and can be costly, especially important individual specimens bearing the signature or monogram of their leading artists and modellers. However, the output was large and by no means all examples are rare or in great demand.

For further information see *Royal Doulton 1815–1965*, by D. Eyles (Hutchinson, 1965); *The Royal Doulton Lambeth Wares*, by D. Eyles (Hutchinson, 1975). There are also very specialist books and price guides, such as J. Lukins's *Doulton Lambeth Advertising Wares* (Venta Books, 1991); Victoria Bergesen's *Encyclopaedia of British Art Pottery* (Barrie & Jenkins, 1991) is also extremely informative. The reader is also referred to the Doulton Burslem section below for details of general books on Royal Doulton wares.

## Burslem

In 1877 Henry Doulton purchased an interest in the Staffordshire earthenware firm of Pinder, Bourne & Co. of Nile Street, Burslem. In 1882 Doulton (of Lambeth) took over complete control and commenced to use the Doulton & Co. name. From 1882 onwards good quality earthenwares as well as superb quality porcelains have been produced by Doultons who over the years have taken over many other firms including Mintons. The present Royal Doulton companies are world leaders.

**DOULTON**

Standard impressed mark on earthenwares (not stonewares) made at the Nile Street, Burslem, factory, c.1882 onwards.

Standard printed or impressed marks, c.1882–1902. 'England' added from 1891.

New 'Royal Doulton' mark c.1902–32.

Revised standard mark, with 'Made in England' added c.1932 onwards.

The words 'Bone China' added on china wares. This was amended to 'English Fine Bone China' in 1959. The description 'ENGLISH TRANSLUCENT CHINA' used from 1960.

Impressed month and year numerals can occur and show the period of manufacture. Other indications of period include the addition of a number added by the standard marks, beginning with '1' in 1928. One therefore adds 27 to that number to discover the year of decoration. The additional wording 'Copyright Doulton & Co. Limited' occurs on most new designs introduced after 1960.

The Doulton Burslem wares, especially the fine porcelains, are very collectable, as are the large range of decorative figures. Numerous price guides have been published giving details on the rarity and desirability of the different models and types.

Specialist reference books include *The Doulton Burslem Wares*, by D. Eyles (Barrie & Jenkins, 1980); *Royal Doulton Figures*, by D. Eyles, R. Dennis & L.

Irvine (Royal Doulton Ltd, revised edition, 1994); *The Doulton Figure Collectors Handbook*, by K. Pearson (K. Francis Publishing, 1986 and later editions); *The Lyle Price Guide to Doulton* (Lyle Publications, 1986 and later editions); *Phillips Collectors Guide to Royal Doulton*, by C. Braithwaite (Boxtree Ltd, 1989); *Doulton for the Collector*, by J. Lukins (Venta Books, 1994); and *Legacy of Sir Henry Doulton: 120 Years of Royal Doulton in Burslem, 1877–1997*, by K. Niblett (Stoke-on-Trent Museum, 1997). There is also a very active Royal Doulton International Collectors' Club which issues an informative magazine and specialist publications. Details of the club from Royal Doulton (UK) Ltd, Minton House, Stoke-on-Trent, Staffordshire.

## CHRISTOPHER DRESSER

Dr Christopher Dresser (1834–1904) was an important late Victorian designer. He produced novel ceramic forms for several pottery firms. His reproduced signature, usually impressed or moulded, adds considerably to the interest and value of even mass-produced articles.

Victoria Bergesen's *Encyclopaedia of British Art Pottery* (Barrie & Jenkins, 1991) gives basic information and details the many published references to his work.

## DUDSON

Various members of the Dudson family potted at Hanley from the 18th century onwards. Marked examples are, however, normally of a post-1850 date. The best known or traditional Dudson wares comprise various coloured fine stoneware type bodies decorated with sprigged relief motifs in the

Wedgwood style. These can be very attractive. Standard impressed marks incorporate the name 'Dudson' with or without 'Hanley'. However, many examples were not marked.

**DUDSON** c.1850–91

**DUDSON
ENGLAND** c.1891+

**DUDSON BROTHERS
ENGLAND** c.1900+

Later marks include:

c.1936–45

c.1945+

The Victorian Dudson wares are decorative and collectable but not unduly costly.

The standard reference book is *Dudson. A Family of Potters since 1800*, by Audrey M. Dudson (Dudson Publications, 1985). Typical Wedgwood-type wares are also featured in *British Pottery. An Illustrated Guide*, by G. Godden (Barrie & Jenkins, 1974), Plate 244. The present title is Dudson Brothers Ltd, specialists in durable Hotel wares.

# FALCON WARE

Like several trade-names 'Falcon' has been used by more than one firm. In this case we have J. H. Weatherby & Sons Ltd of the Falcon Pottery, Hanley (c.1891–present day) and Thomas Laurence Ltd, of the Falcon Pottery at Longton (c.1897–1962) which was continued by Shaw & Copestake (q.v.). The Falcon trade-name, however, probably dates from the 1920s. In 1990 a further complication arose when Ivan Dean established his Falcon China Ltd, at Longton.

In recent years the post-1920s Falcon wares have become collectable. The standard book covering all three above mentioned firms is *The Falcon Ware Story*, by Susan J. Verbeek (Pottery Publications, 1997).

# S. FIELDING & CO. (LTD)

Manufacturers of earthenware at Stoke, c.1879–1982. The trade-name 'Crown Devon' was introduced early in the 20th century, in succession to decorative lines termed 'Royal Windsor', 'Crown Chelsea' or 'Louis Ware'. It was initially associated with a decorative range of vellum-coloured fine quality earthenwares very much in the style of the popular Royal Worcester floral decorated wares.

Post-1891 printed mark, two of several, incorporating initials 'S. F. & Co.' The name 'Fielding' also occurs. Impressed month and year numerals can also occur.

Early printed 'Crown Devon' mark, c.1905–13.

Standard printed marks, c.1913–30.

Standard printed mark, c.1930–9 and 1945–50s.

The following two marks relate (with variations) to the 1950s up to the closure in 1982.

The second mark can occur with added wording 'Potters for over 200 years'. The impressed name 'FIELDING' also often occurs sometimes with date markings, the last two numerals indicating the year.

The 'Crown Devon' earthenwares have become collectable in recent years but only at a modest price range. The range of products made between about 1900 and 1982 was huge. For further information the reader is referred to *Crown Devon. History of S. Fielding & Co.*, by S. Hall (Jazz Publications, 1993) and to Ray Barker's *The Crown Devon Collectors Handbook* (Francis Joseph, 1997).

# G

## W. H. GOSS (LTD)
## (GOSS CHINA CO. LTD)

Manufacturers of porcelain, parian and earthenwares at Falcon Pottery, Stoke, c.1858–1939.

W. H. GOSS

Early impressed or printed marks incorporate the name or the initials 'W. H. G.', c.1858+.

W.H.GOSS.

Printed crest mark, with several slight variations, c.1862–1939.

Whilst the typical mass-produced Goss armorial trinkets featuring the arms or crest of various towns are collectable, the average price is not high. Various special books and price guides have been published. The more modern works include *William Henry Goss,* by L. & N. Pine (Milestone, 1986); *Price Guide to Arms & Decoration of Goss China,* by N. Pine (Milestone, 1990); *The Concise Encyclopaedia & Price Guide to Goss China,* by N. Pine (Milestone, 1992), with later revised editions or updates. A large selection of pieces can be seen at Nicholas Pine's private museum at Horndean, Hampshire. There are also Goss Collectors' Clubs. Doulton now own the Goss trade-name and some of the original pattern books. They have issued modern articles under the Goss name. Some early or special Goss wares and parian wares can be very desirable but by no means all specimens.

## GRAINGER-WORCESTER

Factory worked by Grainger, Wood & Co. (c.1801–12), by Grainger, Lee & Co. (c.1812–39) and by George Grainger (& Co.) (c.1839–1902) when the firm was taken over by the Royal Worcester Porcelain Co. Fine porcelains were produced. The name marks of the Grainger-Wood partnership are very rare.

**GRAINGER LEE & CO.**

Printed or painted name-marks in various forms, c.1812–39.

**G. GRAINGER**

Printed or painted name-marks in various forms, c.1839+.

**G. GRAINGER & CO.**

Printed or painted name-marks with '& Co.' added usually found after c.1850.

**G. G. W.**
**G. G.**

Initial marks in various forms, c.1839+.

Printed or impressed mark, c.1870–89.

Printed mark, c.1889–1902. 'England' added from 1891.

From 1891 to 1902 year letters A to L were added under the later shield marks, to indicate the year of production.

The Grainger-Worcester porcelains are of very good quality and the more important specimens are very collectable and may be costly. Typical specimens are on display in the Worcester works collection. The reader is also referred to the specialist work *Grainger's Worcester Porcelain* by Henry & John Sandon (Barrie & Jenkins, 1989). This work includes details of the factory shape and pattern books.

## A. E. GRAY & CO. LTD

Albert Edward Gray (1871–1959) established the Globe Pottery in Hanley in 1912. The company was mainly devoted to decorating and employed especially in the 1920s and 1930s a talented team of designers and decorators. The company moved to Stoke in about 1936 and continued to 1961. It was then acquired by Portmeirion Potteries Ltd.

The following printed marks were used.

c.1912–31          c.1931–4          c.1934–61

The Gray wares, both earthenware and porcelains, are typical of their period, they can be very smart and are probably undervalued today. In 1982 the Stoke City Museum mounted a splendid exhibition of Gray's Pottery and issued a helpful exhibition catalogue *Hand-Painted Gray's Pottery*. A revised booklet by P. Niblett was published in 1987. The City (now Potteries) Museum has a good collection of Gray's wares.

# H

## JAMES HADLEY & SONS (LTD)

Manufacturers of earthenware and porcelain at Worcester, c.1896–1905. James Hadley was formerly modeller to the Royal Worcester Porcelain Company; his signature may be found on some of their finest figures, groups, vases, etc., c.1875–94.

*Hadley*

The figures, groups and ornaments modelled by James Hadley for the Royal Worcester Company are of fine quality and are usually very desirable and costly. For this aspect of Hadley's work the reader should consult Henry Sandon's standard work *Royal Worcester Porcelain, from 1862 to the Present Day* (Barrie & Jenkins, 1973 and revisions).

Printed or impressed mark, 1896–7.

Printed mark, with variations, c.1897–1902.

Printed mark, 1902–5.

Early in July 1905 Hadley's private company was taken over and amalgamated with the Royal Worcester Company. Many old Hadley forms were continued and these usually include the name 'Hadley' or 'Hadley Ware'.

The Hadley wares of the 1896–1905 period are interesting and are of good quality. They seem rather neglected by most collectors of Worcester porcelains and consequently prices are in the medium range. Good specimens can be seen in the Worcester Works Museum. The reader is also referred to my *Illustrated Encyclopaedia of British Pottery and Porcelain* (Barrie & Jenkins, 1966) and to the *Encyclopaedia of British Porcelain Manufacturers* (Barrie & Jenkins, 1988).

## HERCULANEUM POTTERY

This Liverpool pottery, worked by various owners, produced high-grade earthenware and porcelain, c.1793–1841.

**HERCULANEUM**

Early impressed name-mark usually found on earthenwares and stonewares, very rarely found on porcelain, c.1793–1820.

Two printed or impressed marks, c.1796–1822.

Printed mark, with Liver-bird device, occurs on porcelains, c.1805–20.

**L**

A large impressed 'L' can occur on Herculaneum porcelains, c.1805–20.

**HERCULANEUM LIVERPOOL**

Full name-mark normally impressed, c.1822–33.

The rare and usually unmarked Herculaneum porcelains of the approximate period 1800–20 are very desirable. Unusual specimens will be costly. For further information see my *Encyclopaedia of British Porcelain Manufacturers* (Barrie & Jenkins, 1988). Representative examples of the pottery's varied productions – earthenwares, stonewares and porcelains – are on view in the City Museum & Art Gallery.

## ROBERT HERON (& SON)

Manufacturer of earthenwares. Took over the Fife Pottery, Sinclairtown, Scotland, by September 1837.

**R. H. F. P.**

Printed mark occurs incorporating these initials, c.1837–60.

**R. H. & S.**

**ROBERT HERON & SON**

Printed marks incorporating these initials or the name in full occur c.1850–1929.

**WEMYSS**

Trade name 'Wemyss' or 'Wemyss Ware' on decorative, freely-decorated earthenwares, c.1880 into the 20th century.

Printed mark, c.1920–9. The decorative 'Wemyss' wares often also bear the mark of Goode's, the London retailers.

Whilst the standard Heron earthenwares are not distinguished, the boldly-painted Wemyss wares bearing this trade-name are collectable and can be costly. Specialist books illustrate and discuss these usually

20th-century wares, see *Wemyss Ware 1880–1930*, by R. de Rin (Sotheby's, 1978) or *Wemyss Ware*, by V. de Rin (Scottish Academic Press, 1986). Victoria Bergesen's *Encyclopaedia of British Art Pottery* (Barrie & Jenkins, 1991) also has a helpful entry under 'Fife Pottery'. The reader is warned that later Wemyss-styled wares have been produced and these can bear the Wemyss name.

## HICKS & MEIGH (HICKS, MEIGH & JOHNSON)

Manufacturers of earthenwares, 'Stone China', etc., at Shelton in the Staffordshire Potteries, c.1804–22. Subsequently Hicks, Meigh & Johnson, c.1822–35.

Sample printed Royal Arms marks found on fine-quality Hicks & Meigh's 'Stone China', c.1804–22. The pattern number under the basic mark varies.

H. M. J.
H. M. & J.
H. M. & I.

Rare Hicks, Meigh & Johnson marks, 1822–35.

Although these two partnerships are mainly known for their high-quality and colourful 'Stone China' wares, good earthenwares and mainly unmarked porcelains were also produced. These are all collectable and can be costly depending on their decorative merits. For further information see *Staffordshire Porcelain* (1983), Chapter 17; *Encyclopaedia of British Porcelain Manufacturers* (1988); and specialist books on ironstone-type wares.

# J

## GEORGE JONES (& SONS LTD)

Manufacturers of decorative earthenwares and majolica-style wares at Stoke, c.1861–1951. Porcelain produced from 1872.

Distinguishing monogram found on several relief, impressed or printed marks, c.1861 to late 1873 when '& Sons' was added to marks.

Printed or impressed mark, c.1874–1924. 'England' was added from 1891. 'Crescent China' may occur under mark from c.1893.

Printed or impressed mark, c.1924–51.

George Jones products are usually of good quality and are decorative. Examples are collectable, especially the finer majolica-type colour-glazed earthenwares. Such wares are featured in books on majolica (see Pictorial Glossary). George Jones also produced decorative essays in the Pâte-sur-Pâte technique. The reader is also referred to Godden's *Illustrated Encyclopaedia of British Pottery and Porcelain* or *Staffordshire Porcelain* (1983). The specialist book is *George Jones Ceramics*, by Robert Cluett (Schiffer Publishing, USA, 1998).

# L

## BERNARD LEACH

The Leach Pottery was established by Bernard Leach, CBE (1887–1979), at St Ives, Cornwall, in 1921. At this famous pottery a number of talented studio potters have been trained and have helped to extend the Leach Pottery tradition for fine craftsmanship and good design.

Basic Leach Pottery squared, or circular, impressed seal, c.1921+. The monogram or sign of individual potters often occurs with this mark. This is the standard St Ives seal-mark, not that of individual potters. It occurs on standard tablewares as well as on individual pieces.

Individual painted or incised initial marks used by Bernard Leach, c.1921–79.

Genuine individual pots by Bernard Leach are very sought after and will be costly. Hence some copies have been produced, mainly after the master's death in 1979.

All books on Studio Pottery will feature Leach's work and that of his talented team of potters who worked at the Leach Pottery from time to time. The reader is referred also to the *Encyclopaedia of British Porcelain Manufacturers* and to the host of specialist books which include *The Art of Bernard Leach*, by C. Hogben (Faber & Faber, 1978); *Bernard Leach*.

*Beyond East & West*, by B. Leach (Faber & Faber, 1978); *B. Leach, Hamada & Their Circle*, by T. Birks & C. W. Digby (Phaidon/Christie's, 1990); and *The Leach Legacy. St Ives Pottery and its Legacy*, by M. Whybrow (Sansom & Co., 1996).

## LEEDS POTTERY

This famous Yorkshire pottery produced a wide range of earthenwares, creamware, basalt, etc., under various proprietorships from c.1758 to c.1878. The early pre-c.1775 wares appear to have been unmarked.

LEEDS POTTERY     Standard impressed mark in upper or lower case letters, c.1775–1800+: this style of mark is sometimes stamped twice, one at right angles to the other. It should be noted that this mark is quite rare on genuine pieces but it appears on a host of later pieces made in the old style.

Readers should consult standard specialist reference books such as *Creamware*, by D. Towner (Faber & Faber, 1978); *The Leeds Pottery*, by D. Towner (Cory, Adams & Mackay, 1963); and the Northern Ceramic Society's 1986 exhibition catalogue *Creamware and Pearlware* (City Museum, Stoke-on-Trent), or buy from knowledgeable sources! The Leeds Pottery is mainly known for its often pierced creamware but various other types of ceramic were produced, see G. Godden's *An Illustrated Encyclopaedia of British Pottery and Porcelain* (1966); typical 20th-century reproductions are shown on Plates 346–8. Genuine, preferably marked, Leeds pottery is very collectable but need not be that costly – especially for standard specimens such as creamware plates. The reader should be aware that a current firm the 'Leedsware Pottery Co. Ltd', of Burslem, produces a wide range of old-style Leeds-type creamware. Such decorative, but non-antique, items are widely available.

## WILLIAM LITTLER

William Littler potted at Longton Hall in the Staffordshire Potteries in the 1749–60 period. He subsequently moved to West Pans, near Musselburgh, in Scotland and produced similar types of porcelain, within the approximate period 1764–77, before moving back to Staffordshire.

The often hastily painted blue so-called 'crossed Ls' mark, versions of which are here shown, was formerly believed to relate to Littler's Longton Hall period. Present thinking is that this mark was used at West Pans (c.1764–77), not at Longton Hall.

Littler's porcelains, especially the earlier Longton Hall pieces, are very collectable and can be costly. However, no true Longton Hall mark was used. The reader is referred to G. Godden's *Encyclopaedia of British Porcelain Manufacturers* (1988) and to *Digging for Early Porcelain*, edited by D. Barker and S. Cole (City Museum, Stoke-on-Trent, 1998).

## LIVERPOOL

This was one of the centres of the pottery trade in the 18th and early part of the 19th centuries. Tin-glazed delft-type pottery as well as cream-coloured earthenwares and porcelain were produced by several manufacturers but, as a general rule, the Liverpool wares are unmarked.

J. Sadler

Sadler
Liverpool

John Sadler and the firm of Sadler & Green printed earthenwares and porcelain made by other manufacturers from c.1756, and signatures occur on some of these printed motifs.

The early Liverpool pieces are very collectable, at least to specialist collectors, and unusual examples are in demand. As several potters were involved and as the wares were in general unmarked, I can in this Handbook only refer the reader to the now rather outdated *The Illustrated Guide to Liverpool Herculaneum Pottery*, by A. Smith (Barrie & Jenkins, 1970), which contains some information on 18th-century specimens, and Dr Bernard Watney's more recent specialist book *Liverpool Porcelain of the Eighteenth Century* (Richard Dennis, 1997).

## LOCKE & CO. (LTD)

Manufacturers of porcelain at Worcester, c.1896–1915.

Early examples of the approximate period 1896–8 may bear written or impressed name marks, such as: Locke & Co. Worcester.

Standard printed mark, c.1896–98. 'Ltd' added below 'Locke & Co.', c.1898–1902.

Standard printed mark, 1902–15.

Whilst Locke-Worcester porcelains are interesting and collectable the general price range is not as high as for Royal Worcester, or for George Grainger pieces. The works were, however, on a small scale and examples are by no means common. Some better than average examples are shown in my 1966 book

*An Illustrated Encyclopaedia of British Pottery and Porcelain*, Plates 355–6. An interesting booklet by L. H. Harris and T. Willis was issued by the Dyson Perrins Museum at Worcester in connection with an 1989 exhibition of Locke's porcelains.

## LOWESTOFT PORCELAIN FACTORY

Charming porcelains painted in underglaze blue were made at this small factory at Lowestoft, Suffolk, c.1757–99. Overglaze enamel colours were used from c.1770 but the blue and white specimens outnumber the coloured pieces. The body is soft paste containing bone ash and similar to that used at the Bow factory. Most products are of a useful nature, teawares, etc., rather than ornamental.

Whilst most Lowestoft is unmarked some underglaze blue examples made before about 1775 can bear a painter's number, usually placed on the inside of a footrim, rather than in the middle of the base. Of these numbers 3 and 5 are the most common. Being individually painted they can vary in their rendering but typical examples are shown.

A copy of the Worcester crescent mark can occur on Lowestoft porcelains decorated in the Worcester style. The crescent may be open (no cross-hatching or shading) or shaded (on printed designs). Copies of the Dresden crossed swords mark can also occur on German-styled designs.

**A TRIFLE FROM LOWESTOFT**

The inscription 'A Trifle from Lowestoft' can occur on some later pieces – mugs, etc. The Trifles are normally decorated with simple enamelled designs. Many (now old) reproductions of these Trifle inscribed pieces were later made on the Continent. They therefore tend to be of hard-paste porcelain.

Lowestoft porcelains are very collectable. Specimens (other than the more ordinary items) tend to be costly, the inscribed and dated pieces, extremely so!

As the majority of genuine Lowestoft soft-paste porcelain is unmarked, the reader needs to consult specialist well-illustrated reference books. These include *Lowestoft Porcelain in Norwich Castle Museum*, by S. Smith (2 vols, Norwich Museum Service, 1975 & 1985); *Early Lowestoft*, by C. Spencer (Ainsworth & Nelson, 1981); *Lowestoft Porcelains*, by G. Godden (Antique Collectors' Club, 1985); and *Variety in Lowestoft Porcelain*, by M. Corson (Lilac, 1992). In addition various learned papers have been published on different aspects of Lowestoft porcelain, see my *Encyclopaedia of British Porcelain Manufacturers* (1988).

# M

## JAMES MACINTYRE & CO.

Manufacturers of earthenware at Burslem, c.1860–1928+.

**MACINTYRE**

Several early impressed or printed marks occur incorporating the name with or without the initial 'J'. '& Co.' was added to name-marks from 1867.

Post-1894 printed mark with word 'Limited' or 'Ltd' added. Since 1928 only electrical wares have been produced.

An 1888 advertisement showing typical wares is reproduced in the *Illustrated Encyclopaedia of British Pottery and Porcelain*, Plate 365. See also Victoria Bergesen's *Encyclopaedia of British Art Pottery* (Barrie & Jenkins, 1991) and books on Moorcroft, see below.

Although the standard Macintyre wares are of good quality and are of interest, the main importance to collectors is that William Moorcroft designed and carried out work for this company before setting up his own factory. Pieces bearing a Macintyre mark or name along with a Moorcroft signature are very desirable.

## C. T. MALING & SONS (LTD)

Maling, Newcastle-upon-Tyne earthenwares can date back to the early part of the 19th century but much later specimens have become collectable within recent years, although at modest prices. I reproduce here some of the standard marks, although some patterns or types have their own marks all incorporating the name 'Maling'. Production ceased in 1963.

c.1875–1908                c.1908–24                c.1924+

With recent interest in these Newcastle earthenwares much research has been carried out and the reader is referred to specialist paperback books, such as *Maling. A Tyneside Pottery*, published without credit to an author by Tyne & Wear Museums (1981); *Maling and other Tyneside Pottery*, by R. C. Bell (Shire Publications, 1986); and *Maling. The Trade Mark of Excellence*, by S. Moore & C. Ross (Tyne & Wear Museums, revised 1992 edition).

## MARTIN BROTHERS
The first of the British 'Studio Potters' working together making individually designed stonewares at Fulham and Southall, London, c.1873–1914.

Incised or stamped signature mark with address 'FULHAM', 1873–4.

R. W. MARTIN
LONDON

Incised mark with address 'LONDON', c.1874–8.

SOUTHALL

Various incised or stamped signature marks with address 'SOUTHALL', c.1878–9.

**LONDON &
SOUTHALL**

Signature marks with double address 'LONDON & SOUTHALL' date from 1879.

**BROS
BROTHERS**

From 1882 'BROS' or 'BROTHERS' added to standard signature 'R. W. MARTIN'.

Most Martin Brothers stoneware bears the incised date near the signature mark.

Individual 'Martinware' stonewares are very collectable and good specimens will be costly, especially the famous bird-like pots with loose covers. However, some fakes occur with mock Martin Brothers marks. Various books include illustrations of the brothers at work and their typical pots. See my *Illustrated Encyclopaedia of British Pottery and Porcelain*, Plates 374–8 and more modern specialist works such as *The Martin Brothers Potters*, by M. Haslam (R. Dennis, 1978) and Richard Dennis's 1978 exhibition catalogue. Victoria Bergesen's extremely helpful *Encyclopaedia of British Art Pottery* (Barrie and Jenkins, 1991) is also of value, giving many references to articles and papers on the work of the Martin Brothers.

## MASON

A family of potters trading under various styles (see below) at Lane Delph and Fenton from c.1800 to c.1854. Charles James Mason patented the famous 'PATENT IRONSTONE CHINA' in 1813.

**M. MASON**

Standard impressed mark on porcelain made by Miles Mason, c.1800–13. Specimens are rather rare and collectable and important pieces can be costly.

MILES

MASON

Printed mark on blue printed porcelain of willow-pattern type, c.1805–13.

**PATENT IRONSTONE CHINA**

Impressed mark in various forms with or without the name 'MASON'S', c.1813+.

Standard printed mark on Mason Ironstone wares from c.1815. Very many variations of this mark occur and some have been used by Mason's Ironstone China Ltd, the present owners of many of the original Mason models and patterns.

**G. & C. J. M.**

Several printed marks were used in the 1813–29 period incorporating the initials 'G. & C. J. Mason'.

**C. J. MASON & CO.**
**C. J. M. & Co.**

Many marks were used in the 1829–45 period, incorporating the new style 'C. J. Mason & Co.' or the initials 'C. J. M. & Co'. From 1845 to 1848 and from c.1851 to 1854 Charles Mason traded on his own (without the '& Co.'): the former standard printed 'Mason's Patent Ironstone China' mark was much used.

The Mason patterns, moulds, etc., passed through several firms to G. L. Ashworth & Bros in 1861 and this firm was retitled Mason's Ironstone China Ltd in 1968. It is now part of the Wedgwood group and production continues of traditional old Mason shapes and patterns. Modern versions of the old Mason's Patent Ironstone mark will include 'England' or 'Made in England'. Also a © or ® and probably modern wording relating to the name of the pattern. None of these features occurs on pre-Ashworth products made before the 1850s.

Miles Mason wares and the earlier ironstone wares are highly collectable, especially rare shapes or important specimens.

Several specialist books give good details of the varied Mason products, including *Mason Porcelain & Ironstone 1796–1853*, by R. Haggar & E. Adams

(Faber & Faber, 1977); *Godden's Guide to Mason's China and the Ironstone Wares* (Antique Collectors' Club, 1980); *Mason, a Family of Potters*, by D. Skinner (City Museum & Art Gallery, Stoke-on-Trent, 1982); *Miles Mason Porcelain, a Guide to Patterns and Shapes*, by D. Skinner & V. Young (City Museum & Art Gallery, Stoke-on-Trent, 1992); *Mason's. The First Two Hundred Years*, by G. B. Roberts (Merrell Holperton, 1996); *The Raven Mason Collection at Keele University*, edited by G. B. Roberts and J. Twitchett (Keele University Press, 1997); and *Godden's Guide to Ironstone, Stone and Granite Wares* (Antique Collectors' Club, 1999). Collections of typical Mason wares can be seen at The Potteries Museum in Hanley and at the University of Keele (by prior arrangement). Specialist dealers also stock and exhibit a good range of Mason wares.

## JOHN MEIR & SON

Manufacturers of earthenwares at Tunstall, c.1837–97. Formerly John Meir (c.1812–36). The Meir earthenwares are typical of the middle range of Staffordshire earthenwares. They may be decorative but they are not especially valued. Many were exported.

**J. MEIR & SON**

**J. M. & SON**

**J. M. & S.**

Several different impressed or printed marks occur consisting of, or incorporating, these names or initials, c.1837–97. The initial 'I' sometimes replaces the 'J'. A typical printed mark is also reproduced.

## W. R. MIDWINTER (LTD)

Although the Midwinter pottery was established at Burslem in 1910, it is the later, post-war, modern-style wares that are most collectable. Various printed marks have been used, all featuring the Midwinter surname. The marks here reproduced are merely samples, as different patterns or forms, such as 'Stylecraft', will have their own individual marks. These can include month and year markings as '5. 62' for May 1962. Since 1970 W. R. Midwinter Ltd has been part of the Wedgwood group, although the Midwinter Pottery was closed in 1987.

c.1930–41          c.1953+          c.1950–87

Whilst Midwinter wares have become popular and collectable, standard patterns will not command high prices. Recent specialist books contain a wealth of information on the contemporary and standard Midwinter forms, patterns and designers. These works include *Midwinter. A Collectors' Guide*, by A. Peat (Cameron & Hollis, 1992) and *Midwinter Pottery. A Revolution in British Tableware*, by S. Jenkins (R. Dennis, 1997).

## MINTON

Important manufacturer of porcelain and various types of earthenware at Stoke-on-Trent, under several different partnerships, as listed, 1793 to present day as part of the Doulton Group.

The early earthenwares and pre-1805 porcelains were apparently unmarked. The porcelains may bear pattern numbers that can in some cases be checked with the surviving pattern books.

Painted mark on porcelain, normally in overglaze blue enamel, found with or without pattern number, c.1805–16, mark rather rare.

There was a gap in the production of porcelain between c.1816 and 1824.

Minton porcelains and earthenwares of the approximate period 1824–40 are largely unmarked.

The Dresden crossed-swords mark occurs in underglaze blue on a class of floral-encrusted Minton porcelain of the 1820s. This mock Dresden device can, however, appear on many other types of ceramics.

Several different printed marks of the 1820s and 1830s incorporate the initial 'M'.

Many printed marks of the MINTON & BOYLE period (c.1836–41) incorporate the initials 'M. & B.'

Many different marks of the 1841–73 period incorporate or comprise the initials 'M. & Co.', for MINTON & CO.

**M. & H.**

Many different printed marks of the MINTON & HOLLINS period (c.1845–68) incorporate the initials 'M. & H.'

**B. B.
NEW STONE**

Impressed mark on earthenwares, c.1830–60.

Incised mark found on Minton parian figures and groups, c.1845–60.

Painted or printed ermine device found on fine Minton porcelains, c.1850–70. A similar incised mark occurs on parian and other figures from about 1845.

**MINTON**

**MINTONS**

The name 'Minton' occurs incorporated in many printed marks from 1851 onwards. The basic impressed mark from 1862 to 1872 was the word 'MINTON', and 'S' was added from 1873 so that the post-1873 basic mark was 'MINTONS'.

Standard printed mark, c.1863–72.

Revised basic printed mark with crown above, c.1873–1912. The word 'England' added from 1891.

Basic printed mark, c.1912–50, often with 'Made in England' added below.

New printed trade-mark introduced in 1951. The words 'Bone China. Made in England', may occur under this mark.

**MINTON CHINA**

Impressed mark on porcelain blanks from c.1951 onwards.

**ROYAL DOULTON**

Since 1968 newly engraved marks usually incorporate the Doulton name with the date of introduction of that pattern and the © copyright device.

Minton porcelains are always of high quality. They are very collectable but values depend on many features, age, rarity, condition, type of body, quality of decoration, etc.

Various specialist books and the better general works illustrate a good range of the very varied Minton products. These include my *Minton Pottery and Porcelain of the First Period 1793–1850* (Barrie & Jenkins, 1978); *The Dictionary of Minton*, by P. Atterbury & M. Batkin (Antique Collectors' Club, 1990); *Minton The First Two Hundred Years of Design and Production*, by Joan Jones (Swan Hill Press, 1993); *Regency Minton Porcelain*, by D. Langford (Canterbury Ceramic Circle, 1997); and *Minton Patterns of the First Period c.1796 to 1816* by R. Cumming & M. Berthoud (Micawber, 1997). More specialist publications are cited in my *Encyclopaedia of British Porcelain Manufacturers* (Barrie & Jenkins, 1988). Other aspects of Minton's wares are represented in books on Majolica and on Pâte-sur-Pâte decoration – see the Pictorial Glossary.

## TABLE OF YEAR CYPHERS FOUND IMPRESSED IN THE BODY OF MINTON WARES, SHOWING THE DATE OF PRODUCTION

## MINTON'S ART POTTERY STUDIO

This short-lived venture was established by Mintons of Stoke, at Kensington Gore in London, near the Royal Albert Hall, c.1871–5. It aroused great interest at the time as 'educated women, of good social position, were employed (with some male artists) to decorate blanks sent down from Stoke. The experiment was initially under the direction of the well-known artist, designer, and illustrator W. S. Coleman.

This special printed mark was added to the impressed-marked Minton pottery blanks, c.1871–5.

These 'Art Pottery' Minton wares are interesting and collectable. Good, decorative, examples are in demand and may be costly – in Art Pottery terms. An outline of the enterprise was given in my pioneer book *Victorian Porcelain* (1961) but Victoria Bergesen's *Encyclopaedia of British Art Pottery* (Barrie & Jenkins, 1991) gives an excellent and full account with details of the many artists employed by Mintons at their London Art Pottery Studio.

## W. MOORCROFT (LTD)

Manufacturers of earthenwares, normally decorated with bold floral designs, at Burslem (Cobridge), c.1913 to present day. Various changes of ownership and title (now Moorcroft Plc) have occurred in post-war years.

William Moorcroft (1872–1945) had earlier designed for and worked for James Macintyre (q.v.). These pre-1913 pieces can also bear his signature mark.

**MOORCROFT
BURSLEM**

Standard impressed mark, c.1915+. Modern wares can have the wording 'Made in England' added.

Signature marks also occur. The initials 'W. M.' occur on some examples. Walter Moorcroft succeeded his father William in 1945. The J. Moorcroft signature dates from c.1990.

Moorcroft wares, particularly the earlier examples, have become very collectable and rare or important specimens can be very costly. Various specialist books have been published including *Moorcroft Pottery*, by P. Atterbury (R. Dennis, 1979); *Moorcroft. A Guide to Moorcroft Pottery 1897–1990*, by P. Atterbury (R. Dennis, revised edition, 1993); *Collecting Moorcroft*, by F. Salmon (K. Francis, 1994); and *Moorcroft, The Phoenix Years*, by F. Street (W. M. Publications, 1997).

## MOORE BROS
Manufacturers of decorative porcelains at Longton, c.1870–1905. The firm was continued by Bernard Moore, c.1905–15. In this later period good glaze-effects were produced.

**MOORE**

**MOORE BROS**

Standard impressed marks, c.1870–1905. The word 'England' also occurs from 1891.

Standard printed mark, c.1880–1902. With 'England' from 1891.

Rather rare printed mark, c.1902–5.

Painted or stencilled name-mark on Bernard Moore's Chinese-styled glaze-effects, c.1905–15. A BM initial monogram also occurs.

The cactus, hop or lily relief-decorated Moore porcelains are very popular but good examples of Bernard Moore glaze-effects can also be very desirable. The reader is referred to *Bernard Moore, Master Potter 1850–1935*, by A. Dawson (R. Dennis, 1982).

# N

## NANTGARW PORCELAIN WORKS

Situated at Nantgarw, Glamorgan, Wales, where fine-quality, highly translucent, mellow porcelain was made c.1813–14 and c.1817–22.

NANTGARW

NANT-GARW
C. W.

Standard impressed marks, which are often difficult to see, unless the porcelain is held to a light. The name occurs with, or without, a hyphen.

Painted name-mark in writing letters which should be viewed with great caution, as this overglaze mark is often added to Coalport and other porcelains.

Nantgarw porcelain is rare and highly collectable. Good well-decorated examples, especially when painted by leading decorators, can be costly. The reader is warned that fakes occur and not all porcelain attributed to Nantgarw was necessarily made there! For further information and illustrations, see *The Pottery and Porcelain of Swansea and Nantgarw*, by E. M. Nance (Batsford, 1942); *Nantgarw Porcelain*, by W. D. John (R. H. John, 1948); and *Nantgarw Porcelain 1813–1822*, by R. Williams (Friends of Nantgarw China Works Museum, 1993).

## JAMES NEALE & CO.

Manufacturers of high grade, Wedgwood-type earthenware – creamware, basalt, jasper – and rarely porcelain at Hanley, c.1776–92. Robert Wilson (Neale's partner) succeeded from April 1792 but the old Neale marks may have been continued for a few years. Many specimens were, however, unmarked.

**NEALE & PALMER**

Rare impressed mark used by this early partnership, c.1769–76.

Rare circular impressed or moulded mark on Wedgwood-type black basalt vases, etc., c.1776–80.

**NEALE**

**NEALE & CO.**

**NEALE & WILSON**

Impressed name marks usually found on good quality earthenwares and rare porcelains, c.1776–92.

The attractive and rather rare Neale wares are very collectable, although not excessively expensive. For further information see Diana Edwards's specialist work *Neale Pottery and Porcelain* (Barrie & Jenkins, 1987), and for the porcelains, Chapter 4 of *Staffordshire Porcelain*.

## NEW HALL PORCELAIN WORKS

Worked by several partners and changing partnerships at Shelton from c.1781 to 1835. The early pre-1814 products are a type of hybrid hard-paste porcelain; from c.1814 to 1835 the then standard English bone china was made.

The early porcelains do not bear a factory mark, but the pattern number can be painted on teapots, creamers, etc. (not on cups and saucers) from about 1788 onwards. The pattern was usually painted in larger-sized numerals than on other porcelains. Such numbers can occur with a 'No.' or 'N' prefix or without any prefix. Of course, other firms also used similar pattern numbers so these are only helpful when one knows that the number correctly relates to the patterns. A basic list of New Hall numbers is given by David Holgate in his contribution to *Staffordshire Porcelain* (1983); see also *A Guide to New Hall*

*N 273*

*Porcelain Patterns*, by A. de Saye Hutton (Barrie & Jenkins, 1990).

Painted decorator's (?) sign, found on some otherwise unmarked New Hall porcelain of the 1800–15 period.

**WARBURTON'S PATENT**

Rare painted mark found on New Hall (hybrid hard-paste) porcelains, printed with gold, c.1810–14.

Printed mark, rather occasionally used on New Hall bone china wares, c.1814–20. Later wares of the 1820–35 period are unmarked, except in some cases for pattern numbers which climbed up into the 3,000 range.

New Hall porcelains are very collectable and rare unrecorded patterns or shapes will be costly. Initially New Hall was popular because it was available and inexpensive. Neither of these conditions now applies and many pieces traditionally attributed to the New Hall partnerships are now believed to have been produced by other firms: New Hall being the market-leader, with many followers – all producing unmarked wares. Consequently these porcelains of the c.1781–1820 period are the subject of learned research and endless debate!

The reader is referred to specialist works such as *New Hall & its Imitators*, by D. Holgate (Faber & Faber, 1971); *Staffordshire Porcelain* (1983); *New Hall*, by D. Holgate (Faber & Faber, 1987), and *A Guide to New Hall Porcelain Patterns*, by A. de Saye Hutton (Barrie & Jenkins, 1990). Details of the various and changing partnerships are given in my *Encyclopaedia of British Porcelain Manufacturers* (Barrie & Jenkins, 1988).

# P

## PILKINGTON'S POTTERY (ROYAL LANCASTRIAN)

Pilkington's Tile & Pottery Co. Ltd commenced the manufacture of ornamental wares, vases, etc. in about 1897. Until March 1938 decorative lustre effects were produced often with individual motifs designed by leading artists and designers.

Standard impressed mark, c.1904–14. Roman numerals found below this mark show the year of production, e.g. 'VII' for 1907.

Standard impressed mark, c.1914–35. The words 'England' or 'Made in England' also occur.

The stencilled marks of the various designers and artists are also found on Pilkington's wares; the key to these is given in the *Encyclopaedia of British Pottery and Porcelain Marks* (1964).

The 'Royal Lancastrian' wares, especially the lustre-effects, are very collectable and can be costly, but the technique gives rise to very variable results and care should be taken in choosing pleasing top-quality examples. For further information, see *Pilkington's Royal Lancastrian Pottery & Tiles*, by A. J. Cross (R. Dennis, 1980). Victoria Bergesen's *Encyclopaedia of British Art Pottery* (Barrie & Jenkins, 1991) is also extremely helpful.

## PINXTON

A porcelain factory was established at Pinxton in Derbyshire by John Coke (a local landowner) and William Billingsley (a talented ex-Derby ceramic decorator) in 1796. Billingsley left for Mansfield in 1799 but the Pinxton factory was continued for a number of years, mainly, I believe, as a decorating establishment. Most Pinxton porcelain is unmarked and bears a close likeness, in body, form and styles of decoration, to the contemporary Derby porcelain.

*Pinxton.*

Very rare painted or gilt name-mark in writing letters, c.1796–1805.

*P108*

The painted initial 'P' rarely occurs, sometimes preceding the pattern number, different numbers occurring on each pattern.

**A (etc)**

Printer's type letters can occur impressed into the body, as at Derby.

Pinxton porcelain is rare, having been produced for a relatively short period. The best pieces and the rarer, ornamental, shapes will be costly. The attribution of the unmarked Pinxton porcelains is mainly linked to the knowledge of the body and glaze, plus reference to known patterns and pattern numbers and the key shapes. Recent specialist books give a good guide to shapes and typical patterns, in particular *The Patterns and Shapes of the Pinxton China Factory 1796–1813*, by N. D. Gent (privately published, 1996) and *Pinxton Porcelain 1795–1813*, by C. Barry Sheppard (privately published, 1996). Typical specimens can also be seen at the Victoria & Albert Museum, at the Usher Gallery at Lincoln and at the Derby Museum.

## PLYMOUTH PORCELAIN FACTORY

Hard-paste porcelain was made under William Cookworthy's proprietorship at Plymouth, Devon, c.1768–70. Hard-paste Plymouth porcelain is rare, desirable and costly. It follows that fakes and reproductions have been produced. Some are antique (but not genuine) in their own right.

**MR. WM. COOKWORTHY'S FACTORY. PLYMOUTH.**

Very rare or unique inscription mark, in writing letters, on a sauce boat in the Plymouth Museum and Art Gallery. Included in the *Illustrated Encyclopaedia of British Pottery and Porcelain* (1966), Plate 463. Fakes can bear similar inscriptions.

Standard, but rare, painted mark in underglaze blue or overglaze enamel, c.1768–70.

For further information and illustrations, see *Cookworthy's Plymouth and Bristol Porcelain*, by F. Severne Mackenna (F. Lewis, 1946); *English Blue and White Porcelain*, by B. Watney (Faber & Faber, 1963); *English Porcelain 1745–1850*, edited by R. J. Charleston (Benn, 1965); *Illustrated Encyclopaedia of British Pottery and Porcelain* (1966); and my *Encyclopaedia of British Porcelain Manufacturers* (Barrie & Jenkins, 1988). Typical specimens can be seen in the Victoria & Albert Museum and in the Plymouth Museum collection.

## POOLE POTTERY

Manufactured originally by Carter, Stabler & Adams (Ltd) at Poole, Dorset, from 1921 to the present day. The Pottery is open to visitors on the Quayside at Poole in Dorset and there is now a Poole Pottery Collectors Club, centred on the factory.

Standard impressed or printed name-mark, with or without border lines, c.1921+. A variation with the firm's name above also occurs, with 'Ltd' after 1925.

**POOLE**

**ENGLAND**

Printed trade-mark, c.1950–6.

Poole

English Fine
Bone China

Revised printed mark, c.1956+. Various modern wording such as 'oven tableware' can occur with this and similar Poole marks.

Poole
Studio.

New description introduced c.1963, when new title Poole Pottery Ltd was adopted.

Poole
English Fine
Bone China.

Various printed 'Fine Bone China' marks introduced in 1983.

Poole pottery is very fashionable and collectable but desirability and therefore value varies greatly. Readers are recommended to consult up-to-date specialist works such as *The Poole Potteries*, by J. Hawkins (Barrie & Jenkins, 1980); *Poole Pottery, Carter & Co. and their Successors 1873–1995*, by L. Hayward (R. Dennis, 1995); and *Poole Pottery. Poole in the 1950s*, by P. Atterbury (R. Dennis, 1997).

## F. & R. PRATT

Manufacturers of earthenwares at Fenton, c.1818, continued into 20th century. This Staffordshire firm is best known for its high-quality Victorian multi-colour printing from sets of copper-plates, engraved by Jesse Austin. This technique, perfected by 1851, is widely known from the long series of pot-lid designs. However, the firm produced many other types of ceramics including good terra-cotta.

**F. & R. P.**
**F. & R. P. & Co.**

Several different printed marks occur, incorporating these initials, c.1818–50. '& Co.' added c.1840. These initial marks mainly occur on single-colour printed wares.

**PRATT**
**FENTON.**

F. & R. PRATT & Co.
FENTON

Printed marks occurring, rather rarely, on the colour-printed earthenwares of pot-lid type, for which this firm is famous. These marks generally appear only on later examples, often of 20th-century date. Most multicolour printed wares were unmarked and by no means all pot-lids and related pieces were made by Pratts.

Pot-lids and other multicolour printed wares are very collectable and later reproductions or reissues abound. Rare subjects and uncommon shapes can be costly. Several general and specialist books give information and illustrate typical specimens. To date, the most helpful is the late A. Ball's *The Price Guide to Pot-Lids and other Underglaze Multicolour Prints on Ware* (Antique Collectors' Club, 2nd edition, 1980). The Potteries Museum at Hanley houses an interesting collection. There is also a 'Pot Lid Circle' which publishes newsletters and holds meetings. Specialist sales are conducted by various auctioneers featuring Pratt-type wares.

# R

## SAMUEL & JOHN RATHBONE

Manufacturers of porcelains and probably earthenwares at Tunstall, c.1812–35.

Printed mark, usually in underglaze blue, c.1812–35.

S. & J. R.

S. J. R.

Initials incorporated in various marks, c.1812–35.

For details of these reattributed marks the reader is referred to *Staffordshire Porcelain* (1983) and the *Encyclopaedia of British Porcelain Manufacturers* (Barrie & Jenkins, 1988). The Rathbone porcelains are interesting but not especially valuable.

## RIDGWAY

The various Ridgway partnerships centred on the Cauldon Place Pottery at Shelton (Hanley) in the Staffordshire Potteries are of interest and importance. The various periods from c.1802 onwards are here treated separately. For further information and illustrations of typical wares the reader is referred to G. Godden's standard work *Ridgway Porcelains* (Antique Collectors' Club, 1985) or to *Staffordshire Porcelain*.

## Job Ridgway (& Sons)

**I. RIDGWAY**

Very rare impressed mark, c.1802–8.

**RIDGWAY & SONS**

Rare impressed mark found on some early porcelains, c.1808–13.

### J. & W. Ridgway

From 1813 to 1830 Job's two sons John and William Ridgway traded together at Cauldon Place, producing a wide variety of earthenwares and porcelains.

**J. & W. RIDGWAY.**
**J.& W. R.**
**J. W. R.**
**I. & W. R.**
**I. W. R.**

Various printed or rarely impressed name or initial marks as used in the 1813–30 period. Note the 'J' was often rendered as an 'I' at this period.

In 1830 the two brothers separated, John continued the Cauldon Place Works to 1855 and William Ridgway worked the Bell Works (and other factories) at Shelton (see below).

### John Ridgway (& Co.)

Manufacturer of fine porcelain and earthenwares at Cauldon Place, Shelton, c.1830–55, in succession to J. & W. Ridgway.

**J. R.**
**I. R.**
**JOHN RIDGWAY**

Several printed marks occur incorporating the initials 'J. R.' (or 'I. R.') or the name 'John Ridgway', c.1830–41. The basic mark is the Royal Arms with the initials worked in the ribbon under; two specimen marks are reproduced.

**J. R. & Co**   Similar initial or name-marks with the addition of '& Co.' occur, c.1841–55.

John Ridgway & Co. was succeeded by JOHN RIDGWAY, BATES & CO., c.1856–58, then BATES, BROWN-WESTHEAD, MOORE & CO., c.1859–61, then BROWN-WESTHEAD, MOORE & CO., c.1862–1904 (q.v.); initial and name-marks were used by these different firms.

The Ridgway wares, particularly the J. & W. Ridgway and the John Ridgway wares, are collectable and of a general high quality. Commercial value depends on the object or on the quality of the decoration, the porcelains being in higher regard than the earthenwares.

**William Ridgway (& Co.)**
Manufacturers of earthenwares of various types at Bell Works, Shelton, and Church Works, Hanley, c.1830–54. Also traded under other styles.

**W. R.**
**W. RIDGWAY**   Several printed or impressed marks, incorporating these initials or the name, c.1830–4.

**W. R. & Co.**
**W. RIDGWAY & CO.**   Several printed or impressed marks occur from c.1834 to 1854; note the addition of '& Co.'

**W. R. S. & Co.**   From c.1838 to 1848 the firm of WILLIAM RIDGWAY, SON & CO. worked the Church Works and the Cobden Works (c.1841–6); the initials were incorporated in several printed marks.

## RIDGWAY, MORLEY, WEAR & CO.

Manufacturers of earthenwares at Shelton, c.1836–42. Partnership succeeded Hicks, Meigh & Johnson and was followed by Ridgway & Morley, c.1842–5.

R. M. W. & Co.

Several different printed marks occur incorporating these initials or the name in full, c.1836–42.

Several different printed marks occur incorporating the initials 'R. & M.' or the name of the firm in full, c.1842–5.

## ROBINSON & LEADBEATER (LTD)

Manufacturers of parian figures, etc., at Stoke, c.1864–1924.

Impressed initial mark, found on the back of the base of parian and china figures and groups, c.1885+.

A selection of Robinson & Leadbeater's figures are featured in the *Illustrated Guide to Victorian Parian China*, by C. and D. Shinn (Barrie & Jenkins, 1971) and in *The Parian Phenomenon*, edited by Paul Atterbury (R. Dennis, 1989). This partnership specialized in the production of parian wares. Much is of average quality but some very fine examples were produced, some of which were tinted. As with all parian, the desirability is mainly dependent on the attractiveness of the composition, the quality and condition!

## ROCKINGHAM WORKS

Situated on the Earl Fitzwilliam's Rockingham estate, near Swinton in Yorkshire. From 1806 to 1842 the works were managed by the Bramelds. A wide range of earthenwares were produced; also decorative porcelain from 1826.

B
BRAMELD
BRAMELD & CO.

Several printed, impressed and moulded marks were used on earthenwares from 1806, incorporating the initial 'B' or the name 'Brameld' (often with crosses or numerals, after the name).

Cl. CL6. CCL.

Painted, printed or gilt 'class marks' of small size, found on otherwise unmarked Rockingham porcelains, c.1826–40.

Printed griffin mark (the crest of Earl Fitzwilliam) in *red* (or rarely in underglaze blue), c.1826–30. The mark occurs *impressed* on some figures. After 1830 the basic mark occurs printed in puce; different wording appears under the crest: 'Royal Rock(ingham) Works' and/or 'China Manufacturers to the King'. The wording 'Manufacturers to the Queen' probably denotes wares decorated by Alfred Baguley after the closure of the factory in 1842.

Rockingham porcelain has always enjoyed a high reputation. It is certainly very decorative and collectable. Rare or especially fine quality examples will be costly. Fakes have been produced and these bear copies of the Griffin crest mark. However, genuine examples are seldom marked – in a teaset only the saucers were marked. Many unmarked porcelains produced by other makers of the 1820–40 period tend to be attributed to Rockingham in error.

The reader is recommended to consult the several specialist books, which include *Rockingham Ornamental Porcelain*, by D. G. Rice (Adam Publishing, 1965); *The Illustrated Guide to Rockingham Pottery & Porcelain*, by D. G. Rice (Barrie & Jenkins, 1971); *The Rockingham Pottery*, by A. E. Eaglestone & T. A. Lockett (revised edition, David & Charles, 1973); *Rockingham Pottery & Porcelain 1745–1842*, by A. & A. Cox (Faber & Faber, 1983); or the more modern general books such as my *Encyclopaedia of British Porcelain Manufacturers* (Barrie & Jenkins, 1988). The Rotherham Museum in Yorkshire has a good collection of their local wares.

It should be noted that the description 'Rockingham Glaze' is a generic term, which relates to a brownish treacle-like glaze effect found on domestic wares, mainly teapots of many makes and periods.

## RUSKIN POTTERY
Manufacturers of earthenwares under the proprietorship of W. Howson Taylor, at Smethwick, near Birmingham, from 1898 to July 1935.

**TAYLOR**    Early impressed name-mark, c.1898+.

    Painted or incised marks, c.1898+.

**RUSKIN**    Several impressed or printed marks incorporating
**RUSKIN POTTERY**    the name 'RUSKIN', in various forms; the name 'W. HOWSON TAYLOR' also occurs. The wording 'Made in England' added to most marks from c.1920.

Ruskin pottery is very collectable and good examples can be very costly, especially the high temperature Oriental-style glaze-effect examples. Victoria Bergesen's *Encyclopaedia of British Art Pottery* (Barrie & Jenkins, 1991) gives a good account (under William Howson Taylor) and lists the more important specialist papers and articles that have featured these decorative wares. The reader is also referred to *Ruskin Pottery*, by P. Atterbury & J. Henson (R. Dennis, 1993).

# S

## SHAW & COPESTAKE (LTD)

This Longton partnership rose from small beginnings in about 1901 to become large producers of mainly inexpensive 'Vases and Fancy Wares', at firstly the Drury Pottery and then the Sylvan Works at Longton. Production ceased in 1982.

The early earthenwares were seemingly unmarked but in the 1930s trade names such as 'Scello' and 'SylvaC', 'SylvaC Ware' or 'SylvaC Ceramics' were employed. The first so-called Daisy-mark was perhaps introduced before 1920, without the name.

'SylvaC' marks date from c.1935. Typical examples, one pre-war, one post-war, are here reproduced.

The 'SylvaC' earthenwares are currently very popular and at a modest price level and a 'SylvaC Collectors Circle' is active. For further information the reader should consult *The SylvaC Companion*, by S. Verbeek (Pottery Publications, 1991); *Shaw & Copestake. The Collectors Guide to Early SylvaC 1894–1939*, by A. Van Der Woerd (Pottery Publications, 1992); or *SylvaC Collectors Handbook* by the same authority (Georgian Publications, 1997). Fakes of popular 1950s 'SylvaC' wares have been reported recently.

## SHELLEY POTTERIES LTD

This company at Foley, Fenton was established in 1929 although the Shelley trade-name was used previously by Wileman & Co. (q.v.) and by Shelley's, c.1925–9. Shelley China Ltd since 1966.

The main post-1929 Shelley printed marks as found on bone china wares are shown below, although some other versions may be found.

c.1925–40

c.1940–66

c.1940–66

The Shelley porcelains are of very high quality and are tasteful and typical of their period c.1929–1965.

The pre-war products, in particular, are now collectable and prices have risen as interest grows in quality porcelains of the 1930s. The standard works on these porcelains are *Shelley Potteries. The History and Production of a Staffordshire Family of Potters*, by C. Watkins, W. Harvey & R. Senft (Barrie & Jenkins, 1980); *Wileman. A Collectors' Guide*, by R. Knight & S. Hill (Jazz Publications, 1995); and *Shelley Pottery. The Later Years*, by C. Davenport (Heather Publications, 1997). There is also 'The Shelley Group' of collectors with its quarterly magazine and The Shelley Group's annual Fair. Doultons now own the 'Shelley' trade-name.

## JOSIAH SPODE

Manufacturer, with his sons, of fine-quality earthenwares and porcelains, at Stoke, c.1770 to April 1833, when Copeland & Garrett succeeded (see p. 67). Josiah Spode is credited with introducing English bone china in about 1800, but perhaps earlier essays can bear the impressed mark STOKE CHINA.

Spode        Rare early impressed mark in upper and lower case letters, c.1780–1810.

SPODE or Spode        Standard name-marks, impressed, printed or written, c.1790–1833.

Typical hand-painted name and pattern number marks, normally found on porcelains, from about 1810 onwards. The pattern number naturally changes with each design.

One of several printed marks found on Spode's high-quality 'Stone China', c.1813–33.

One of several large printed marks commemorating the new 'Felspar' body. Some early examples incorporate the date 1821. This and related marks usually appear on high quality products, c.1821–30.

Two typical printed marks, incorporating the names of special bodies, c.1820–33.

It should be noted that several later Copeland marks can incorporate the old name 'Spode'. Also, the Copeland firm reverted to the 'Spode' name in 1970.

Spode earthenwares and porcelains are highly collectable although the commercial value will vary considerably depending on period, type of ware, decoration, quality, rarity and condition. Spode wares are not in general rare and not all examples are of great value.

The standard specialist book is still L. Whiter's *Spode* (Barrie & Jenkins, revised edition, 1989). The reader should also consult Robert Copeland's Chapter 8 in *Staffordshire Porcelain* and my *Encyclopaedia of British Porcelain Manufacturers* (Barrie & Jenkins, 1988). Good details of the various marks and pattern numbers will be found in Robert Copeland's *Spode & Copeland Marks* (Studio Vista, revised edition, 1998).

## STOCKTON POTTERY (or 'STAFFORD POTTERY')

A wide range of earthenwares was made at this Yorkshire pottery under various managements (as listed below), from c.1825.

### William Smith (& Co.), c.1825–55

W. S. & Co.

W. SMITH & CO.

W. S. & Co.
QUEEN'S WARE
STOCKTON

Many printed or impressed marks incorporating the initials 'W. S. & Co.', often with the place-name 'STOCKTON'. The word 'WEDGWOOD' or 'WEDGEWOOD' was also incorporated before 1848 and sometimes the description 'Queen's Ware'.

### George Skinner & Co., c.1855–70

G. S. & Co.

Several printed or impressed marks incorporate these initials, c.1855–70.

### Skinner & Walker, c.1870–80

S. & W.

Several printed or impressed marks incorporate these initials, often with the place-name 'STOCK-TON' and the description of the body, 'PEARL WARE', etc., c.1870–80.

Stockton pottery is collectable, especially some of the interesting multicoloured printed wares produced by William Smith in the 1840s. Prices, however, should be modest.

## SUNDERLAND POTTERIES

The potteries at Sunderland are associated with a type of 'splash-lustre'. Several different potteries were working in the Sunderland area, and many pieces are unmarked. The marks met with include:

'DAWSON'; 'I. DAWSON'; 'J. DAWSON'; 'DAW-SON & CO.'
These name-marks relate to the Ford and South Hylton Potteries, c.1799–1864.

'J. PHILLIPS'; 'PHILLIPS & CO.'; 'DIXON, AUSTIN & CO.'; 'DIXON & CO.'; 'DIXON, PHILLIPS & CO.'
These name-marks, sometimes incorporated in printed designs, relate to the 'Sunderland' or 'Garrison' Pottery, c.1807–65.

'MOORE & CO.'; 'S. MOORE & CO.': 'S. M. & CO.'
These marks relate to Moore's Wear Pottery.

'A. SCOTT'; 'A. SCOTT & CO.'; 'SCOTT & SONS'; 'SCOTT BROS.'
These name-marks (and the relevant initials) relate to Scott's Southwick Pottery, c.1800–97.

The Sunderland earthenwares are in general of interest and unusual specimens may be costly. This centre is particularly noted for a type of splash-lustre or 'Sunderland-lustre'. This aspect of the output of various factories in or around Sunderland is featured in *Collecting Lustrewares*, by G. Godden & M. Gibson (Barrie & Jenkins, 1991). The reader is also referred to *Sunderland Ware. The Potteries of Wearside*, by J. C. Baker (County Borough of Sunderland, revised edition, 1984).

## SWANSEA

Pottery as well as fine porcelain (c.1814–22) was produced at Swansea in Wales under the management of various firms. Swansea earthenwares before the 1780s were not marked.

**SWANSEA**

**CAMBRIAN**

**CAMBRIAN POTTERY**

Three early impressed or painted marks found on earthenwares; the 'Cambrian Pottery' mark is rare, c.1783–c.1810.

**DILLWYN & CO.**

**DILLWYN SWANSEA**

**IMPROVED STONE WARE DILLWYN**

Three basic 'DILLWYN' marks (on pottery) incorporating the name of this proprietor. Several different printed marks incorporate this name or the initial 'D' or 'D. & Co.', c.1811–17 and 1824–50.

**SWANSEA**

Basic name-mark on fine translucent *porcelain*, impressed, printed over the glaze, or painted, c.1814–22. Reproductions also bear this name-mark. A variation has crossed tridents below the word 'Swansea'; this mark is normally impressed into the porcelain.

**BEVINGTON & CO. SWANSEA**

Rare impressed or painted mark, c.1817–24.

**EVANS & GLASSON SWANSEA**

Several different printed or impressed marks of the 1850–62 period incorporate the names 'Evans & Glasson', found on earthenwares only.

**D. J. EVANS & CO.**    Many different printed or impressed marks of the 1862–70 period incorporate or comprise the name 'D. J. Evans & Co.', found on earthenwares only.

The varied Swansea wares, especially the finer porcelains, are very collectable, particularly in Wales, but not all specimens are marked. The reader is recommended to consult the standard reference books, which include E. Morton Nance's *The Pottery and Porcelain of Swansea and Nantgarw* (Batsford, 1942); W. D. John's *Swansea Porcelain* (Ceramic Book Co., 1957); the *Illustrated Encyclopaedia of British Pottery and Porcelain* (1966); *Swansea Porcelain, Shapes and Decoration*, by A. E. Jones and Sir L. Joseph (D. Brown & Sons, 1988); and *The Glamorgan Pottery, Swansea 1814–38*, by H. Hallesy (Gower Press, 1995). The National Museum of Wales in Cardiff and the Glynn Vivian Art Gallery at Swansea have particularly fine and interesting collections.

**SylvaC**, see Shaw & Copestake

T

## 'TEBO' TOULOUSE

The name given to a modeller or 'repairer' who used the impressed mark 'To' or, rarely, 'T'.

This impressed (or relief moulded) mark is found on various 18th-century English porcelains; Bow porcelain, c.1750–60; Worcester porcelain, c.1760–9; Plymouth porcelain, c.1769–70; Bristol porcelain, c.1770–3. The mark is also found (very rarely) on Caughley porcelain, c.1775–80 and on Chamberlain Worcester porcelains of the 1790s. Recent research suggests that this mark may relate to a modeller named John Toulouse. See *Chamberlain-Worcester Porcelain 1788–1852* by G. A. Godden (Barrie & Jenkins, 1982).

## TOOTH & CO. (LTD)

This company succeeded Tooth & Ault (c.1883–6), in 1887 at the Bretby Art Pottery, Woodville, Derbyshire.

The Bretby sun-burst trade-mark was registered in 1884. The word 'England' was added c.1891; this gave way to 'Made in England' after about 1914.

The initials of Henry Tooth can also occur on Bretby earthenwares. Various trade-names, such as 'Clanta Ware' (c.1914+), also occur in different types or bodies.

The Bretby art wares can be decorative and collectable. Values vary greatly depending on the importance of the specimen. Victoria Bergesen's

Encyclopaedia of British Art Pottery (Barrie & Jenkins, 1991) gives a good account of the Tooth earthenwares and lists many magazine articles dealing with the Bretby wares. The firm is still in production but the items currently of interest to collectors can be said to be restricted to the earlier products, c.1887–c.1920.

## JOHN TURNER

Manufacturer of earthenwares – creamwares, basalt, jasper, porcelain, etc. – at Lane End, c.1762–c.1806.

Very early wares are apparently unmarked.

**TURNER**

Standard impressed mark, c.1770+. Very rarely found on porcelain.

**TURNER & CO.**

Standard impressed mark, c.1780–6 and 1803–6, but the single name 'TURNER' is also used at these periods. From 1784 the Prince of Wales's feather plumes may appear with the standard name-mark.

**TURNER'S PATENT**

Rather rare written mark on special bodies patented in January 1800; used to c.1805.

The Turner wares are of a uniformly high quality and are very collectable by the discerning! They are, however, not of high value. All but very exceptional examples should be available for less than £250.

The standard book is *The Turners of Lane End*, by B. Hillier (Cory, Adams & Mackay, 1965). Other aspects of Turner's output are featured in *Black Basalt*, by D. Edwards (Antique Collectors' Club, 1994), *Staffordshire Porcelain*, edited by G. Godden (1983); and *English Dry-Bodied Stoneware. Wedgwood and Contemporary Manufacturers 1774 to 1830*, by D. Edwards & R. Hampson (Antique Collectors' Club, 1998).

## VEDGWOOD

Misleading mock-Wedgwood mark found impressed on earthenwares of the 1830–60 period. Mark probably used by several manufacturers, including Carr & Patton (Newcastle-on-Tyne) c.1838–47, and William Smith & Co. (Stockton-on-Tees) c.1825–55. The earthenwares bearing this misleading name-mark are of ordinary quality and have little commercial value.

'**VICTORIA**' ironstone or stoneware, see Blakeney Pottery Ltd

## CHARLES VYSE

Modeller of earthenware figures and groups 1920s and 1930s and Chinese glaze-effect wares to 1963.

**C. V.**

Painted or incised initials, c.1919–63, often with place-name 'CHELSEA'.

**VYSE**
or
**C. VYSE**
or
**CHARLES VYSE**

Several different name-marks occur with the place-name 'CHELSEA' and often the year of production.

The Vyse figures and groups are decorative and scarce. They are collectable and of higher than average value. The glaze-effect and studio pottery is also collectable and of value, depending on the importance of the specimen.

Typical Vyse figures are shown in my *British Pottery* (1974), Plate 548. The reader is also directed to Richard Dennis's 1974 exhibition catalogue *Charles Vyse 1882–1971*.

## W(★★★)

An interesting grouping of English ceramics, earthenwares as well as porcelain, bears this unhelpful impressed mark. These wares of the approximate period c.1790–1815 are collectable and being researched by specialists seeking to attribute these wares. For further information see *Staffordshire Porcelain* (1983), Appendix V1 or my *Encyclopaedia of British Porcelain Manufacturers* (Barrie & Jenkins, 1988), p. 743.

## GEORGE WADE (& SON LTD)

George Wade commenced potting at the Manchester Pottery, Burslem c.1899. In June 1919 the firm's title was amended to George Wade & Son Ltd. This continued to 1958 when the new name The Wade Group of Potteries was adopted to embrace A. J. Wade, George Wade & Son Ltd, and Wade (Ulster) Ltd. The present title is Wade Ceramics Ltd.

The three marks given below are standard marks used by George Wade & Sons Ltd, from the mid-1930s. Earlier wares were seldom marked.

c.1936+

c.1936+

c.1947+

The following basic marks relate to a separate but linked company, Wade Heath & Co. (Ltd) of Burslem, c.1927–69. Many different marks were used relating to individual styles and types.

c.1927+

c.1934+

c.1939+
with or with out the
word FLAXMAN

c.1953+

In general the Wade wares and novelties were of an inexpensive nature. They are, however, now collectable on an international scale and several books feature these articles. Such well-illustrated works include *The World of Wade*, by I. Warner & M. Posgay (USA, 1988 and 1994); *Wade Whimsical Collectables. The Charlton Price Guide*, by P. Murray (USA, 3rd edition, 1996); *Wade Collectors' Handbook. Complete Listing and Prices to Wade Collectables*, by F. Salmon (F. Joseph, 1996); *Wade Price Trends. The World of Wade and the World of Wade Book*, by I. Warner & M. Posgay (USA, 1996); and the *Charlton Standard Catalogue of Wade Tableware* (USA, 1997). There is also a Wade Collectors' Club.

## JOHN WALTON

Manufacturer of earthenware figures and groups at Burslem, c.1818–35.

WALTON

Moulded or impressed name-mark found on the back of figures, etc., c.1818–35.

The Walton Staffordshire earthenware figures are one of the very few groups that bear a maker's mark. They are in general above average quality and are collectable. Their value is above that of the unmarked types but many later copies have been produced, with the 'Walton' name-mark. Typical examples are shown in my *Illustrated Encyclopaedia of British Pottery and Porcelain*, Plates 591–2, also in most books on Staffordshire figures, notably P. A. Halfpenny's *English Earthenware Figures 1740–1840* (Antique Collectors' Club, 1991).

## WATCOMBE POTTERY CO.
Manufacturers of ornamental terra-cotta wares at Watcombe, South Devon, c.1867–1901, continued as ROYAL ALLER VALE & WATCOMBE POTTERY CO., c.1901–62.

**WATCOMBE**

Basic impressed marks incorporate the word 'Watcombe' with or without the place-name 'TORQUAY', c.1867–1901.

Printed mark, c.1875–1901.

The Watcombe earthenwares are usually of good quality and of interest. They are collectable, mainly in the West Country, but prices are reasonable. Victoria Bergesen's *Encyclopaedia of British Art Pottery* (Barrie & Jenkins, 1991) gives a good account of the Watcombe wares and artists.

## JOSIAH WEDGWOOD (& SONS LTD)
Celebrated manufacturers of earthenwares and porcelain at Burslem, Etruria and Barlaston, Staffordshire, c.1759 to present day.

**wedgwood**

**WEDGWOOD**

Basic impressed name-mark on earthenwares, c.1759+. Early specimens show individually impressed upper and lower case letters; subsequently all letters are of the same style, sans serif type from c.1929. The word 'ENGLAND' should be added from 1891 or 'MADE IN ENGLAND' from c.1910.

Four impressed 'WEDGWOOD & BENTLEY' marks found on ornamental basalt, jasper and marbled wares, c.1769–80. Examples are rare. The desirable circular mark has in recent years been added to unmarked objects; these fake marks are relatively soft and can consequently be marked by a pin, knife, etc.

**WEDGWOOD & BENTLEY**

W. & B.

**WEDGWOOD**

*Printed* name-mark on rare *porcelains*, c.1812–22.

**WEDGWOOD ETRURIA**

Impressed mark with place-name 'ETRURIA', c.1840–5.

From 1860 Wedgwood creamwares, etc., bear impressed letters which show the month and year that a specimen was potted. The table opposite shows the year letters and relevant dates. The year letter is normally the last of the set of three.

Typical signature mark found on the Wedgwood earthenwares painted by the celebrated French artist Emile Lessore, c.1858–76. Examples of this artist's work are shown in Colour Plate XV of the *Illustrated Encyclopaedia of British Pottery and Porcelain*.

**WEDGWOOD**

Basic printed mark on *porcelain*, c.1878+. The word 'ENGLAND' was added after 1891 and 'MADE IN ENGLAND' after about 1910. The description 'BONE CHINA' also appears.

**WEDGWOOD**

Basic impressed name-mark in *sans serif* type, from 1929.

# WEDGWOOD'S IMPRESSED YEAR LETTERS

Occurring in sets of three (from 1860), the *last* date letter shows
the year of manufacture

| | | | | |
|---|---|---|---|---|
| O = 1860 | U = 1866 | Z = 1871 | E = 1876 | J = 1881 |
| P = 1861 | V = 1867 | A = 1872 | F = 1877 | K = 1882 |
| Q = 1862 | W = 1868 | B = 1873 | G = 1878 | L = 1883 |
| R = 1863 | X = 1869 | C = 1874 | H = 1879 | M = 1884 |
| S = 1864 | Y = 1870 | D = 1875 | I = 1880 | N = 1885 |
| T = 1865 | | | | |

| | | |
|---|---|---|
| O = 1886 | | |
| P = 1887 | | A = 1898 | From 1898 to |
| Q = 1888 | | B = 1899 | 1906 the letters |
| R = 1889 | From 1886 to 1897 | C = 1900 | used from |
| S = 1890 | the earlier (1860–71) | D = 1901 | 1872 to 1880 |
| T = 1891★ | letters are repeated | E = 1902 | re-occur, but |
| U = 1892 | | F = 1903 | 'ENGLAND' |
| V = 1893 | ★ From 1891 'ENGLAND | G = 1904 | should also |
| W = 1894 | should occur on specimens. | H = 1905 | appear |
| X = 1895 | | I = 1906 | |
| Y = 1896 | | | |
| Z = 1897 | | | |

From 1907 the sequence was continued, but a '3' replaces the first letter.
From 1924 a '4' replaces the '3'. After 1930 the month is numbered in
sequence and the last two numbers of the year are given, i.e. 1A 32 =
January 1932, 'A' being the workman's mark.

Standard printed mark from c.1940. Note the then
new Barlaston address.

Several different versions of the standard Portland vase mark have been employed since the early 1970s. These usually occur printed in two colours – the vase device being in black. Various pattern names and reference numbers also appear on different designs.

The trade mark registration letter ® was added from 1973.

**WEDGWOOD®**
Bone China
MADE IN ENGLAND

Black & gold
c.1973–80

**WEDGWOOD®**
Bone China
MADE IN ENGLAND

Black & sepia
c.1980–91

WEDGWOOD®
Bone China
MADE IN ENGLAND

Black & sepia
c.1991–7

New trade mark introduced in November 1997.

The Wedgwood wares are of uniformly high quality and are of course collectable. The earlier examples, particularly marked examples of the Wedgwood & Bentley period, are rightly costly. The reader should remember, however, that the output of this large factory working for more than 200 years has been huge and not all specimens are rare or valuable.

Many books give good information on this famous firm: examples include The Story of Wedgwood, by A. Kelly (Faber & Faber, 1975); Wedgwood Portrait Medallions, by R. Reilly and G. Savage (Barrie & Jenkins, 1973); The Dictionary of Wedgwood, by R. Reilly and G. Savage (Antique Collectors' Club, 1980); 18th Century Wedgwood, by D. Buten (Buten Museum of Wedgwood, USA, 1980); Wedgwood Ceramics 1846–1959), by M. Batkin (R.

Dennis, 1982); Wedgwood, by R. Reilly (2 vols, Macmillan, 1989); Josiah Wedgwood 1730–1795, by R. Reilly (Macmillan, 1992); Wedgwood Jasper, by R. Reilly (Thames & Hudson, 1994); The Green Frog Service, by M. Raeburn (Cacklegoose Press, 1995); and English Dry-Bodied Stoneware. Wedgwood and Contemporary Manufacturers 1774 to 1830, by D. Edwards & R. Hampson (Antique Collectors' Club, 1998).

There are also Wedgwood Societies in England and in the USA. The Wedgwood factory site at Barlaston in Staffordshire includes a fine museum and collection of old Wedgwood as well as an interesting Visitors' Centre.

## WEDGWOOD & CO. (LTD)

Manufacturers of earthenwares at Tunstall, c.1860–1965, then retitled 'Enoch Wedgwood (Tunstall) Ltd', it subsequently became part of the Wedgwood group but the old name was discontinued. The 'Wedgwood & Co.' earthenwares are not of special value.

**WEDGWOOD & CO.**   Standard name-mark, found incorporated in several printed marks, or used alone impressed, c.1860–1900; 'Ltd' added from about 1900. Impressed mark also rarely found on wares of the 1790–1801 period, produced at the Ferrybridge Pottery in Yorkshire or in Staffordshire by Ralph Wedgwood.

 Printed mark, one of several incorporating the name Wedgwood & Co., c.1860+.

The marks and wares of this firm are often mistaken for those of Josiah Wedgwood & Sons who used the simple word 'Wedgwood', not 'Wedgwood & Co.' or 'Wedgwood & Co. Ltd'.

## WILEMAN & CO.

Manufacturers of china and earthenware at Foley Works, Fenton, c.1890–1925.

Printed mark, c.1890, note trade name 'FOLEY'.

Printed trade marks, two of several incorporating the trade name 'Shelley', c.1911+.

The Wileman porcelains are collectable but generally in the lower price ranges. The reader is also referred to the Shelley section, and to *Wileman, A Collectors' Guide*, by R. Knight & S. Hill (Jazz Publications, 1995).

## WILTSHAW & ROBINSON (LTD)

Manufacturers of earthenware and china at Carlton Works, Stoke, c.1890–1957, retitled Carlton Ware Ltd in January 1958.

Three sample printed marks, of which several occur incorporating the initials 'W. & R.' or the trade-name 'Carlton Ware', c.1890+.

Carlton ware has become collectable, within modest price levels. The reader is referred to *Collecting Carlton Ware*, by Francis Salmon (Kevin Francis Publishing, 1993). See also under Carlton Ware.

## ENOCH WOOD (& SONS)

Celebrated modeller and manufacturer of earthenwares at Burslem, c.1784–90. In partnership under the style 'Wood & Caldwell' from c.1790 to 1818. Traded as Enoch Wood & Sons from July 1818 to 1846.

**E. W.**

**E. WOOD**

Rather rare impressed initial or name-marks found on fine creamwares, basalt, jasper, etc., c.1790–1818.

**WOOD & CALDWELL**

Standard impressed mark, c.1790–1818, rather rare.

Standard impressed mark of the 1818–46 period with the new-style 'Enoch [or 'E'] Wood & Sons'. Fine blue-printed earthenwares were made especially for the American market.

**E. W. & S.**

**E. & E. W.**

**E. WOOD & SONS**

Several printed marks of the 1818–46 period incorporate these initials, as on the sample printed mark reproduced below, or the name in full.

Enoch Wood's products are varied and interesting. A large assortment of blue-printed tablewares were produced, much for our export markets. Most examples are of modest price but rare or special items are obviously in demand. Good examples are in The Potteries Museum at Hanley. For further information and illustrations, see *The Wood Family of Burslem*, by F. Falkner (1912). Typical examples are also shown in the *Illustrated Encyclopaedia of British Pottery and Porcelain*, Plates 639–43. For a review of his rare porcelains see my *Encyclopaedia of British Porcelain Manufacturers* (Barrie & Jenkins, 1988).

## WORCESTER PORCELAIN FACTORY

Established in 1751 by Dr John Wall and partners, after acquiring the Bristol works of Benjamin Lund. Worcester porcelain is justly celebrated for its charm and quality. The glaze is perfect, not discoloured or crazed; some early wares were decorated with overglaze prints and with attractive underglaze-blue designs.

### Dr Wall Period

Many early specimens decorated in underglaze-blue bear various workmen's signs on the base or under the handle: four typical marks are reproduced, see also the *Encyclopaedia of British Porcelain Manufacturers*, p. 797. Porcelains bearing these devices would date c.1752–65.

The first standard Worcester mark is the blue crescent device, filled in (or with cross-hatching) on printed designs, open (outlines only) crescent on hand-painted examples, c.1758–83.

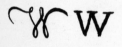

Blue painted or printed examples sometimes bear the rather rare 'W' mark, which occurs in various differing forms, c.1760–80.

Many different factory Oriental-style marks also occur painted in underglaze-blue, often on colourful Japanese-type patterns, c.1760–75. Such mock oriental marks are not confined to Worcester.

Two typical examples of the 'square' or 'seal' mark found painted by hand in underglaze-blue on Worcester porcelains, often in conjunction with colourful 'scale blue' patterns. Many variations occur, c.1760–75. Reproductions often bear such 'square' marks.

  Two examples of the Worcester version of the Dresden crossed-swords mark found on overglaze printed specimens as well as ornate and colourful designs.

  Printed Worcester numeral marks, disguised with Oriental-styled flourishes, formerly attributed to the Caughley factory in error, c.1770–83.

The first or 'Dr Wall' period of Worcester porcelain came to an end in September 1783. The factory, moulds, etc., were purchased by Thomas Flight and the works were continued under various partnerships, using different marks, as listed.

### Flight Period

 Early standard crescent mark continued but now very small, c.1783–92.

 Rather rare blue mark, c.1783–8.

 Rather rare blue mark with crown, c.1788–92.

FLIGHT'S Other rare marks comprise or incorporate the name 'Flight' or 'Flight's', c.1788–92.

### Barr, also Flight & Barr Period

  Standard incised 'B' marks, often with a small cross, c.1792–1807.

**F. & B.**
**FLIGHT & BARR**

Other rather rare marks incorporate or comprise the name 'Flight & Barr', or the initials 'F. & B.'

### Barr, Flight & Barr Period
Standard impressed or incised BFB marks (with or without crown), c.1807–13.

**BARR FLIGHT**
**& BARR**
**ROYAL PORCELAIN**
**WORKS**
**WORCESTER**

One of several printed or written marks incorporating the name 'Barr, Flight & Barr', c.1807–13.

### Flight, Barr & Barr Period
Standard impressed mark, the initials 'FBB' under a crown, c.1813–40.

**FLIGHT, BARR & BARR**

Several different printed or written marks occur with the title in full, c.1813–40.

Messrs Chamberlains (q.v.) continued the works from 1840 to 1852.

### Kerr & Binns Period
Standard impressed or printed mark, *without* crown above, c.1852–62.

Rare printed shield-mark on fine-quality specimens: the last two numerals of the year occur in the central bar, 57 for 1857, etc.

**W. H. KERR & CO**

Some rare marks incorporate the title 'W. H. Kerr & Co.', c.1856–62.

### Royal Worcester
Standard printed or impressed mark, with crown above, c.1862–75 (numerals under the main mark are the last two of the year of decoration, 73 for 1873, etc.).

Amended printed or impressed mark, note crescent instead of 'C' in centre and filled-in crown settling on circle, c.1876–91.

Post-1891 standard printed mark, note wording around, not found on earlier versions. The dots each side of the crown are year markings starting with one in 1892.

Revised printed mark, c.1944–55; from 1956 the words are placed below the main device.

Version with words 'Bone China' below 'Royal Worcester', c.1956+

Revised version, c.1959+. Year-marks occur with these marks up to the early 1970s, when the year-marks were discontinued

Standard mark c.1970 onwards but special marks can relate to special issues or projects.

Methods of dating Royal Worcester porcelain to the year are given by G. A. Godden in the *Encyclopaedia of British Pottery and Porcelain Marks* (1964) and in Henry Sandon's specialist book *Royal Worcester Porcelain from 1862 to the Present Day* (Barrie & Jenkins, 3rd edition, 1978).

Worcester porcelains are of an uniformly high quality. All periods are collectable but the price varies greatly – ranging up to over £10,000 for very special pieces. The reader is warned that fakes exist, mainly but not exclusively relating to copies of 18th-century types.

Many specialist books have been written on the various aspects of Worcester porcelain. The following will be found helpful: *Worcester Porcelain* by F. A. Barrett (1953, revised edition, 1966); *Coloured Worcester Porcelain of the First Period*, by H. Rissik Marshall (Ceramic Book Co., 1954); *Victorian Porcelain*, by G. A. Godden (H. Jenkins, 1961); *English Blue and White Porcelain of the 18th Century*, by B. Watney (Faber & Faber, 1963, revised edition 1973); *Illustrated Encyclopaedia of British Pottery and Porcelain*, by G. A. Godden (1966); *Caughley and Worcester Porcelains, 1775–1800*, by G. A. Godden (Antique Collectors' Club, 1981); *The Illustrated Guide to Worcester Porcelain*, by H. Sandon (Barrie & Jenkins, 1969); the same author's *Flight and Barr Worcester Porcelain 1783–1840* (Antique Collectors' Club, 1978); his *Royal Worcester Porcelain from 1862 to the Present Day* (Barrie & Jenkins, 1978); *Worcester Blue & White Porcelain 1751–1790*, by L. Branyan, N. French & J. Sandon (Barrie & Jenkins, 1989); *The Dictionary of Worcester Porcelain, Vol 1, 1751–1851*, by John Sandon (1993); and *Worcester Porcelain 1751–1790. The Zorensky Collection*, by Simon Spero & John Sandon (Antique Collectors' Club, 1997).

Most major museum collections feature a representative selection of Worcester porcelain but the splendid, comprehensive, collection on display at the Worcester Porcelain Works, Severn Street, Worcester is a must!

# Potters' Initial Marks

This helpful section lists the initials used as a mark, or part of a mark, by various 19th-century potters or partnerships, with their approximate working period. An asterisk indicates an entry in the main marks section.

| | | |
|---|---|---|
| **A. Bros** | *G. L. Ashworth & Bros, Hanley | 1861–1968 |
| **A. & Co.** | Edward Asbury & Co., Longton | c.1875–1925 |
| **A. B.** | Adams & Bromley, Hanley | c.1873–86 |
| **A. B. & C.** | Allman, Broughton & Co., Burslem | c.1861–8 |
| **A. B. & Co.** | Allman, Broughton & Co., Burslem | c.1861–8 |
| **A. B. & Co.** | A. Bullock & Co., Hanley | c.1895–1902 |
| **A. & B.** | Adams & Bromley, Hanley | c.1873–86 |
| **A. B. J.** | A. B. Jones, Longton | c.1900 |
| **A. B. J. & S.** | A. B. Jones & Sons, Longton | c.1900 + |
| **A. B. J. & Sons** | A. B. Jones & Sons, Longton | c.1900 + |
| **A. & C.** | Adams & Cooper, Longton | c.1850–77 |
| **A. F. & S.** | A. Fenton & Son, Hanley | c.1887–1901 |
| **A. G.** | A. Godfrey, Hanley | c.1829–37 |
| **A. G. H. J.** | A. G. Harley Jones, Fenton | c.1907–34 |
| **A. G. R.** | A. G. Richardson, Cobridge | c.1920–1 |
| **A. G. R. & Co. Ltd** | A. G. Richardson & Co. Ltd, Tunstall | c.1915 + |
| **A. J. M.** | A. J. Mountford, Burslem | c.1897–1901 |
| **A. J. W.** | A. J. Wilkinson, Burslem | c.1885 + |
| **A. M. L.** | A. Mackee, Longton | c.1892–1906 |
| **A. P. Co.** | Anchor Porcelain Co., Longton | c.1901–18 |
| **A. P. Co. L.** | Anchor Porcelain Co. Ltd, Longton | c.1901–18 |
| **A. S.** | A. Shaw, Tunstall | c.1853–85 |
| **A. & S.** | Arkinstall & Sons, Stoke | c.1904–24 |
| **A. S. B.** | A. Stanyer, Burslem | c.1916–41 |
| **A. S. & Co.** | Ambrose Smith & Co., Burslem | c.1784–6 |
| **A. S. W.** | Rye Pottery, Sussex | c.1920–3 |
| **A. W. L.** | Arthur Wood, Longport | c.1904–28 |
| | | |
| **B.** (incised) | *Worcester, Barr period | c.1792–1807 |
| **B.** (impressed) | J. & E. Baddeley, Shelton | c.1784–1806 |
| | Thomas Barlow, Longton | c.1849–82 |
| | T. W. Barlow & Son Ltd, Longton | c.1882–1940 |
| **B.** (painted) | *Bow, London | c.1747–76 |
| | *Bristol (porcelains) | c.1770–81 |
| **B.** (printed) | *Rockingham (earthenwares) | c.1810–42 |
| **B. & Co.** | Barrow & Co., Fenton | c.1853–4 |
| | L. A. Birks & Co., Stoke | c.1896–1900 |
| | Bodley & Co., Burslem | c.1865 |
| | Boulton & Co., Longton | c.1892–1902 |
| **B. Ltd** | Barlows (Longton) Ltd, Longton | c.1920–52 |
| **B. & Son** | Bodley & Son, Burslem | c.1874–5 |
| **B. A. & B.** | Bradbury, Anderson & Betteney, Longton | c.1844–52 |
| **B. A. J.** | A. B. Jones, Longton | c.1900 + |

| | | |
|---|---|---|
| **B. A. J. & S(ons)** | A. B. Jones, Longton | c.1900 + |
| **B. B.** | *Minton, Stoke | c.1830–60 |
| **B. B. B.** | Booths Ltd, Tunstall | c.1891–1948 |
| **B. B. B.** | Bridgett, Bates & Beech, Longton | c.1875–82 |
| **B. B. C.** | J. Shaw & Sons Ltd, Longton | c.1931–63 |
| **B. B. & Co.** | *Baker, Bevans & Irwin, Swansea | c.1813–38 |
| **B. & B.** | Baggerley & Ball, Longton | c.1822–36 |
| | Bailey Ball, Longton | c.1843–9 |
| | Bailey & Batkin, Lane End | c.1814–27 |
| | Bates & Bennett, Cobridge | c.1868–95 |
| | Blackhurst & Bourne, Burslem | c.1880–92 |
| | L. A. Birks, Stoke | c.1896–1900 |
| | Bridgett & Bates, Longton | c.1882–1915 |
| **B. B. Ltd** | Barker Bros Ltd, Longton | c.1876 + |
| **B. B. & I.** | *Baker, Bevans & Irwin, Swansea | c.1813–38 |
| **B. B. W. & M.** | Bates, Brown-Westhead & Moore, Shelton | c.1859–61 |
| **B. & C.** | Bridgwood & Clarke, Burslem | c.1857–64 |
| **B. C. Co.** | Britannia China Co., Longton | c.1895–1906 |
| **B. C. G.** | B. C. Godwin, Burslem | c.1851 |
| **B. & E.** | Beardmore & Edwards, Longton | c.1856–8 |
| **B. E. & Co.** | Bates, Elliott & Co., Burslem | c.1870–5 |
| **B. F.** | B. Floyd, Lane End | c.1843 |
| **B. F. (monogram)** | *Burmantofts, Leeds | c.1882–1904 |
| **B. F. B.** | *Worcester, Barr, Flight & Barr | c.1807–13 |
| **B. G.** | B. Godwin, Cobridge | c.1834–41 |
| **B. G. P. Co.** | Brownfield's Guild Pottery Society Ltd, Cobridge | c.1891–1900 |
| **B. G. & W.** | Bates, Gildea & Walker, Burslem | c.1878–81 |
| **B. H. & Co.** | Beech Hancock & Co., Tunstall | c.1851–5 |
| **B. & H.** | Bednall & Heath, Hanley | c.1879–99 |
| | Beech & Hancock, Tunstall | c.1855–76 |
| | Blackhurst & Hulme, Longton | c.1890–1932 |
| | Bodley & Harrold, Burslem | c.1863–5 |
| **B. & K.** | Barkers & Kent, Fenton | c.1889–1941 |
| **B. & K. L.** | Barkers & Kent, Longton | c.1889–1941 |
| **B. & L.** | Bourne & Leigh, Burslem | c.1892–1941 |
| **B. & L.** | *Burgess & Leigh, Burslem | c.1862 + |
| **B. & L. Ltd** | *Burgess & Leigh, Burslem | c.1889 + |
| **B. M. & Co.** | Bayley Murray, Glasgow | c.1875–84 |
| **B. M. & T.** | Boulton, Machin & Tennant, Tunstall | c.1889–99 |
| **B. N. & Co.** | Bourne, Nixon & Co., Tunstall | c.1828–30 |
| **B. P.** | Bovey Pottery & Co. Ltd, Devon | c.1894–1957 |
| **B. P. Co.** | Blyth Porcelain Co. Ltd, Longton | c.1905–35 |
| | Bovey Tracey Pottery Co., Devon | c.1894–1957 |
| | Bridge Products Co., Somerset | c.1954–63 |
| | Brownhills Pottery Co., Tunstall | c.1872–96 |
| **B. P. Co. Ltd** | Blyth Porcelain Co. Ltd, Longton | c.1905–35 |
| | Britannia Pottery Co. Ltd, Glasgow | c.1920–35 |
| **B. R. & Co.** | Birks, Rawlins & Co., Stoke | c.1900–33 |
| **B. R. & T.** | Baxter, Rowley & Tams, Longton | c.1882–5 |
| **B. & S.** | Barker & Son, Burslem | c.1850–60 |
| | Beswick & Son, Longton | c.1916–30 |

| | | |
|---|---|---|
| | *Bishop & Stonier, Hanley | c.1891–1939 |
| | Brown & Stevenson, Burslem | c.1900–23 |
| **B. S. & T.** | Barker, Sutton & Till, Burslem | c.1834–43 |
| **B. & T.** | Barker & Till, Burslem | c.1843–50 |
| | Blackhurst & Tunnicliffe, Burslem | c.1879 |
| **B. T. P. Co.** | Bovey Tracey Pottery Co., Devon | c.1894–1957 |
| **B. T. & S. F. B.** | B. Taylor & Sons, Ferrybridge Pottery, Yorks | c.1852–6 |
| **B. & W.** | Birch & Whitehead, Shelton | c.1796 |
| | Boughley & Wiltshire, Longton | c.1892–5 |
| **B. W. & B.** | Batkin, Walker & Broadhurst, Lane End | c.1840–5 |
| **B. W. & Co.** | Bates Walker & Co., Burslem | c.1875–8 |
| | Buckley, Wood & Co., Burslem | c.1875–85 |
| **B. W. M.** | *Brown-Westhead, Moore & Co., Hanley | c.1862–1904 |
| **B. W. M. & Co.** | *Brown-Westhead, Moore & Co., Hanley | c.1862–1904 |
| | | |
| **C.** | *Caughley, Shropshire | c.1775–99 |
| **C. & Co.** | Calland & Co., Swansea | c.1852–6 |
| | Clokie & Co., Castleford, Yorks. | c.1888–1961 |
| | Colclough & Co., Longton | c.1887–1928 |
| | J. H. Cope & Co., Longton | c.1887–1947 |
| **C. A. L.** | C. Amison, Longton | c.1889–1962 |
| **C. A. & Co. Ltd** | Ceramic Art Co. Ltd, Hanley | c.1892–1903 |
| **C. A. & Sons** | *C. Allerton & Sons, Longton | c.1859–1942 |
| **C. B.** | *Charles Bourne, Fenton | c.1807–30 |
| | Christie & Beardmore, Fenton | c.1807–30 |
| | Collingwood Bros, Longton | c.1887–1957 |
| **C. B. D.** | *Coalport, Shropshire | c.1851 + |
| **C. & B.** | Carter & Barker, Hanley | c.1834–41 |
| | Christie & Beardmore, Fenton | c.1902–3 |
| | Cotton & Barlow, Longton | c.1850–5 |
| **C. B. & C.** | Cyples, Barlow & Cyples, Lane End | c.1841–4 |
| | C. Collinson & Co., Burslem | c.1867–75 |
| | Cockson and Chetwyn, Colridge | c.1867–75 |
| **C. D.** | *Coalport, Shropshire | c.1815–30 |
| **C. & D.** | Cooper & Dethick, Longton | c.1876–88 |
| **C. & E.** | Cartwright & Edwards, Longton | c.1857 + |
| | Cope & Edwards, Longton | c.1844–57 |
| **C. & E. Ltd** | Cartwright & Edwards, Longton | 1857 + |
| **C. E. & M.** | Cork, Edge & Malkin, Burslem | c.1860–71 |
| **C. F.** | Charles Ford, Hanley | c.1874–1904 |
| **C. & F.** | Cockran & Fleming, Glasgow | c.1896–1920 |
| **C. & F. G.** | Cockran & Fleming, Glasgow | c.1896–1920 |
| **C. & G.** | Collingwood & Greatbatch | c.1870–87 |
| | *Copeland & Garrett, Stoke | c.1833–47 |
| **C. H.** | Charles Hobson, Burslem | c.1865–73 |
| **C. H. Co.** | Hanley China Co., Hanley | c.1899–1901 |
| **C. H. & G.** | Copestake, Hazzall & Gerard | c.1828–30 |
| **C. H. & S.** | C. Hobson & Son, Burslem | c.1873–80 |
| **C. & H.** | Cockson & Harding, Shelton | c.1856–62 |
| | Coggins & Hill, Longton | c.1892–8 |
| | Coombs & Holland, Wales | c.1855–8 |

|  | Cumberlidge & Humphreys, Tunstall | c.1886–95 |
|---|---|---|
| C. J. M. & Co. | *C. J. Mason, Fenton | c.1829–45 |
| C. J. W. | Wileman & Co., Fenton | c.1892–1925 |
| C. K. | Charles Keeling, Shelton | c.1922–5 |
| C. M. | Carlo Manzoni, Hanley | c.1895–8 |
|  | Charles Meigh, Hanley | c.1835–49 |
| C. & M. | Clokie & Masterman, Castleford, Yorks. | c.1888–1961 |
| C. M. & S. | Charles Meigh & Son, Hanley | 1851–61 |
| C. M. S. & P. | Meigh & Pankhurst, Hanley | 1850–1 |
| C. & P. | Carr & Patton, North Shields | c.1838–47 |
| C. P. Co. | Campbellfield Pottery, Glasgow | c.1850–1905 |
|  | Clyde Pottery, Greenock | c.1850–1903 |
| C. P. P. Co. | Crystal Porcelain Pottery Co., Cobridge | c.1882–6 |
| C. & R. | Chesworth & Robinson, Lane End | c.1825–40 |
|  | Chetham & Robinson, Longton | c.1822–37 |
| C. T. M. | *C. T. Maling, Newcastle | c.1859–90 |
| C. T. M. & Sons | *C. T. Maling & Sons, Newcastle | 1890–1963 |
| C. V. | *Charles Vyse, London | c.1919–63 |
| C. W. | C. Waine, Longton | c.1891–1920 |
| C. & W. | Capper & Wood, Longton | c.1895–1904 |
| C. & W. K. H. | C. & W. K. Harvey, Longton | c.1835–53 |
| C. Y. & J. | Clementson, Young & Jameson | c.1844 |
| C. & Y. | Clementson & Young, Shelton | c.1845–47 |
|  |  |  |
| D. | *Derby | c.1750–1848 |
|  | T. J. Dimmock & Co., Shelton | c.1828–59 |
|  | Dillwyn & Co., Swansea | c.1811–17 |
| D. & B. | Deakin & Bailey, Lane End | c.1828–32 |
|  | Deaville & Badderley, Hanley | c.1853–4 |
| D. B. & Co. | Davenport Banks & Co., Hanley | c.1860–73 |
|  | Davenport Beck & Co., Hanley | c.1873–80 |
|  | Dunn Bennett & Co., Burslem | c.1875 + |
| D. & C. L. | Dewes & Copestake, Longton | c.1894–1915 |
| D. D. & Co. | D. Dunderdale & Co., Castleford, Yorks. | c.1790–1820 |
| D. L. & Co. | D. Lockhart & Co., Glasgow | c.1865–98 |
| D. L. & S. | D. Lockhart & Sons, Glasgow | c.1898–1953 |
| D. M. | *W. De Morgan, London | c.1872–1907 |
| D. M. & S. | D. Methven & Sons, Kirkcaldy | c.1875–1930 |
| D. P. Co. | Diamond Pottery Co., Hanley | c.1908–35 |
|  | Dresden Porcelain Co., Longton | c.1896–1904 |
| D. R. | Della Robbia Co., Birkenhead | c.1894–1901 |
| D. & S. | Dimmock & Smith, Hanley | c.1826–59 |
|  |  |  |
| E. & Co. | Edgerton & Co., Lane End | c.1823–7 |
| E. B. | E. Bailey, Lane | c.1827–30 |
|  | *E. Bingham, Castle Hedingham, Essex | c.1864–1901 |
| E. & C. | Edgerton & Co., Lane End | c.1823–7 |
| E. B. & B. | Edge, Barker & Barker, Fenton | c.1836–40 |
| E. B. & Co. | *E. Brain & Co., Fenton | c.1903–63 |
|  | Edge, Barker & Co., Fenton | c.1835–6 |
| E. & B. | Evans & Booth, Burslem | c.1856–69 |
| E. & B. L. | Edwards & Brown, Longton | c.1882–1933 |

| | | |
|---|---|---|
| **E. B. & S.** | E. Booth & Son, Stoke | c.1791–1802 |
| **E. B. & J. E. L.** | Bourne & Leigh, Burslem | c.1892–1941 |
| **E. C.** | E. Challinor, Tunstall | c.1842–67 |
| **E. & C. C.** | E. & C. Challinor, Fenton | c.1862–91 |
| **E. & E. W.** | ★Enoch Wood & Sons, Burslem | c.1818–46 |
| **E. & F.** | Elsmore & Forster, Tunstall | c.1853–71 |
| | Evans & Foulkes, Hanley | c.1876 |
| **E. F. B.** | E. F. Bodley & Co., Burslem | c.1862–5 |
| **E. F. B. & Co.** | F. Bodley & Co., Burslem | c.1862–5 |
| **E. F. B. & Son** | E. F. Bodley & Son, Longport | c.1881–98 |
| **E. G. & C.** | Everard Glover & Colclough, Lane End | c.1847 |
| **E. & G. P.** | E. & G. Phillips, Longport | c.1822–34 |
| **E. & H.** | Eardley & Hammersley, Tunstall | c.1862–6 |
| **E. I. B.** | E. J. Birch, Shelton | c.1796–1814 |
| **E. J.** | Elijah Jones, Cobridge | c.1831–40 |
| **E. J. D. B.** | E. J. D. Bodley, Burslem | c.1875–92 |
| **E. K. B.** | Elkin, Knight & Bridgwood, Fenton | c.1827–40 |
| **E. K. & Co.** | Elkin Knight & Co., Fenton | c.1822–6 |
| **E. M. & Co.** | Edge, Malkin & Co., Burslem | c.1871–1903 |
| **E. & N.** | Elkin & Newton, Longton | c.1844–5 |
| **E. P. Co.** | Empire Porcelain Co., Stoke | c.1896–1967 |
| **E. S. & Co.** | Eardley, Spear & Co., Tunstall | c.1873 |
| **E. W.** | Edward Walley, Cobridge | c.1845–60 |
| | ★Enoch Wood, Burslem | c.1790–1818 |
| **E. W. & M.** | Ellis, Unwin & Mountford, Hanley | c.1860–1 |
| **E. W. & S.** | ★Enoch Wood & Sons, Burslem | 1818–46 |
| | | |
| **F. & Co.** | T. Fell & Co., Newcastle | c.1817–90 |
| **F. & Sons** | Ford & Sons, Burslem | c.1893–1938 |
| **F. & Sons Ltd** | Ford & Sons Ltd, Burslem | c.1908–38 |
| **F. B.** | Frederick Booth, Bradford, Yorks. | c.1881 |
| | Ferrybridge Pottery, Yorks. | 19th–20th century |
| **F. B. & Co.** | ★F. Beardmore & Co., Fenton | c.1903–14 |
| **F. & B.** | ★Worcester, Flight & Barr | c.1792–1807 |
| **F. B. B.** | ★Worcester, Flight, Barr & Barr | c.1813–40 |
| **F. C.** | F. Cartlidge & Co., Longton | c.1889–1904 |
| **F. C. & Co.** | Ford Challinor & Co., Tunstall | c.1865–80 |
| **F. & C.** | Ford, Challinor & Co., Tunstall | c.1865–80 |
| **F. G. B.** | G. F. Bowers, Tunstall | c.1842–68 |
| **F. & H.** | Forester & Hulme, Fenton | c.1887–93 |
| **F. M.** | F. Malcolm, Stoke | c.1859–60 |
| | F. Mills, Hanley | c.1884–92 |
| | Francis Morley, Hanley | c.1845–9 |
| **F. M. & Co.** | F. Morley & Co., Hanley | c.1849–58 |
| **F. & P.** | Ford & Pointon, Hanley | c.1917–36 |
| **F. & R.** | Ford & Riley, Burslem | c.1882–93 |
| **F. & R. P.** | ★F. & R. Pratt & Co., Fenton | 1818 + |
| **F. & R. P. & Co.** | F. & R. Pratt & Co., Fenton | 1818 + |
| **F. & S.** | Ford & Son, Burslem | c.1893–1964 |
| **F. T. & R.** | Flacket, Toft & Robinson, Longton | c.1858 |
| **F. W. & Co.** | F. Winkle & Co., Stoke | c.1890–1931 |

| | | |
|---|---|---|
| **G. & Co.** | Gallimore & Co., Longton | c.1906–34 |
| | ★Grainger & Co., Worcester | c.1839–1902 |
| | Grove & Co., Stoke | c.1867–9 |
| **G. & A.** | Galloway & Atkinson, Newcastle | c.1870 |
| **G. Bros** | J. & R. Godwin, Cobridge | c.1834–66 |
| | Grimwade Bros, Hanley and Stoke | c.1886–1900 |
| | Gelson Brothers | c.1868–75 |
| **G. B.** | George Baguley, Hanley | c.1850–4 |
| | Grimwades Ltd, Stoke | c.1900 + |
| **G. B. & Co.** | G. Bennett & Co., Stoke | c.1894–1902 |
| **G. & B.** | Goodwin & Bullock, Longton | c.1852–6 |
| **G. B. H.** | Goodwin, Bridgwood & Harris, Lane End | c.1829–31 |
| **G. B. & H.** | Goodwin, Bridgwood & Harris, Lane End | c.1829–31 |
| **G. B. O.** | Goodwin, Bridgwood & Orton, Lane End | c.1827–9 |
| **G. B. & O.** | Goodwin, Bridgwood & Orton, Lane End | c.1827–9 |
| **G. & C. J. M.** | ★Mason, Lane Delph | c.1813–29 |
| **G. C. P. Co.** | Clyde Pottery Co., Greenock | c.1850–1903 |
| **G. & D.** | Guest & Dewsbury, Llanelly | c.1877–1927 |
| **G. &. E.** | Goodwin & Ellis, Lane End | c.1839–40 |
| **G. F. B.** | ★G. F. Bowers, Tunstall | c.1842–68 |
| **G. F. B. B. T.** | ★G. F. Bowers, Tunstall | c.1842–68 |
| **G. F. S.** | G. F. Smith, Stockton | c.1855–60 |
| **G. G.** | George Guest, Tunstall | c.1875–92 |
| **G. G. & Co.** | ★G. Grainger, Worcester | c.1839–1902 |
| **G. G. W./S. P.** | ★G. Grainger, Worcester | c.1848–65 |
| **G. H. & Co.** | Gater Hall & Co., Tunstall and Burslem | c.1895–1943 |
| **G. & H. H.** | Godwin & Hewitt, Hereford | c.1889–1910 |
| **G. J.** | ★George Jones, Stoke | c.1861–73 |
| **G. J. & S(ons)** | ★George Jones & Sons, Stoke | c.1874–1951 |
| **G. L. A.** | ★G. L. Ashworth & Bros, Hanley | c.1862 + |
| **G. L. A. & Bros** | ★G. L. Ashworth & Bros, Hanley | c.1862 + |
| **G. L. B. & Co.** | G. L. Bentley & Co., Longton | c.1898–1912 |
| **G. M. C.** | Creyke & Sons Ltd, Hanley | c.1920–48 |
| **G. P.** | George Phillip, Longport | c.1834–47 |
| | George Procter, Longton | c.1840–2 |
| **G. P. Co.** | ★Baker, Bevans & Irwin, Swansea | c.1813–38 |
| | George Proctor & Co., Longton | c.1892–1940 |
| **G. R.** | George Ray, Longton | c.1846–52 |
| | G. Rogers, Hanley | c.1829–32 |
| **G. P. Co.** | ★Baker, Bevans & Irwin, Swansea | c.1813–38 |
| **G. P. & Co.** | George Proctor & Co., Longton | c.1891–1940 |
| **G. R. & Co.** | Godwin Rowley & Co., Burslem | c.1828–31 |
| **G. S. & Co.** | George Skinner & Co., Stockton | c.1855–70 |
| **G. S. & S.** | George Shaw & Sons, Rotherham | c.1887–85 |
| **G. & S.** | Grove & Stark, Longton | c.1871–85 |
| **G. & S. Ltd** | Gibson & Sons, Burslem | c.1885 + |
| **G. T. M.** | G. T. Mountford, Stoke | c.1888–98 |
| **G. T. & S.** | G. W. Turner & Sons, Tunstall | c.1873–95 |
| **G. W.** | ★George Grainger, Worcester | c.1839–1902 |
| | George Weston, Lane End | c.1807–30 |
| | G. Wooliscroft, Tunstall | c.1851–54 |
| **G. W. & Co.** | G. Wood & Co., Shelton | c.1853 |

| | | |
|---|---|---|
| **G. W. & S.** | G. Warrilow & Sons, Longton | c.1887–1940 |
| **G. W. & Sons Ltd** | G. Warrilow & Sons, Longton | c.1887–1940 |
| **G. W. T. S.** | G. W. Turner & Sons, Tunstall | c.1873- |
| **G. W. T. & S.** | G. W. Turner & Sons, Tunstall | c.1873–95 |
| **G. & W.** | Gildea & Walker, Burslem | c.1881–5 |
| **G. & W. S. & Co.** | G. & W. Smith & Co., Stockton | c.1860 |
| | | |
| **H.** | Hackwood, Hanley | 19th century |
| | W. & J. Harding, Shelton | c.1862–72 |
| | F. Hughes & Co., Fenton | c.1889–1953 |
| | W. Hulme, Burslem | c.1891–1941 |
| **H. & Co.** | Hackwood & Co., Hanley | c.1807–27 |
| | Hammersley & Co., Longton | c.1887–1932 |
| | Hill & Co., Longton | c.1898–1920 |
| **H. A. & Co.** | H. Alcock & Co., Cobridge | c.1861–1910 |
| | H. Adams & Co., Longton | c.1870–85 |
| | H. Aynsley & Co., Longton | c.1873 + |
| **H. & A.** | Hammersley & Astbury, Longton | c.1872–5 |
| | Hulse & Adderley, Longton | c.1869–75 |
| **H. B.** | H. Burgess, Burslem | c.1864–92 |
| | Hawley Bros, Rotherham, Yorks. | c.1868–1903 |
| | Hines Bros, Fenton | c.1886–1907 |
| **H. B. & Co.** | Harvey, Bailey & Co., Lane End | c.1833–5 |
| | Heath, Blackhurst & Co., Burslem | c.1859–77 |
| **H. & B.** | Hampson & Broadhurst, Longton | c.1847–53 |
| | Harrap & Burgess, Hanley | c.1894–1903 |
| | Heath & Blackhurst, Burslem | c.1859–77 |
| | Hibbert & Boughey, Longton | c.1889 |
| **H. & C.** | Harding & Cockson, Cobridge | c.1834–60 |
| | Hope & Carter, Burslem | c.1862–80 |
| | Hulme & Christie, Fenton | c.1893–1902 |
| **H. C. Co.** | Hanley China Co., Hanley | c.1899–1901 |
| **H. & D.** | Hallam & Day, Longton | c.1880–5 |
| **H. F.** | F. Hughes & Co., Fenton | c.1889–1953 |
| **H. F. W. & Co. Ltd** | H. F. Wedgwood & Co. Ltd, Longton | c.1954–9 |
| **H. & G.** | Heath & Greatbatch, Burslem | c.1891–3 |
| | Holland & Green, Longton | c.1853–82 |
| | Hollinshead & Griffiths, Burslem | c.1890–1909 |
| | Hulse & Ginder, Fenton | c.1827–33 |
| **H. & H.** | Hilditch & Hopwood, Lane End | c.1835–59 |
| **H. H. & M.** | Holdcraft, Hill & Mellor, Burslem | c.1860–70 |
| **H. J.** | A. G. Harley Jones, Fenton | c.1907–34 |
| **H. J. C.** | H. J. Colclough, Longton | c.1897–1937 |
| **H. J. W.** | H. J. Wood, Burslem | c.1884 + |
| **H. & K.** | Hackwood & Keeling, Hanley | c.1835–6 |
| | Hollinshead & Kirkham, Tunstall | c.1870–1956 |
| **H. L. & Co.** | Hancock, Leigh & Co., Tunstall | c.1860–2 |
| **H. & M.** | Hamilton & Moore, Longton | c.1840–58 |
| | *Hicks & Meigh, Shelton | c.1806–22 |
| | Hilditch & Martin | c.1815–32 |
| **H. M. I.** | *Hicks, Meigh & Johnson, Shelton | c.1822–35 |
| **H. M. & I.** | *Hicks, Meigh & Johnson, Shelton | c.1822–35 |

| | | |
|---|---|---|
| **H. M. J.** | *Hicks, Meigh & Johnson, Shelton | c.1822–35 |
| **H. M. & J.** | *Hicks, Meigh & Johnson, Shelton | c.1822–35 |
| **H. M. W. & Sons** | H. M. Williamson & Sons, Longton | c.1879–1941 |
| **H. N. & A.** | Hulse, Nixon & Adderley, Longton | c.1853–68 |
| **H. P.** | H. Palmer, Hanley | c.1760–80 |
| **H. P. Co.** | Hanley Porcelain Co., Hanley | c.1892–9 |
| **H. & P.** | Harrison & Phillips, Burslem | c.1914–15 |
| **H. P. & M.** | Holmes, Plant & Maydew, Burslem | c.1876–85 |
| **H. & R.** | Hall & Read, Burslem | c.1882–8 |
| | Hughes & Robinson | |
| **H. & R. J.** | H. & R. Johnson, Cobridge and Tunstall | c.1902 + |
| **H. & S.** | Hart & Son (Retailers), London | c.1826–69 |
| | Hilditch & Sons, Lane End | c.1819–35 |
| | Holmes & Son, Longton | c.1898–1903 |
| **H. T.** | Tooth & Co., Derbyshire | c.1887–1900 |
| **H. W. & Co.** | Hancock, Whittington & Co., Burslem | c.1863–72 |
| | Hawley, Webberley & Co., Longton | c.1895–1902 |
| **H. & W.** | Hancock & Whittingham, Stoke | c.1873–9 |
| | Holdcroft & Wood, Tunstall | c.1864–71 |
| | | |
| **I. D. B.** | J. D. Baxter, Hanley | c.1823–7 |
| **I. E. B.** | J. & E. Baddeley, Shelton | c.1784–1806 |
| **I. H.** | J. Heath, Hanley | c.1770–1800 |
| **I. H. & Co.** | J. Heath & Co., Tunstall | c.1828–41 |
| **I. K.** | J. Kishere, London | c.1800–43 |
| **I. M.** | *J. Meir, Tunstall | c.1812–36 |
| **I. M. & Co.** | J. Miller & Co., Glasgow | c.1869–75 |
| **I. M. & S.** | *J. Meir & Sons, Tunstall | c.1837–97 |
| **I. R.** | J. Ridgway, Shelton | c.1830–41 |
| **I. R. & Co.** | *Coalport, Shropshire | c.1820–50 |
| **I. T.** | J. Twigg, Kilnhurst | c.1822–81 |
| **I. W. & Co.** | I. Wilson & Co., Yorks. | c.1852–87 |
| **I. W. R.** | *Ridgway, Hanley | c.1813–30 |
| **I. W. & R.** | *Ridgway, Hanley | c.1813–30 |
| | | |
| **J. & Co.** | Jackson & Co., Yorks | c.1870–87 |
| **J. A.** | J. Alcock, Colridge | c.1848–60 |
| | J. Amison, Longton | c.1882–99 |
| | J. Aynsley, Longton | c.1864–73 |
| **J. B.** | J. Beech, Burslem | c.1877–89 |
| | J. & M. P. Bell & Co., Glasgow | c.1842–1928 |
| | J. Bevington, Hanley | c.1872–92 |
| | J. Broadhurst & Sons, Fenton | c.1862 + |
| **J. B. & Co.** | J. Bennett & Co., Hanley | c.1896–1900 |
| | Bennett & Shenton, Hanley | c.1900–3 |
| | J. Bevington & Co., Hanley | c.1869–7 |
| **J. B. & S.** | J. Beech & Son, Longton | c.1860–98 |
| | J. Broadhurst & Sons, Fenton | c.1862 + |
| **J. B. W.** | J. B. Wathen, Fenton | c.1864–9 |
| **J. C.** | J. Clementson, Shelton | c.1839–64 |
| **J. C. L.** | J. Chew, Longton | c.1903–4 |
| **J. C. & Co.** | J. Carr & Co., North Shields | c.1845–1900 |

| | | |
|---|---|---|
| | J. Cartlidge & Co., Longton | c.1864–7 |
| | J. Chetham & Co., Stoke | c.1870–2 |
| **J. & C. W.** | J. & C. Wileman, Fenton | c.1864–9 |
| **J. D.** | J. Deaville, Hanley | c.1854 |
| | J. Drewry, Lane End | c.1812–25 |
| | J. Dudson, Hanley | c.1838–88 |
| **J. D. & Co.** | J. Dimmock & Co., Hanley | c.1862–1904 |
| **J. D. B.** | J. D. Baxter, Hanley | c.1823–7 |
| **J. E.** | Jones Edwards, Burslem | c.1842–51 |
| | John Edwards, Longton | c.1847–53 |
| **J. E. B.** | J. & E. Baddeley, Shelton | c.1784–1806 |
| **J. E. & Co.** | J. Edwards & Co., Fenton | c.1847–1900 |
| **J. E. & S.** | J. Edwards & Son, Burslem | c.1851–82 |
| **J. F. A.** | J. F. Adderley, Longton | c.1901–5 |
| **J. F. & Co.** | J. Furnival & Co., Cobridge | c.1845–70 |
| **J. F. & C. W.** | J. & C. Wileman, Fenton | c.1864–7 |
| **J. F. E.** | J. F. Elton & Co. Ltd, Burslem | c.1901–10 |
| **J. F. E. & Co. Ltd** | J. F. Elton & Co. Ltd, Burslem | c.1901–10 |
| **J. F. W.** | J. F. Wileman, Fenton | c.1869–92 |
| **J. G.** | J. Gerrard, Hanley | c.1846–53 |
| | John Goodwin, Longton | c.1845–51 |
| | J. Gosling, Burslem | c.1896–8 |
| | J. Grove, Hanley | c.1852–61 |
| | ★George Jones, Stoke | c.1861–1951 |
| **J. & G. L.** | Jackson & Gosling, Longton | c.1866 + |
| **J. & G. A.** | J. & G. Alcock, Cobridge | c.1839–46 |
| **J. G. S. & Co.** | J. Goodwin, Stoddard & Co., Longton | c.1898–1940 |
| **J. & G. V.** | J. & G. Vernon, Burslem | c.1880–9 |
| **J. H.** | J. Holdcroft, Longton | c.1865–1939 |
| | J. Holland, Turnstall | c.1852–4 |
| **J. H. & Co.** | J. Heath & Co., Tunstall | c.1828–41 |
| | J. Hollins & Co., Hanley | c.1888–92 |
| **J. H. B.** | J. H. Baddeley, Hanley | c.1841–53 |
| **J. H. C. & Co.** | J. H. Cope & Co., Longton | c.1887–1947 |
| **J. H. W.** | J. H. Walton, Longton | c.1912–21 |
| **J. H. W. & Sons** | J. H. Weatherby & Sons, Hanley | c.1891 + |
| **J. J. & Co.** | J. Jackson & Co., Rotherham | c.1870–87 |
| **J. K.** | J. Kent, Longton | c.1897 + |
| **J. K. L.** | J. Kent, Longton | c.1897 + |
| **J. K. K.** | J. K. Knight, Longton | c.1846–55 |
| **J. L. C.** | J. L. Chetham, Longton | c.1841–62 |
| **J. M.** | ★J. Meir, Tunstall | c.1812–36 |
| | J. Miller, Glasgow | c.1869–75 |
| **J. M. & Co.** | ★James Macintyre & Co., Burslem | c.1860 |
| | John Marshall & Co., Bo'ness | c.1860–99 |
| | J. Maudesley & Co., Tunstall | c.1862–4 |
| | J. Miller & Co., Glasgow | c.1869–75 |
| **J. M. & S.** | ★J. Meir & Son, Tunstall | c.1837–97 |
| **J. & M. P. B. & Co.** | J. & M. P. Bell & Co., Glasgow | c.1842–1928 |
| **J. P.** | J. Proctor, Longton | 1843–6 |
| **J. P. & Co.** | J. Pankhurst & Co., Hanley | c.1852–83 |
| **J. P. & Co.** (contd) | J. Plant & Co., Stoke | c.1891–1902 |

|  | J. Pratt & Co., Lane Delph | c.1851–72 |
|---|---|---|
| **J. P. & Co. (L)** | J. Pratt & Co. Ltd, Fenton | c.1872–8 |
| **J. P. Ltd** | J. Pearson Ltd, Brampton | c.1907 + |
| **J. & P.** | Jackson & Patterson, Newcastle | 1830–45 |
| **J. R.** | James Reeves, Fenton | c.1870–1948 |
|  | *J. Ridgway, Shelton | c.1830–55 |
|  | J. Robinson, Burslem | c.1876–98 |
| **J. R. & Co.** | J. Ridgway & Co., Shelton | c.1830–55 |
|  | *Coalport, Shropshire | c.1820–60 |
| **J. R. B. & Co.** | J. Ridgway, Bates & Co., Shelton | c.1856–58 |
| **J. R. & F. C.** | J. R. & F. Chetham, Longton | c.1846–69 |
| **J. & R. G.** | J. & R. Godwin, Cobridge | c.1834–66 |
| **J. R. H.** | J. & R. Hammersley, Hanley | c.1877–1917 |
| **J. R. & S.** | J. Robinson & Son, Castleford | c.1905–33 |
| **J. S. & Co.** | Jones, Shepherd & Co., Longton | c.1867–8 |
|  | J. Shore & Co., Longton | c.1887–1905 |
| **J. S. H.** | Hill Pottery & Co., Burslem | c.1861–7 |
| **J. S. S. B.** | J. Sadler & Sons, Burslem | c.1899 + |
| **J. S. W.** | J. S. Wild, Longton | c.1904–27 |
| **J. & S. A.** | J. & S. Alcock, Colridge | c.1848–9 |
| **J. T.** | J. Tams (& Sons Ltd), Longton | c.1875 + |
|  | J. Twenlow, Shelton | c.1795–7 |
|  | J. Twigg, Kilnhurst, Yorks. | c.1822–81 |
| **J. T. Ltd** | J. Tams Ltd, Longton | c.1912 + |
| **J. T. & S(ons)** | J. Tams & Sons, Longton | c.1903–12 |
|  | J. Thompson & Sons, Glasgow | c.1816–84 |
| **J. & T. B.** | J. & T. Bevington, Hanley | c.1865–78 |
| **J. & T. E.** | J. & T. Edwards, Burslem | c.1839–41 |
| **J. & T. F.** | J. & T. Furnival, Shelton | c.1843 |
| **J. & T. L.** | J. & T. Lockett, Longton | c.1836–49 |
| **J. T. H.** | J. T. Hudden, Longton | c.1859–85 |
| **J. V.** | James Vernon, Burslem | c.1860–80 |
| **J. V. junr** | James Vernon, Burslem | c.1860–80 |
| **J. V. & S.** | James Vernon, Burslem | c.1860–80 |
| **J. W.** | J. Woodward, Swadlincote | c.1859–88 |
| **J. & W.** | Jones & Walley, Cobridge | c.1841–3 |
| **J. W. D.** | Ashby Potters Guild, Woodville, Derbys. | c.1909–22 |
| **J. W. P. & Co.** | J. W. Pankhurst & Co., Hanley | c.1850–82 |
| **J. W. R.** | *Ridgway, Shelton | c.1814–30 |
| **J. & W. R.** | *Ridgway, Shelton | c.1814–30 |
| **J. W. & S.** | J. Wilson & Sons, Fenton | c.1898–1926 |
| **J. Y.** | J. Yates, Hanley | c.1784–1835 |
|  |  |  |
| **K. & Co.** | Keeling & Co., Burslem | c.1886–1936 |
|  | W. Kirby & Co., Fenton | c.1879–85 |
|  | Kirkland & Co., Etruria | c.1892 + |
| **K. & B.** | *Worcester, Kerr & Binns | 1852–62 |
|  | King & Barratt, Burslem | c.1898–1940 |
|  | Knapper & Blackhurst, Tunstall | c.1867–88 |
| **K. & Co. B.** | Keeling & Co., Burslem | c.1886–1936 |
| **K. E. & Co.** | Knight, Elkin & Co., Fenton | c.1826–46 |
| **K. E. B.** | King, Edge & Barratt, Burslem | c.1896–7 |

| | | |
|---|---|---|
| | Knight, Elkin & Bridgwood, Fenton | c.1829–40 |
| **K. & E.** | Knight & Elkin, Fenton | c.1826–47 |
| **K. F. A. P. Co.** | Kensington Fine Art Pottery Co., Hanley | c.1892–9 |
| **K. & M.** | Keys & Mountford, Stoke | c.1850–7 |
| **K. P. B.** | Kensington Pottery Ltd, Hanley | 1922 + |
| **K. P H.** | Kensington Pottery Ltd, Hanley | 1922 + |
| | | |
| **L.** | Herculaneum Pottery, Liverpool | c.1793–1841 |
| **L. & Sons** | Lancaster & Sons, Hanley | c.1900–44 |
| **L. & A.** | Lockhart & Arthur, Glasgow | c.1855–64 |
| **L. B. & C.** | Lockett, Baguley & Cooper, Hanley | c.1855–61 |
| **L. E. & S.** | Liddle, Elliot & Son, Burslem | c.1862–70 |
| **L. H.** | Lockett & Hulme, Lane End | c.1822–6 |
| **L. & L.** | Lovatt & Lovatt, Langley Mill, Notts. | c.1895 + |
| **L. & M.** | Ynysmedw Pottery, Swansea | c.1860–70 |
| **L. & P.** | Lakin & Poole, Burslem | c.1791–5 |
| **L. P. & Co.** | Livesley, Powell & Co., Hanley | c.1851–66 |
| **L. P. Co. Ltd** | Longton Pottery Co. Ltd, Longton | c.1946–55 |
| **L. S.** | Lancaster & Sons, Hanley | c.1900–44 |
| **L. W.** | Lewis Woolf & Sons, Ferrybridge, Yorks. | c.1856–83 |
| **L. W. & S.** | Lewis Woolf & Sons, Ferrybridge, Yorks. | c.1856–83 |
| | | |
| **M.** | J. Maddock, Burslem | c.1842–55 |
| | *Maling, Newcastle | c.1817–30 |
| | *Minton, Stoke | c.1793 + |
| | Royal Albion China Co., Longton | c.1921–48 |
| **M. & Co.** | *Minton, Stoke | c.1841–73 |
| | Moore & Co., Hanley | c.1898–1903 |
| | Moore & Co., Fenton | c.1872–92 |
| **M. & A.** | Morley & Ashworth, Hanley | c.1859–61 |
| **M. & B.** | *Minton, Stoke | c.1836–41 |
| **M. & C. L.** | Matthews & Clark, Longton | c.1902–6 |
| **M. & E.** | Mayer & Elliott, Longport | c.1856–61 |
| **M. E. & Co.** | *Middlesbrough Earthenware Co., Yorks. | c.1844–52 |
| **M. F. & Co.** | Morley, Fox & Co., Fenton | c.1906–44 |
| **M. H. & Co.** | Mason, Holt & Co., Longton | c.1857–84 |
| | Minton, Hollins & Co., Stoke | c.1845 + |
| **M. & H.** | Marsh & Heywood, Tunstall | c.1818–36 |
| | Mason & Holt, Longton | c.1857–84 |
| | Middleton & Hudson, Longton | c.1877–88 |
| | *Minton, Stoke | c.1845–68 |
| **M. J. B.** | *Blakeney Pottery Ltd., Stoke | c.1969 + |
| **M. L. & Co.** | Moore, Leason & Co., Fenton | c.1892–6 |
| **M. & M.** | Mayer & Maudesley, Tunstall | c.1837–8 |
| | Price Bros, Burslem | c.1896–1903 |
| **M. & N.** | Mayer & Newbold, Lane End | c.1817–33 |
| **M. P. & Co.** | Middlesbrough Pottery Co., Yorks. | c.1834–44 |
| **M. & P.** | Meigh & Pankhurst, Hanley | c.1850–1 |
| **M. & S.** | Maddock & Seddon, Burslem | c.1839–42 |
| | Mayer & Sherratt, Longton | c.1906–41 |
| | *C. Meigh & Son, Hanley | c.1851–61 |
| **M. S. & Co.** | Myott Son & Co., Stoke, Cobridge | c.1898 + |

| | | |
|---|---|---|
| **M. T. & Co.** | Marple, Turner & Co., Hanley | c.1851–3 |
| **M. & T.** | Machin & Thomas, Burslem | c.1831–2 |
| **M. & U.** | Mogridge & Underhay (retailers) Ltd | c.1912 + |
| **M. V. & Co.** | Mellor, Venables & Co., Burslem | c.1834–51 |
| **M. W. & Co.** | Massey & Wildblood & Co., Longton | c.1887–9 |
| | Morgan, Wood & Co., Burslem | c.1860–70 |
| **M. W. H.** | Malkin, Walker & Hulse, Longton | c.1858–64 |
| | | |
| **N. H.** | *New Hall, Shelton | c.1820–35 |
| **N. H. & Co.** | Neale, Harrison & Co., Hanley | c.1875–85 |
| **N. S.** | *Spode (on 'New Stone' wares), Stoke | c.1805–25 |
| **N. W. P. Co.** | New Wharf Pottery Co., Burslem | c.1878–94 |
| | | |
| **O. H. E. C.** | Old Hall Earthenware Co., Hanley | c.1861–86 |
| **O. P.** | Ollivant Potteries Ltd, Stoke | 1948–54 |
| **O. P. L.** | Ollivant Potteries Ltd, Stoke | 1948–54 |
| | | |
| **P.** | Pennington, Liverpool | c.1770–85 |
| | *Pilkingtons, nr Manchester | c.1897–1957 |
| | *Pinxton Porcelain Works, Derbys. | c.1796–1813 |
| | J. H. Proctor, Longton | c.1857–84 |
| **P. & Co.** | Pearson & Co., Chesterfield | c.1805 + |
| | Pountney & Co., Bristol | c.1849–89 |
| **P. & Co. Ltd** | Pountney & Co. Ltd, Bristol | c.1889 + |
| **P. & A.** | Pountney & Allies, Bristol | c.1815–35 |
| **P. A. B. P.** | Pountney & Allies, Bristol | c.1815–35 |
| **P. B.** | Poulson Bros, Ferrybridge, Yorks. | c.1884–1927 |
| **P. & B.** | Powell & Bishop, Hanley | c.1876–8 |
| **P. B. & Co.** | Pinder Bourne & Co., Burslem | c.1862–82 |
| **P. B. & H.** | Pinder, Bourne & Hope, Burslem | 1851–62 |
| **P. B. L.** | Plant Bros, Longton | c.1898–1906 |
| **P. B. & S.** | Powell, Bishop & Stonier, Hanley | c.1878–91 |
| **P. & C.** | Physick & Cooper, Hanley | c.1899–1900 |
| **P. & F. W.** | P. & F. Warburton, Cobridge | c.1795–1802 |
| **P. G.** | Sampson Bridgwood & Son, Longton | c.1870 + |
| **P. H. Co.** | Hanley Porcelain Co., Hanley | c.1892–9 |
| **P. H. & Co.** | P. Holdcroft & Co., Burslem | c.1846–52 |
| **P. H. G.** | Pratt, Hassall & Gerrard, Fenton | c.1822–34 |
| **P. L.** | R. H. & S. L. Plant (Ltd), Longton | c.1898 + |
| **P. P.** | Pearl Pottery Co. Ltd, Hanley | c.1894–1912 |
| **P. P. Co. Ltd** | Pearl Pottery Co. Ltd, Hanley | c.1912–36 |
| | Plymouth Pottery Co. Ltd | c.1856–63 |
| **P. & S.** | Pratt & Simpson, Fenton | c.1878–83 |
| **P. & S. L.** | R. Plant & Sons, Longton | c.1895–1901 |
| **P. & U.** | Poole & Unwin, Longton | c.1871–6 |
| **P. W.** | P. Warburton, Cobridge | c.1802–12 |
| **P. W. & Co.** | Podmore, Walker & Co., Tunstall | c.1834–59 |
| **P. W. & W.** | Podmore, Walker & Co., Tunstall | c.1834–59 |
| | | |
| **R.** | S. & J. Rathbone, Tunstall | c.1812–35 |
| | *J. Ridgway, Hanley | c.1830–55 |
| **R. & Co.** | Reid & Co., Longton | c.1913–46 |

| | | |
|---|---|---|
| **R. & A.** | Ridgway & Abington, Hanley | c.1847–60 |
| **R. B.** | Robinson Bros, Castleford | c.1897–1904 |
| **R. B. & Co.** | R. Britton & Co., Leeds | c.1850–3 |
| **R. B. & S.** | R. Britton & Son, Leeds | c.1872–8 |
| **R. C. & A.** | Read, Clementson & Anderson, Hanley | c.1836 |
| **R. C. & Co.** | R. Cockran & Co., Glasgow | c.1846–1918 |
| **R. & C.** | Read & Clementson, Hanley | c.1833–5 |
| **R. (C) Ltd** | A. G. Richardson, Cobridge | c.1920–1 |
| **R. C. R.** | S. & E. Collier, Reading | c.1870–1957 |
| **R. & D.** | Redfern & Drakeford, Longton | c.1892–1933 |
| **R. F. & S.** | R. Floyd & Sons, Stoke | c.1907–30 |
| **R. G.** | R. Gallimore, Longton | c.1906–34 |
| | R. Garner, Fenton | 18th century |
| **R. G. S.** | R. G. Scrivener & Co., Hanley | c.1870–83 |
| **R. G. S. & Co** . | R. G. Scrivener & Co., Hanley | c.1870–83 |
| **R. H.** | R. Hammersley, Burslem | c.1860–83 |
| **R. H. & Co.** | R. Hall & Co., Tunstall | c.1841–9 |
| **R. H. F. P.** | *R. Heron (& Son) Scotland | c.1837–60 |
| **R. H. & S.** | R. Hammersley & Son, Burslem | c.1884–1905 |
| | *R. Heron & Son, Scotland | c.1850–60 |
| **R. H. P. & Co.** | R. H. Plant & Co., Longton | c.1881–98 |
| **R. H. & S. L. P.** | R. H. & S. L. Plant, Longton | c.1898 + |
| **R. & L.** | *Robinson & Leadbeater, Stoke | c.1864–1924 |
| **R. & M.** | *Ridgway & Morley, Hanley | c.1842–5 |
| **R. & M.** | Roper & Meredith, Longton | c.1913–24 |
| **R. M. A.** | R. M. Astbury, Lane End | c.1790 |
| **R. M. & S.** | R. Malkin & Sons, Fenton | c.1882–92 |
| **R. M. W. & Co.** | *Ridgway, Morley, Wear & Co., Hanley | c.1836–42 |
| **R. & N.** | Rowley & Newton Ltd, Longton | c.1896–1901 |
| **R. & P.** | Rhodes & Proctor, Burslem | c.1883–5 |
| **R. S.** | S. Radford, Fenton | c.1879–1957 |
| | R. Stevenson & Son, Cobridge | c.1810–32 |
| **R. & S.** | Rigby & Stevenson, Hanley | c.1894–1954 |
| | Robinson & Son, Longton | c.1881–1903 |
| **R. S. & Co.** | Rathbone, Smith & Co., Tunstall | c.1883–97 |
| **R. S. R.** | Ridgway, Sparkes & Ridgway, Hanley | c.1873–9 |
| **R. S. & S.** | R. Stevenson & Son, Cobridge | c.1832–5 |
| **R. S. W.** | Stevenson & William, Cobridge | c.1825 |
| | Rye Pottery, Sussex | c.1869–1920 |
| **R. & T.** | Reed & Taylor, Ferrybridge Pottery, Yorks. | c.1843–50 |
| **R. T. & Co.** | Reed & Taylor, Ferrybridge Pottery, Yorks. | c.1843–50 |
| **R. V. W.** | R. V. Wildblood, Longton | c.1887–8 |
| **R. & W.** | Ray & Wynne, Lane End | c.1837–46 |
| | Robinson & Wood, Hanley | c.1832–6 |
| **R. W. & B.** | Robinson, Wood & Brownfield, Cobridge | c.1838–41 |
| **R. W. M.** | *Martin Brothers, London | c.1873–1914 |
| **S.** (printed) | *Caughley, Shropshire | c.1775–99 |
| **S.** (impressed) | *Spode, Stoke | c.1777–1805 |
| **S. Bros** | Stubbs Bros, Fenton | c.1899–1904 |
| **S. & C.** | Shore & Coggins, Longton | c.1911 + |
| **S. Ltd** | Swinnertons Ltd, Hanley | c.1906 + |

| | | |
|---|---|---|
| **S. & Sons** | Southwick Pottery, Sunderland | c.1829–38 |
| **S. A. & Co.** | ★S. Alcock & Co., Burslem | c.1830–59 |
| **S. B. & S.** | S. Barker & Son, Swinton, Yorks. | c.1834–93 |
| | S. Bevington & Son, Hanley | c.1851–63 |
| | S. Boyle & Sons, Hanley | c.1850–2 |
| | S. Bridgwood & Son, Longton | c.1853 + |
| **S. & B.** | Sefton & Brown, Ferrybridge | c.1897–1919 |
| | Shorter & Boulton, Stoke | c.1878–1905 |
| **S. & B. T.** | Smith & Binnall, Tunstall | c.1897–1900 |
| **S. C.** | S. Clive, Tunstall | c.1875–80 |
| **S. & C.** | Shore & Coggins, Longton | c.1911 + |
| **S. C. C.** | Star China Co., Longton | c.1900–19 |
| **S. C. & Co.** | S. Clive, Tunstall | c.1875–80 |
| **S. C. H. L.** | Shore, Coggins & Holt, Longton | c.1905–10 |
| **S. E.** | S. Elkin, Longton | c.1856–64 |
| **S. & E.** | Swift & Elkin, Longton | c.1840–3 |
| **S. & F.** | Smith & Ford, Burslem | c.1895–8 |
| **S. F. & Co.** | ★S. Fielding & Co., Stoke | c.1879 + |
| **S. H.** | S. Hallen, Burslem | c.1851–4 |
| | S. Hancock, Tunstall and Stoke | 1858–90 |
| | ★Derby, King Street | c.1861–1935 |
| **S. H. & S.** | S. Hancock & Sons, Stoke | c.1891–35 |
| | S. Hughes & Son, Burslem | c.1853–5 |
| **S. J.** | S. Johnson, Burslem | c.1887–1912 |
| **S. J. B.** | S. Johnson, Burslem | c.1887–1912 |
| **S. & J. B.** | S. & J. Burton, Hanley | c.1832–45 |
| **S. J. R.** | ★S. & J. Rathbone, Tunstall | c.1812–35 |
| **S. & J. R.** | S. & J. Rathbone, Tunstall | c.1812–35 |
| **S. K. & Co.** | S. Keeling & Co., Hanley | c.1840–50 |
| **S. L.** | S. Longbottom, Nafferton, Yorks. | Late 19th cent. |
| **S. & L.** | Stanley & Lambert, Longton | c.1850–4 |
| **S. M. & Co.** | ★Sunderland Potteries | c.1803–74 |
| **S. & N. L.** | Salt & Nixon, Longton | c.1897–1904 |
| **So.** (printed) | ★Caughley, Shropshire | c.1775–99 |
| **S. P. Ltd** | Sylvan Pottery Ltd, Hanley | c.1946 + |
| **S. S.** | S. Smith Ltd, Longton | c.1846–1963 |
| | Southwick Pottery, Sunderland | c.1872–82 |
| **S. & S.** | D. Sutherland & Sons, Longton | c.1865–75 |
| **S. & S. S.** | Shaw & Sons, Tunstall | c.1892–1910 |
| **S. & V.** | Sant & Vodrey, Cobridge | c.1887–93 |
| **S. & W.** | Stockton Pottery | c.1870–80 |
| **S. W. P.** | South Wales Pottery, Llanelly | c.1839–58 |
| **Sx.** (printed) | ★Caughley, Shropshire | c.1775–99 |
| | | |
| **T.** | See mark list under 'Tebo' Toulouse | c.1750–90 |
| **T. A.** | T. Ainsworth, Stockton | c.1858–67 |
| **T. A. & S. G.** | T. A. & S. Green, Fenton | c.1876–89 |
| **T. B.** | T. Bevington, Hanley | c.1877–91 |
| **T. & B.** | Tomkinson & Billington, Longton | c.1868–70 |
| **T. B. & Co.** | T. Booth & Co., Burslem | c.1868–72 |
| **T. B. & S.** | T. Boote & Son, Burslem | c.1842 + |
| **T. B. & S.** (contd) | T. Brown & Sons, Ferrybridge | c.1919 + |

| T. B. G. | T. & B. Godwin, Burslem | c.1809–34 |
|---|---|---|
| T. & B. G. | T. & B. Godwin, Burslem | c.1809–34 |
| T. C. | T. Cone, Longton | c.1892 + |
| T. & C. F. | T. & C. Ford, Hanley | c.1854–71 |
| T. C. W. | T. Wild & Co., Longton | c.1896–1904 |
| T. D. & Co. | T. Dimmock & Co, Shelton | c.1828–67 |
| T. E. | T. Edwards, Burslem | c.1844–8 |
| T. F. | T. Ford, Hanley | c.1853–74 |
| | T. Forester, Longton | c.1880–3 |
| | T. Fradley, Stoke | c.1875–85 |
| T. F. & Co. | T. Fell & Co., Newcastle | c.1830–90 |
| | T. Forester & Co., Longton | c.1888 |
| | T. Furnival & Co., Hanley | c.1844–6 |
| T. F. & S. | T. Forester & Sons, Longton | c.1883–1959 |
| T. F. & Sons | T. Furnival & Sons, Cobridge | c.1871–90 |
| T. F. & S. Ltd | T. Forester & Sons Ltd, Longton | c.1891–1959 |
| T. G. | T. Godwin, Burslem | c.1834–54 |
| | T. Goodfellow, Tunstall | c.1828–60 |
| | T. Green, Fenton | c.1848–58 |
| T. G. B. | T. G. Booth, Tunstall | c.1876–83 |
| T. G. & F. B. | T. G. & F. Booth, Tunstall | c.1883–91 |
| T. G. G. & Co. | T. G. Green & Co. Ltd, Church Gresley, Derbys. | c.1864 + |
| T. I. & Co. | T. Ingleby & Co., Tunstall | c.1834–5 |
| T. I. & J. E. | T. I. & J. Emberton, Tunstall | c.1869–82 |
| T. J. & J. M. | T. J. & J. Mayer, Burslem | c.1843–55 |
| T. & K. L. | Taylor & Kent, Longton | c.1867 + |
| T. & L. | Tams & Lowe, Longton | c.1865–74 |
| T. L. K. | Taylor & Kent Ltd, Longton | c.1867 + |
| T. M. | ★Blakeney Pottery, Stoke | c.1969 + |
| | T. Mayer, Stoke | c.1956 + |
| | T. Morris, Longton | c.1897–1901 |
| T. M. R. | T. M. Randall (decorator), Madeley | c.1825–40 |
| T. N. & Co. | T. Nicholson & Co., Castleford | c.1854–71 |
| To. | See mark list under 'Tebo' Toulouse | c.1750–90 |
| T. P. | T. Peake, Tunstall | c.1830–51 |
| | T. Pinder, Burslem | c.1848–51 |
| | T. Plant, Lane End | c.1825–50 |
| T. P. L. | T. P. Ledgar, Longton | c.1900–5 |
| T. P. & S. | T. Phillips & Son, Burslem | c.1845–6 |
| T. R. & Co. | T. Rathbone & Co., Tunstall | c.1898–1923 |
| | T. Rathbone & Co., Portobello | c.1810–45 |
| T. & R. B. | T. & R. Boote, Burslem | c.1842 + |
| T. R. & P. | Tundley, Rhodes & Proctor, Burslem | c.1873–83 |
| T. S. & C(oy) | T. Shirley & Co., Greenock | c.1840–57 |
| T. T. | Taylor, Tunnicliffe & Co., Hanley | c.1868 + |
| | T. Till, Burslem | c.1850 |
| T. T. & Co. | Taylor, Tunnicliffe & Co., Hanley | c.1868 + |
| T. & T. | Turner & Tomkinson, Tunstall | c.1860–72 |
| T. T. & S. | Thomas Till & Sons, Burslem | c.1850–1929 |
| T. U. & Co. | U. Thomas & Co., Hanley | c.1888–1905 |
| T. W. & Co. | T. Wood & Co., Burslem | c.1885–96 |

| | | |
|---|---|---|
| **T. W. & S.** | T. Wood & Sons, Burslem | c.1896–7 |
| **U. C. & N.** | U. Clark & Nephews, Dicker, Sussex | c.1900–20 |
| **U. H. P. Co.** | Upper Hanley Pottery Co., Hanley | c.1895–1910 |
| **U. H. & W.** | Unwin, Holmes & Worthington, Hanley | c.1865–8 |
| **U. M. & T.** | Unwin, Mountford & Taylor, Hanley | c.1864 |
| **U. T. & Co.** | U. Thomas & Co., Hanley | c.1888–1905 |
| **V. & B.** | Venables & Baines, Burslem | c.1851–2 |
| **V. M. & Co.** | Venables, Mann & Co. | c.1853–6 |
| **W.** | E. Walley, Cobridge | c.1845–56 |
| | Wardle & Co., Hanley | c.1871–1935 |
| | T. Wolfe, Stoke | c.1784–1818 |
| | *E. Wood, Burslem | c.1784–92 |
| | *Worcester porcelains` | c.1760–75 |
| **W(***)** | See mark list | c.1790–1815 |
| **W. & C.** | Wade & Co., Burslem | c.1887–1927 |
| | Whittaker & Co., Hanley | c.1886–92 |
| | *Wileman & Co., Longton | c.1892–1925 |
| **W. & Sons** | H. M. Williamson & Son, Longton | c.1874–1941 |
| **W. & A.** | Wardle & Ash, Hanley | c.1859–62 |
| | Warren & Adams, Longton | c.1853–64 |
| | Wild & Adams, Longton | c.1909–27 |
| **W. A. & Co.** | *William Adams, Tunstall and Stoke | c.1893–1917 |
| **W. A. & S.** | *William Adams, Tunstall and Stoke | c.1819–64 |
| **W. A. A.** | W. A. Adderley (& Co.), Longton | c.1876–1905 |
| **W. A. A. & Co.** | W. A. Adderley & Co., Longton | c.1876–1905 |
| **W. B.** | W. Baker (& Co.), Fenton | c.1839–68 |
| | W. Beech, Burslem | |
| | W. Bennett, Hanley | c.1882–1937 |
| **W. & B.** | Wagstaff & Brunt, Longton | c.1880–1927 |
| | *J. Wedgwood (& Sons Ltd) | c.1769–80 |
| | Wood & Baggaley, Burslem | c.1870–80 |
| | Wood & Bowers, Burslem | c.1839 |
| | Wood & Brownfield, Cobridge | c.1838–50 |
| **W. & B. Ltd** | Wood & Barker Ltd, Burslem | c.1897–1903 |
| **W. B. & S.** | *W. Brownfield & Sons, Cobridge | c.1871–91 |
| **W. B. & Sons** | *W. Brownfield & Sons, Cobridge | c.1871–91 |
| **W. & C.** | Walker & Carter, Longton | c.1872–89 |
| | Wood & Challinor, Tunstall | c.1828–43 |
| | Wood & Clarke (& Co.), Burslem | c.1871–2 |
| **W. C. & Co.** | *Chamberlain & Co., Worcester | c.1845–52 |
| | Wood, Challinor & Co., Tunstall | c.1860–4 |
| **W. & Co.** | Wardle & Co., Hanley | c.1882–1909 |
| **W. D. M.** | *W. De Morgan, London | c.1872–1907 |
| **W. E.** | W. Emberton, Tunstall | c.1851–69 |
| **W. & E. C.** | W. & E. Corn, Longport | c.1864–1904 |
| **W. E. W.** | W. E. Withinshaw, Burslem | c.1873–8 |
| **W. F.** | W. Fifield (decorator), Bristol | c.1810–55 |
| **W. F. & Co.** | Whittingham, Ford & Co., Burslem | c.1868–73 |
| **W. F. & R.** | Whittingham, Ford & Riley, Burslem | c.1876–82 |
| **W. & G.** | W. & G. Harding, Burslem | c.1851–5 |

| W. H. | W. Hackwood, Hanley | c.1827–43 |
|---|---|---|
| | W. Hudson, Longton | c.1889–1941 |
| W. & H. | Wildblood & Heath, Longton | c.1889–99 |
| | Wood & Hulme, Burslem | c.1882–1905 |
| | Worthington & Harrop, Hanley | c.1856–73 |
| W. H. & Co. | Whittaker, Heath & Co., Hanley | c.1892–8 |
| W. H. & S. | W. Hackwood & Sons, Hanley | c.1846–9 |
| | Wildblood, Heath & Sons, Longton | c.1899–1927 |
| W. H. G. | ★W. H. Goss, Stoke | c.1858–1944 |
| W. H. L. | W. H. Lockitt, Hanley | c.1901–19 |
| W. H. & W. | Wood, Hulse & Winkle, Hanley | c.1882–5 |
| W. & J. B. | W. & J. Butterfield, Tunstall | c.1854–61 |
| W. & J. H. | W. & J. Harding, Hanley | c.1862–72 |
| W. K. & Co. | W. Kirkby & Co., Fenton | c.1879–85 |
| W. L. L. | W. Lowe, Longton | c.1874–1930 |
| W. & L. | Wildblood & Ledgar, Longton | c.1896–1900 |
| W. & L. L. | Wathen & Lichfield, Fenton | c.1862–4 |
| W. & P. | Wood & Piggott, Tunstall | c.1869–71 |
| W. P. Co. | Wellington Pottery Co., Hanley | c.1899–1901 |
| W. R. | ★W. Ridgway, Hanley | 1830–54 |
| W. & R. | ★Carlton Ware, Stoke | c.1958 + |
| | Wilkinson & Richhuss, Hanley | c.1856–62 |
| | Wiltshaw & Robinson, Stoke | c.1890–1957 |
| | Wittman & Roth, London | c.1880 + |
| | Wright & Rigby, Cobridge | c.1882–4 |
| W. R. & Co. | ★W. Ridgway & Co., Hanley | c.1834–54 |
| W. R. S. & Co. | ★W. Ridgway, Son & Co., Hanley | c.1838–48 |
| W. S. | W. Smith & Co., Stockton, Yorks | c.1845–84 |
| W. S. & Co. | ★Stockton Pottery | c.1825–55 |
| W. S. Junr & Co. | W. Smith & Co., Stockton, Yorks | c.1845–55 |
| W. S. K. | W. S. Kennedy, Burslem | c.1844–55 |
| W. & Sons | H. M. Williamson & Sons, Longton | c.1879–1941 |
| W. & S. E. | W. & S. Edge, Lane Delph | c.1841–8 |
| W. & T. A. | W. & T. Adams, Tunstall | c.1860–90 |
| W. T. H. | W. T. Holland, South Wales Pottery | c.1860s |
| W. W. | J. Wedg-Wood, Burslem | c.1841–60 |
| | Wilkinson & Wardle, Denby, Yorks | c.1864–6 |
| W. & W. B. | Wooldridge & Walley, Burslem | c.1898–1901 |
| W. & W. Co. | W. Wood & Co., Burslem | c.1873–1932 |
| Y. | Yale & Barker, Longton | c.1841–53 |
| Y. M. P. | Ynysmendw Pottery, Swansea | c.1850 |
| Y. P. | Ynysmendw Pottery, Swansea | c.1850 |
| Z. B. | Z. Boyle, Hanley | c.1823–8 |
| Z. B. & S. | Z. Boyle & Son, Hanley | c.1828–50 |

Further details of many of the marks listed in this section will be found in the *Encyclopaedia of British Pottery and Porcelain Marks* (Herbert Jenkins Ltd, 1964). The reader is also referred, in the case of initials found on porcelains, to my *Encyclopaedia of British Porcelain Manufacturers* (Barrie & Jenkins, 1988), Section V, pages 817–29.

# Registered Designs 1839–1883 and Registration Numbers 1884–1999

The British Government passed various Acts to give copyright protection to new designs. The Sculpture Copyright Act of 1797 and the updated 1814 version gave protection to modelled forms provided that the proprietor marked his productions with the words 'Published by', followed by his name, a simple address and the date of first issue. Obviously such clear markings are self-explanatory but few ceramic objects, apart from jugs, bear this form of marking.

From 1839 to 1842 new designs were required to be registered at the Board of Trade in London, under Acts 2 & 3 Victoria c. 17. Again the name, address and date of the initial publication had to be given on the copies. A relatively few ceramic designs were registered, see following list.

**1839**

| | | |
|---|---|---|
| Nov 19 | no. 106 | John Ridgway |

**1840**

| | | |
|---|---|---|
| Mar 5 | 273 | John Ridgway |
| Mar 5 | 274 | John Ridgway |
| Oct 28 | 444 | John Ridgway |

**1841**

| | | |
|---|---|---|
| May 10 | 692 | John Ridgway & Co. |
| Sept 2 | 808–9 | J. & T. Edwards |
| Sept 10 | 832 | J. & T. Edwards |
| Sept 27 | 849 | John Ridgway & Co. |
| Dec 31 | 1002–5 | Kidston & Co. (Glasgow) |

**1842**

| | | |
|---|---|---|
| Mar 17 | 1141–2 | Charles Meigh |
| May 30 | 1266–8 | James Edwards |

The dates of these registrations, together with the allocated number, can occur as part of the printed mark on these 1839–42 designs.

In 1842 a system was introduced whereby a new design or form could be registered at the Design Office, in London. To secure the copyright protection a rendering of the new unique form, or pattern, had to be sent to the office in Whitehall, together with the required registration fee. The relevant facts were then entered in ledgers, under various 'classes'. There were thirteen classes, of which class IV covered ceramic objects (glass wares were class III).

Each day several designs would have been received for registration. These were entered in the first register under the date of receipt and allocated a reference number and a 'parcel number'. This parcel number indicated the entry number for that day but each entry could cover several objects registered by any one firm. The drawings or other representation of the article were filed in separate books.

Once entered, a special coded device was issued by the Registrar and sent to the manufacturer. Exact copies of this device had to be affixed to the protected product. This British Registered Design mark took the basic diamond shape shown opposite.

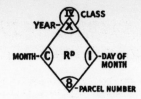

The class number IV appears at the top. The initials R$^D$ appear in the centre, standing for registered. The inner angles showed the coded letter for the year, at twelve o'clock; the day of the month, given in clear numbers, at three o'clock; the parcel number at six o'clock; and the code letter for the month at nine o'clock.

The above placing applies to the period 1842 to 1867. From 1868 to 1883 the order was amended, so that the year letter appears in the three o'clock position; the coded month letter at six o'clock; the parcel number at nine o'clock; and the day number at twelve o'clock. I here show this amended device as used from 1868.

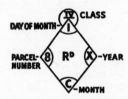

Below are given the year and month letters for the two periods.

## YEARS

1842–67
*Year Letter at Top*

| | | | |
|---|---|---|---|
| A = 1845 | N = 1864 |
| B = 1858 | O = 1862 |
| C = 1844 | P = 1851 |
| D = 1852 | Q = 1866 |
| E = 1855 | R = 1861 |
| F = 1847 | S = 1849 |
| G = 1863 | T = 1867 |
| H = 1843 | U = 1848 |
| I = 1846 | V = 1850 |
| J = 1854 | W = 1865 |
| K = 1857 | X = 1842 |
| L = 1856 | Y = 1853 |
| M = 1859 | Z = 1860 |

1868–83
*Year Letter at Right*

| | |
|---|---|
| A = 1871 | L = 1882 |
| C = 1870 | P = 1877 |
| D = 1878 | S = 1875 |
| E = 1881 | U = 1874 |
| F = 1873 | V = 1876 |
| H = 1869 | W = March 1–6 1878 |
| I = 1872 | X = 1868 |
| J = 1880 | Y = 1879 |
| K = 1883 | |

## MONTHS (BOTH PERIODS)

| | | |
|---|---|---|
| A = December | E = May | K = November (and December 1860) |
| B = October | G = February | M = June |
| C or O = January | H = April | R = August (and September 1–19 1857) |
| D = September | I = July | W = March |

Once decoded, the present-day owner can discover the date, month and year of registration. This of course only represents the earliest possible date of the piece. The initial fee gave protection for a three-year period but in practice the mark can occur on pieces made after this period had lapsed.

Having discovered the date of registration, the reader can further ascertain the name of the person or firm concerned in the registration, with the assistance of the following list. In most cases this will be the manufacturer but in a few instances the registration was made by other persons or firms, such as the designer or a retailer. I have marked such non-ceramic names with an asterisk. In a very few cases a design was registered by two firms and, of course, there was nothing to stop the copyright owner selling on the rights to another manufacturer. Such provisions are, however, very rare and in most cases the name given in this listing will relate to the manufacturer. It is, of course, vital to read and decode the mark correctly!

As some registrations relate to the form of the piece (or part of a piece, such as a moulded-edged design) and other entries relate to the added decoration it is possible to have two separate registration marks on a single piece. In general terms an impressed or moulded mark will relate to the basic shape of the piece, whilst a printed mark will relate to the decoration.

I have in this unique listing been at pains to give some helpful basic indication of the subject of the registration: the form or added pattern. As the listing exceeds 4,000 entries each description has to be brief. For this reason also I have not quoted the official entry number as this does not normally appear on the piece. I have also needed to abbreviate the place-name of the manufacturer's town or city.

By far the largest number of firms were situated in the group of Staffordshire towns which make up the district we know as The Potteries, now embraced by the City of Stoke-on-Trent. These Staffordshire townships were Burslem (B); Cobridge (C); Fenton (F); Hanley (H); Lane End (LE); Longport (Lpt); Longton (L); Shelton (Sh), part of Hanley; Stoke (S); and Tunstall (T). To these Staffordshire place-names one can add Etruria (E), the name of the Wedgwood factory, and Newcastle-under-Lyme (N). Other place-names and my abbreviations included in this comprehensive list are: Belleek (Bel); Birmingham (Bir); Broseley (Br); Burton-on-Trent (BT); Cambridge (Cam); Cardiff (Cf); Coalport (Cpt); Derby (D); Devon (De); Dublin (Du); France (Fr); Germany (Ger); Glasgow (G); Great Yarmouth (GY); Hastings (Hgs); Ireland (Ire); Jackfield (J); Leeds (Lds); Liverpool (Liv); Llanelly (Ll); London (Ln); Manchester (M); New York (NY); Newcastle-upon-Tyne (NT); Norwich (No); Prescot (P); Scotland (Sc); Sheffield (Sd); Shropshire (Shrop); Sunderland (Su); Swadlincote (Sw); Swinton (Sn); Tamworth (Tam); Wales (Ws); Wareham (Wm); Watcombe (Wat); Weston-super-Mare (WsM); Winchester (Win); Worcester (W); Wordsley (Wy); and Yorkshire (Y).

The original files covering the 1839–42 and the 1842–83 systems are held at the Public Record Office at Kew. The general references are BT43 for the representations of the designs or shapes and BT44 for the registers of names and addresses with the reference number. It should be noted that some of these records are in a very bad state and some are not available for public study.

The Potteries Museum (at Bethesda Street, Hanley) has a good selection of British ceramics of registered forms or bearing registered patterns and marks.

The copyright in the following unique listing is twofold. The basic list of names and dates has been extracted from the original official documents retained at the Public Record Office at Kew. These are covered by Crown Copyright and have been published here by kind permission of the authorities. The additional information on the manufacturers and their registered products plus the format of the listing is covered by my copyright. This listing must not therefore be copied without written permission from both parties.

As mentioned earlier, an asterisk in the list below refers to non-manufacturing persons or firms, mainly situated away from pottery producing areas.

| Date | Parcel | Manufacturer | Town | Object |
|------|--------|--------------|------|--------|
| **1842 (X at top)** | | | | |
| Sep 22 | 1 | James Dixon & Son★ | Sd | Jug, for mounting |
| Nov 2 | 1 | Joseph Wolstenholme★ | Sd | Tray |
| Nov 3 | 1 | Joseph Wolstenholme★ | Sd | Covered jug |
| Nov 26 | 3 | Henry Hunt★ | Ln | Flower pot |
| Nov 26 | 3 | Henry Hunt★ | Ln | Flower pot |
| Dec 2 | 3 | Joseph Clementson | Sh | Lucerne design |
| Dec 2 | 3 | Joseph Clementson | Sh | Rustic scenery design |
| Dec 30 | 2 | James Edwards | B | Toiletwares |
| | | | | |
| **1843 (H at top)** | | | | |
| Jan 24 | 2 | John Ridgway & Co. | Sh | Candlestick |
| Jan 24 | 2 | John Ridgway & Co. | Sh | Candlestick |
| Feb 3 | 4 | T. Woodfield★ | Ln | Water closet |
| Feb 21 | 1 | Samuel Alcock & Co. | B | Vase form |
| Feb 21 | 1 | Samuel Alcock & Co. | B | Flared vase |
| Feb 21 | 1 | Samuel Alcock & Co. | B | Two-handled vase |
| Feb 21 | 1 | Samuel Alcock & Co. | B | Celery vase |
| Feb 21 | 1 | Samuel Alcock & Co. | B | Inkstand |
| Mar 21 | 5 | Josiah Wedgwood & Sons | E | Fluted ewer |
| Mar 21 | 5 | Josiah Wedgwood & Sons | E | Moulded ewer |
| Mar 31 | 6 | Samuel Alcock & Co. | B | Pierced vase |
| May 2 | 4 | Josiah Wedgwood & Sons | E | Printed design |
| May 5 | 1 | W. S. Kennedy | B | Bell pull |
| May 11 | 2 | W. S. Kennedy | B | Door knob |
| May 13 | 4 | Jones & Wolley | C | Moulded jug |
| Jun 14 | 5 | Samuel Alcock & Co. | B | Teawares |
| Aug 30 | 8 | James Edwards | B | Dinnerwares |
| Oct 6 | 2 | James Edwards | B | Dinner ware |
| Nov 10 | 3 | Minton & Co. | S | Plate form |
| Nov 28 | 5 | Thomas Dimmock & Co. | Sh | Indian festoon print |
| Dec 14 | 10 | G. F. Bowers & Co. | T | Teawares |
| | | | | |
| **1844 (C at top)** | | | | |
| Feb 15 | 9 | Samuel Alcock & Co. | B | Vases |
| Feb 20 | 4 | Samuel Alcock & Co. | B | Vases |
| Mar 1 | 6 | Hamilton & Moore | L | Teawares |
| Mar 5 | 3 | Mellor, Venables & Co. | B | Teawares |
| Mar 7 | 4 | J. & T. Lockett | LE | Teawares |
| April 3 | 3 | Thomas Edwards | B | Dinnerwares |
| April 11 | 4 | Hilditch & Hopwood | LE | Teawares |
| May 7 | 4 | T. Dimmock, jnr & Co. | Sh | Rhine pattern |
| Jun 29 | 3 | T. Dimmock, jnr & Co. | Sh | Lily pattern |
| July 20 | 5 | John Ridgway & Co. | Sh | Tureen form and printed patterns |
| July 30 | 2 | Herbert Minton & Co. | S | Cup forms |
| Aug 15 | 3 | Knight & Elkin | S | Baronial Halls pattern |

| Aug 21 | 7 | Herbert Minton & Co. | S | Figures & ewer |
|--------|---|----------------------|-----|----------------|
| Sept 9 | 7 | Cyples, Barlow & Cyples | LE | Teawares |
| Sept 19 | 4 | John Ridgway & Co. | Sh | Dinnerwares |
| Sept 21 | 2 | Henry Hunt★ | Ln | Hyacinth pot |
| Sept 30 | 7 | Charles Meigh | H | Moulded jug |
| Oct 14 | 4 | Copeland & Garrett | S | Floral design |
| Oct 17 | 3 | Clementson, Young & Jameson | Sh | Aleppo pattern |
| Oct 23 | 4 | Thomas Davenport | Bir | Button |
| Oct 30 | 4 | Herbert Minton & Co. | S | Dinnerwares & figure |
| Nov 6 | 4 | Herbert Minton & Co. | S | Toiletwares |
| Nov 11 | 5 | James Edwards | B | Printed design |
| Nov 13 | 4 | John Ridgway & Co. | Sh | Dinnerwares |
| Nov 22 | 4 | Thomas Dimmock, junr & Co. | Sh | Bohemia pattern |
| Nov 26 | 3 | Ray & Wynne | LE | Teawares |
| Dec 2 | 3 | Copeland & Garrett | S | Printed patterns |
| Dec 7 | 4 | Thomas Edwards | B | Fluted tea wares |
| Dec 16 | 6 | W. Ridgway, Son & Co. | H | Catshill moss pattern |
| Dec 24 | 2 | John Meir & Son | T | Mazara pattern |

## 1845 (A at top)

| Jan 11 | 6 | George Phillips | Lpt | Corinth pattern |
|--------|---|-----------------|-----|-----------------|
| Jan 15 | 2 | Clementson, Young & Jameson | Sh | Jug form |
| Jan 21 | 6 | T. J. & J. Mayer | Lpt | Moulded jug |
| Jan 27 | 5 | John Rose & Co. | Cpt | Moulded edging |
| Feb 26 | 5 | W. S. Kennedy | B | Forms |
| Feb 27 | 3 | George Phillips | Lpt | Dinnerwares |
| Mar 5 | 1 | Copeland & Garrett | S | Moulded edging |
| Mar 6 | 5 | H. Minton & Co. | S | Figure |
| Mar 17 | 10 | H. Minton & Co. | S | Printed design |
| Mar 20 | 1 | H. Minton & Co. | S | Moulded jug |
| Mar 31 | 4 | Thomas Pearce★ | Ln | Figure – Wesley |
| April 10 | 1 | Thomas Pearce★ | Ln | Figure – Fletcher |
| April 25 | 2 | Copeland & Garrett | S | Printed pattern |
| April 26 | 1 | George Pearce★ | Ln | Figure – J. Wesley |
| April 26 | 3 | T. & R. Boote with Edward Walley and E. Jones | B C H | Dinnerwares |
| April 30 | 2 | Jacob Furnival | C | Printed design |
| May 8 | 2 | Herbert Minton & Co. | S | Moulded jug |
| May 10 | 3 | E. Walley and T. & R. Boote | C | Moulded jug |
| May 31 | 1 | Francis Morley | Sh | Dinnerwares |
| Jun 19 | 1 | George Phillips | Lpt | Lobelia pattern |
| Jun 26 | 3 | Minton & Co. | S | Moulded cup |
| July 5 | 1 | George Phillips | Lpt | Six forms |
| July 5 | 2 | Enoch Wood | B | Lucerne pattern |
| July 26 | 1 | William Adams & Sons | S | Habrana pattern |
| Aug 28 | 3 | Joseph Clementson | Sh | Printed design |
| Sept 4 | 3 | Copeland & Garrett | S | Tartan designs |
| Sept 11 | 2 | Thomas Phillips & Son | B | Floral pattern |
| Sept 19 | 1 | Minton & Co. | S | Moulded font |
| Oct 6 | 1 | H. Minton & Co. | S | Open work border & printed pattern |

| Oct 21 | 1 | Copeland & Garrett | S | Printed design |
| Oct 22 | 2 | Clementson & Young | Sh | Dinnerwares |
| Nov 15 | 2 | Bayley & Ball | L | Printed jug |
| Nov 22 | 2 | Minton & Co. | S | Moulded jug |
| Dec 4 | 4 | John Ridgway | Sh | Dinnerwares |
| Dec 24 | 2 | W. Pigott* | Ln | Button |
| Dec 27 | 3 | James Edwards | B | Jug shape |
| Dec 29 | 2 | Joseph Clementson | Sh | Dinnerwares |
| Dec 30 | 3 | Furnival & Clark | H | Falstaff jug |

## 1846 (I at top)

| Jan 7 | 2 | Joseph Clementson | Sh | Tessino pattern |
| Jan 24 | 2 | Jacob Furnival & Co. | C | Printed design |
| Feb 26 | 5 | T. J. & J. Mayer | Lpt | Covered bowl |
| Mar 2 | 4 | Minton & Co. | S | Moulded jug |
| Mar 11 | 2 | W. S. Kennedy | B | Finger plates |
| April 7 | 1 | W. S. Kennedy | B | Finger plates |
| April 17 | 3 | Copeland & Garrett | S | Finger plate |
| May 21 | 3 | H. Minton & Co. | S | Ewer & basin |
| May 26 | 2 | H. Minton & Co. | S | Moulded jugs |
| Jun 6 | 1 | W. Chamberlain & Co. | W | Moulded edge |
| Jun 26 | 2 | H. Minton & Co. | S | Moulded edge |
| Jun 30 | 3 | John Goodwin | L | Printed design |
| July 11 | 1 | J. K. Knight | L | Printed design |
| July 16 | 1 | W. Ridgway Son & Co. | H | Moulded jug |
| July 17 | 1 | John Ridgway & Co. | H | Aladdin design |
| July 21 | 1 | Francis Morley & Co. | Sh | Printed design |
| Aug 1 | 2 | Josiah Wedgwood & Sons | E | Toiletwares |
| Aug 3 | 1 | Josiah Wedgwood & Sons | E | Floral design |
| Aug 3 | 2 | H. Minton & Co. | S | Toiletwares |
| Sept 3 | 2 | George Phillips | Lpt | Printed design |
| Sept 3 | 3 | Francis Morley & Co. | Sh | Printed design |
| Sept 14 | 4 | Copeland & Garrett | S | Printed design |
| Sept 26 | 2 | John Ridgway & Co. | Sh | Forms |
| Sept 29 | 3 | T. J. & J. Mayer | B | Moulded jug |
| Sept 30 | 2 | Copeland & Garrett | S | Finger plate |
| Oct 26 | 1 | Francis Morley & Co. | Sh | Dinnerwares |
| Oct 26 | 5 | James Edwards | B | Jug form |
| Nov 3 | 1 | Ridgway & Abington | H | Rustic teapot |
| Nov 5 | 2 | George Phillips | Lpt | Friburg pattern |
| Nov 12 | 3 | Charles Meigh | H | Gothic jug |
| Nov 16 | 2 | H. Minton & Co. | S | Floral design |
| Nov 16 | 2 | H. Minton & Co. | S | Moulded edge |
| Nov 21 | 2 | Thomas Furnival & Co. | H | Printed pattern |
| Nov 21 | 2 | Thomas Furnival & Co. | H | Jug form |
| Dec 3 | 4 | Ridgway & Abington | H | Moulded jug |
| Dec 4 | 2 | H. Minton & Co. | S | Printed design |
| Dec 4 | 4 | T. R. Swaine | P | Chimney top |
| Dec 10 | 3 | Joseph Clementson | SL | Toiletwares |
| Dec 14 | 3 | James Edwards | B | Coffee pot |
| Dec 14 | 4 | Minton & Co. | S | Floral pattern |
| Dec 16 | 1 | John Goodwin | L | Printed design |

| Dec 17 | 2 | Copeland & Garrett | S | Border designs |
|--------|---|--------------------|----|----------------|
| Dec 29 | 2 | Edward Challiner | T | Printed design |
| Dec 31 | 3 | Josiah Wedgwood & Sons | E | Printed design |

## 1847 (F at top)

| Jan 9 | 4 | John Ridgway & Co. | Sh | Dinnerwares |
|-------|---|--------------------|----|--------------|
| Jan 9 | 7 | Copeland & Garrett | S | Dinnerwares |
| Feb 2 | 7 | T. & R. Boote | B | Jug form |
| Feb 8 | 5 | T. J. & J. Mayer | B | Pot & cruet |
| Feb 12 | 5 | George Greatback | E | Hearth stone |
| Feb 15 | 4 | Copeland & Garrett | S | Border design |
| Feb 15 | 4 | Copeland & Garrett | S | Nightlightholder |
| Mar 11 | 4 | Stock & Sharp★ | Bir | Pump case |
| Mar 17 | 3 | John Wedge Wood | T | Printed design |
| Mar 17 | 6 | John Ridgway & Co. | Sh | Printed designs |
| Mar 19 | 4 | Batty & Co.★ | Ln | Cruet |
| Mar 22 | 2 | Bailey & Ball | L | Moulded plate |
| Mar 23 | 7 | H. Minton & Co. | S | Inkstand |
| Mar 30 | 1 | James Edwards | B | Jug form |
| April 3 | 6 | S. Alcock & Co. | B | Rustic jug |
| April 27 | 1 | S. Alcock & Co. | B | Jug –Maomi |
| May 12 | 4 | Copeland & Garrett | S | Garden border |
| May 14 | 1 | H. Minton & Co. | S | Dolphin ornament |
| May 14 | 1 | H. Minton & Co. | S | Moulded jug |
| May 19 | 1 | C. Heaton & Co.★ | Ln | Anchovey pot |
| Jun 5 | 2 | Joseph Mappin★ | Sd | Knife handle |
| Jun 11 | 4 | James Edwards | B | Dinnerwares |
| Jun 11 | 6 | Joseph Alexander★ | No | Plate design |
| Jun 21 | 5 | J. Rose & Co. | Cpt | Moulded jug |
| Jun 25 | 2 | James Edwards | B | Dinnerwares |
| Jun 25 | 5 | Edmund Sharpe | Dshire | Spittoon |
| July 5 | 5 | Mellor, Venables & Co. | B | Dinnerwares |
| July 5 | 5 | Mellor, Venables & Co. | B | Medici design |
| July 15 | 1 | Mellor, Venables & Co. | B | Dinnerwares |
| July 16 | 5 | James Edwards | B | Shapes (4) |
| July 27 | 3 | T. J. & J. Mayer | B | Dinnerwares |
| Aug 3 | 3 | J. Rose & Co. | Cpt | Jug form |
| Aug 16 | 2 | James Edwards | B | Covered dish |
| Aug 17 | 2 | W. T. Copeland | S | Plate form |
| Aug 17 | 2 | W. T. Copeland | S | Portland vase jug |
| Aug 19 | 3 | H. Minton & Co. | S | Una & lion |
| Aug 26 | 2 | James Edwards | B | Plate form |
| Sept 9 | 3 | W. T. Copeland | S | Floral print |
| Sept 16 | 3 | W. T. Copeland | S | Floral print |
| Sept 25 | 5 | John Wedge Wood | T | Fluted teapot |
| Oct 1 | 4 | Thomas Peake | T | Tile |
| Oct 2 | 5 | John Ridgway & Co. | Sh | Dinnerwares |
| Oct 4 | 3 | H. Minton & Co. | S | Dorathea figure |
| Oct 8 | 4 | John Wedge Wood | T | Dinnerwares |
| Oct 13 | 1 | W. T. Copeland | S | Toiletwares |
| Oct 23 | 2 | H. Minton & Co. | S | Jug form |
| Oct 23 | 2 | H. Minton & Co. | S | Vandyke pattern |

| Oct 27 | 1 | John Ridgway & Co. | Sh | Dinnerwares |
|---|---|---|---|---|
| Nov 11 | 4 | H. Minton & Co. | S | Border form |
| Nov 23 | 2 | E. P. Willock & Co. | M | Wall bracket |
| Nov 23 | 4 | Josiah Wedgwood & Co. | E | Printed design |
| Dec 1 | 2 | J. Rose & Co. | Cpt | Moulded borders |
| Dec 1 | 2 | J. Rose & Co. | Cpt | Teaware forms |
| Dec 10 | 3 | H. Minton & Co. | S | Children figures |
| Dec 15 | 4 | H. Minton & Co. | S | Printed design |
| Dec 23 | 2 | E. P. Willock & Co. | M | Wall bracket |

## 1848 (U at top)

| Jan 1 | 4 | Barker & Till | B | Dinnerwares |
|---|---|---|---|---|
| Jan 6 | 4 | G. Grainger | W | Plate form |
| Jan 18 | 2 | W. T. Copeland | S | Floral design |
| Feb 11 | 3 | H. Minton & Co. | S | Garden seat? |
| Feb 11 | 3 | H. Minton & Co. | S | Jardinere |
| Feb 17 | 2 | E. P. Willock | M | Wall bracket |
| Feb 18 | 3 | E. P. Willock | M | Wall bracket |
| Feb 29 | 12 | H. Minton & Co. | S | Knife handle |
| Mar 4 | 4 | H. Minton & Co. | S | Bread dish |
| Mar 7 | 1 | Ridgway & Abington | H | Moulded jugs |
| Mar 14 | 2 | W. T. Copeland | S | Printed design |
| Mar 15 | 2 | W. T. Copeland | S | Covered dish |
| Mar 20 | 7 | Wood & Brownfield | C | Plate form |
| Mar 27 | 8 | J. & S. Alcock, junr | C | Dinnerwares |
| April 15 | 4 | J. Ridgway & Co. | Sh | Dinnerwares |
| April 22 | 3 | Josiah Wedgwood & Sons | E | Cheese dish |
| April 27 | 4 | Josiah Wedgwood & Sons | E | Tureen form |
| May 30 | 3 | Thomas Peake | T | Ridge tile |
| Jun 20 | 4 | G. F. Bowers & Co. | T | Teawares |
| Jun 30 | 2 | W. T. Copeland | S | Printed designs |
| Jun 30 | 3 | Ridgway & Abington | H | Moulded design |
| July 26 | 5 | F. Hands★ | Bir | Frame |
| July 27 | 2 | Thomas Peake | T | Tile |
| Aug 10 | 3 | G. Grainger | W | Tureen form |
| Aug 14 | 3 | John Campbell★ | G | Bear design |
| Aug 16 | 8 | Thomas Pinder | B | Printed design |
| Aug 23 | 2 | John Wedge Wood | T | Printed design |
| Aug 26 | 2 | John Meir & Son | T | Roselle design |
| Sept 12 | 1 | Hart & Sons★ | Ln | Finger plate |
| Sept 15 | 3 | W. T. Copeland | S | Printed design |
| Sept 18 | 4 | Charles Meigh | H | Moulded jug |
| Sept 20 | 1 | Hart & Sons★ | Ln | Finger plate |
| Sept 30 | 7 | John Ridgway & Co. | Sh | Dinnerwares |
| Oct 17 | 3 | T. & R. Boote | B | Moulded jug |
| Nov 4 | 2 | W. T. Copeland | S | Moulded jug |
| Nov 13 | 4 | W. T. Copeland | S | Moulded jug |
| Nov 15 | 3 | Henry Meadows★ | Ln | Moulded jug |
| Nov 21 | 5 | H. Minton & Co. | W | Moulded jug |
| Nov 21 | 5 | H. Minton & Co. | W | Printed design |
| Nov 27 | 2 | John Ridgway & Co. | Sh | Printed design |
| Dec 16 | 3 | James Edwards | B | Dinnerwares |
| Dec 28 | 2 | John Ridgway | Sh | Teaware forms |

## 1849 (S at top)

| | | | | |
|---|---|---|---|---|
| Jan 3 | 2 | W. Adams & Sons | T | Athens design |
| Jan 20 | 2 | W. Davenport & Co. | Lgt | Teaware forms |
| Feb 2 | 4 | Mellor, Venables & Co. | B | Dinnerwares |
| Feb 16 | 5 | Minton & Co. | S | Printed design |
| Feb 16 | 11 | Ridgway & Abington | H | Moulded design |
| Feb 26 | 2 | J. Rose & Co. | Cpt | Moulded jug |
| Mar 13 | 2 | Joseph Clementson | Sh | Printed design |
| Mar 26 | 5 | Minton & Co. | S | Moulded bowl |
| Mar 27 | 2 | Cope & Edwards | L | Moulded teapot |
| Mar 31 | 2 | J. Ridgway & Co. | Sh | Moulded teawares |
| April 2 | 5 | Podmore, Walker & Co. | T | California pattern |
| April 10 | 4 | W. T. Copeland | S | Moulded edge |
| April 16 | 6 | C. J. Mason | L | Plate form |
| May 24 | 1 | Mr Wedge Wood | T | Printed design |
| Jun 7 | 3 | T. J. & J. Mayer | Lpt | Printed design |
| July 5 | 3 | Hart & Son★ | Ln | Finger plate |
| July 16 | 2 | Ridgway & Abington | H | Moulded design |
| Aug 11 | 4 | W. T. Copeland | S | Moulded pot |
| Aug 15 | 2 | H. Minton & Co. | S | Moulded jug |
| Aug 17 | 2 | W. T. Copeland | S | Printed design |
| Aug 27 | 5 | Mellor, Venables & Co. | B | Windsor design |
| Sept 14 | 6 | F. & R. Pratt & Co. | F | Moulded jar |
| Sept 28 | 6 | J. Ridgway | Sh | Moulded forms |
| Oct 10 | 2 | J. Ridgway | Sh | Printed design |
| Oct 12 | 4 | Minton & Co. | S | Plate form |
| Oct 26 | 5 | J. Hollinshead | Sh | Wesley design |
| Nov 9 | 4 | W. T. Copeland | S | Moulded jug |
| Nov 17 | 2 | Minton & Co. | S | Moulded jug |
| Nov 22 | 2 | W. T. Copeland | S | Printed design |
| Nov 30 | 5 | J. Rose & Co. | Cpt | Moulded edge |
| Dec 6 | 3 | W. T. Copeland | S | Printed holly design |
| Dec 15 | 4 | T. J. & J. Mayer | Lpt | Moulded jar |

## 1850 (V at top)

| | | | | |
|---|---|---|---|---|
| Jan 3 | 1 | W. Davenport & Co. | Lpt | Dinnerwares |
| Jan 14 | 4 | J. Ridgway | Sh | Hand basins |
| Jan 26 | 6 | George Grainger | W | Printed design |
| Feb 13 | 1 | George Grainger | W | Printed design |
| Feb 13 | 3 | J. & M. P. Bell & Co. | G | Ionia print |
| Feb 27 | 4 | George Grainger | W | Moulded edge |
| Mar 9 | 3 | W. T. Copeland | S | Printed design |
| Mar 12 | 5 | John Isaac★ | Liv | Ink bottle |
| Mar 30 | 9 | J. Rose & Co. | Cpt | Teaware forms |
| April 2 | 11 | William Pierce★ | L | Fireplace |
| April 3 | 5 | James King★ | L | Pomatuim pot |
| April 4 | 4 | T. J. & J. Mayer | B | Printed design |
| April 8 | 1 | J. Clementson | Sh | Siam design |
| April 13 | 7 | Minton & Co. | S | Fluted teawares |
| April 18 | 11 | J. Rose & Co. | Cpt | Teaware forms |
| April 25 | 3 | Minton & Co. | S | Floral design |
| May 25 | 8 | James Moon | M | Smoke conductor |

| Jun 4 | 1 | J. & M. P. Bell & Co. | G | Vase print |
| Jun 5 | 3 | Barker & Son | B | Missouri print |
| Jun 21 | 4 | Edward Walley | C | Moulded jug |
| July 2 | 2 | T. J. & J. Mayer | B | Moulded jug |
| July 16 | 5 | C. & W. K. Harvey | L | Dinnerwares |
| July 30 | 3 | Charles Young | Ln | Loaf casket |
| Aug 16 | 3 | E. P. Willock & Co. | M | Wall bracket |
| Aug 23 | 2 | J. Wedge Wood | T | Printed design |
| Sept 9 | 5 | Thomas Till | B | Moulded jug |
| Sept 16 | 8 | J. & M. P. Bell & Co. | G | Fluted teawares |
| Sept 16 | 9 | J. Ridgway | Sh | Printed design |
| Sept 19 | 2 | W. T. Copeland | S | Printed design |
| Sept 21 | 1 | Mellor, Venables & Co. | B | Dinnerwares |
| Sept 28 | 2 | E. P. Willock & Co. | M | Wall bracket |
| Oct 9 | 2 | Minton & Co. | S | Toiletwares |
| Oct 17 | 6 | W. T. Copeland | S | Moulded bracket |
| Oct 23 | 6 | Crosse & Blackwell★ | L | 1851 Exh. meat pot |
| Oct 31 | 5 | Gabriel Benda★ | L | Tobacco jar |
| Nov 4 | 4 | Josiah Wedgwood & Sons | E | Cambridge ale jug |
| Nov 20 | 7 | Francis Morley & Co. | Sh | Dinnerwares |
| Nov 22 | 3 | J. Rose & Co. | Cpt | Moulded border |
| Dec 5 | 3 | Francis Morley & Co. | Sh | Dinnerwares |
| Dec 19 | 5 | J. Rose & Co. | Cpt | Moulded edge |
| Dec 19 | 6 | T. J. & J. Mayer | Lpt | Moulded jug |
| Dec 20 | 6 | W. T. Copeland | S | Floral design |

## 1851 (P at top)

| Jan 7 | 4 | James Green★ | Ln | 1851 exhibition print |
| Feb 10 | 9 | William Brownfield | C | Moulded border |
| Feb 26 | 8 | J.C. Quince★ | Ln | 1851 exhibition print |
| Mar 14 | 4 | J.C. Quince★ | Ln | Houses of Parliament |
| Mar 17 | 13 | John Ridgway & Co. | Sh | Teawares |
| Mar 17 | 13 | John Ridgway & Co. | Sh | Dinnerwares |
| Mar 17 | 13 | John Ridgway & Co. | Sh | Fountains |
| Mar 17 | 13 | John Ridgway & Co. | Sh | Wash basins |
| Mar 31 | 4 | J. & M. P. Bell & Co. | G | Jug form |
| April 8 | 5 | J. Gardner★ | Ln | Punch inkstand |
| April 9 | 2 | T. Till & Son | B | Moulded jar |
| April 11 | 4 | J. & M. P. Bell & Co. | G | Toiletwares |
| April 11 | 6 | W. S. Kennedy | B | Finger plate |
| April 14 | 7 | J. & M. P. Bell & Co. | G | Dinnerwares |
| April 14 | 7 | J. & M. P. Bell & Co. | G | Teapot |
| April 26 | 3 | Edward Walley | Co | Ceres jug |
| April 29 | 2 | T. S. Bale | Sh | Marble designs |
| May 30 | 4 | W. S. Copeland | S | Printed designs |
| Jun 7 | 4 | J. Ridgway & Co. | Sh | Staircase |
| Jun 11 | 2 | W. T. Copeland | S | Printed design |
| Jun 11 | 3 | Ralph Scragg (modeller) | H | Dinnerwares |
| Jun 19 | 5 | W. T. Copeland | S | Printed design |
| July 10 | 3 | R. Britton & Co. | Lds | Printed design |
| July 14 | 3 | W. T. Copeland | S | Moulded floral pot |
| July 21 | 7 | T. & R. Boote | B | Teawares |

| July 24 | 2 | T. Till & Son | B | Teapot form |
|---|---|---|---|---|
| July 26 | 3 | C. Collinson & Co. | B | Floral design |
| Aug 5 | 4 | J. H. Maw | W | Tile |
| Aug 16 | 2 | Ridgway & Abington | H | Moulded jug |
| Sept 2 | 4 | T. J. & J. Mayer | B | Dinnerwares |
| Sept 19 | 3 | T. & R. Boote | B | Dinnerwares |
| Sept 29 | 4 | James Edwards | Lpt | Dinnerwares |
| Sept 30 | 3 | James Edwards | Lpt | Dinnerwares |
| Oct 1 | 1 | W. T. Copeland | S | Floral print |
| Oct 7 | 3 | Chamberlain & Co. | W | Moulded borders |
| Oct 10 | 4 | William Brownfield | C | Toiletwares |
| Oct 10 | 6 | T. & R. Boote | B | Plate form |
| Oct 14 | 4 | T. Till & Son | B | Woodbine print |
| Oct 16 | 4 | William Brownfield | C | Moulded jug |
| Oct 17 | 3 | George Bowden Sander★ | Ln | Moulded jug |
| Oct 21 | 3 | William Ridgway | Sh | Moulded jug |
| Nov 1 | 5 | George Bowden Sander★ | Ln | Printed designs |
| Nov 10 | 4 | Ralph Scragg (modeller) | H | Teapot form |
| Nov 12 | 6 | Minton & Co. | S | Printed designs |
| Nov 12 | 6 | Minton & Co. | S | Jug form |
| Nov 13 | 2 | Charles Meigh & Son | H | Moulded jug |
| Nov 14 | 4 | George Bowden Sander★ | Ln | Dinnerwares |
| Nov 17 | 8 | Thomas Jackson★ | M | Pot lid print |
| Dec 2 | 2 | Messrs. Mayer | B | Moulded jug |
| Dec 4 | 3 | Minton & Co. | S | Jardinere |
| Dec 4 | 3 | Minton & Co. | S | Garden seat |
| Dec 5 | 5 | John Ridgway & Co. | Sh | Dinnerwares |
| Dec 8 | 8 | W. T. Copeland | S | Printed design |
| Dec 15 | 6 | George Bowden Sander★ | Ln | Printed border |
| Dec 16 | 1 | T. Till & Son | B | Printed design |

**1852 (D at top)**

| Jan 27 | 1 | W. & G. Harding | B | Printed design |
|---|---|---|---|---|
| Jan 30 | 6 | Thomas Jackson★ | M | Covered pot |
| Feb 17 | 1 | Venables & Baines | B | Union print |
| Mar 4 | 2 | William Brownfield | C | Toiletwares |
| Mar 13 | 3 | William Ridgway | Sh | Printed design |
| Mar 22 | 7 | Ralph Scragg (modeller) | H | Moulded jug |
| Mar 24 | 3 | James Edwards | B | Anchor crest |
| Mar 24 | 4 | Minton & Co. | S | Moulded pot |
| Mar 25 | 1 | John Milner★ | C | Jug cover |
| Mar 26 | 3 | J. & M. P. Bell & Co. | G | Moulded jug |
| Mar 29 | 3 | Thomas Jackson★ | M | Printed pot lid designs |
| April 1 | 1 | T. Till & Son | B | Moulded jug |
| April 8 | 4 | T. Till & Son | B | Moulded candlestick |
| April 21 | 4 | George Ray (modeller) | L | Polka jug |
| May 5 | 5 | J. M. Blashfield | Ln | Vase forms |
| May 6 | 5 | George Bowden Sander★ | Ln | Teawares |
| May 7 | 2 | J. M. Blashfield | Ln | Garden vases |
| May 7 | 2 | J. M. Blashfield | Ln | Flower troughs |
| May 14 | 5 | W. T. Copeland | S | Moulded designs |
| May 18 | 1 | Minton & Co. | S | Moulded bowl |

| | | | | | |
|---|---|---|---|---|---|
| Jun 1 | 2 | J. M. Blashfield | Ln | Tazza & bowl |
| Jun 5 | 5 | Minton & Co. | S | Fluted jug |
| Jun 14 | 4 | W. T. Copeland | S | Printed design |
| Jun 21 | 2 | J. & T. Lockett | L | Moulded jug |
| July 1 | 2 | Thomas Jackson★ | M | Printed pot lid |
| July 5 | 3 | J. Parkhurst & Co. | H | Moulded jug |
| July 23 | 3 | Minton & Co. | S | Moulded jugs |
| Aug 4 | 3 | W. T. Copeland | S | Printed designs |
| Aug 13 | 5 | T. Till & Co. | B | Moulded jug |
| Aug 25 | 4 | C. Meigh & Son | H | Moulded design |
| Aug 25 | 5 | George Bowden Sander★ | Ln | Floral printed design |
| Sept 3 | 7 | Minton & Co. | S | Moulded designs |
| Sept 15 | 5 | T. Till & Co. | B | Moulded jug |
| Sept 16 | 1 | Minton & Co. | S | Moulded jug |
| Sept 24 | 1 | Minton & Co. | S | Moulded edge |
| Sept 27 | 3 | Warburton & Britton | Lds | Moulded jug |
| Oct 1 | 6 | W. T. Copeland | S | Printed design |
| Oct 7 | 5 | Ralph Scragg (modeller) | H | Tureen form |
| Oct 23 | 4 | Davenports & Co. | Lpt | Dinnerwares |
| Oct 25 | 2 | William Brownfield | C | Moulded jug |
| Oct 30 | 3 | Marple, Turner & Co. | H | Printed design |
| Nov 4 | 5 | John Holland | T | Printed design |
| Nov 11 | 3 | Minton & Co. | S | Printed design |
| Nov 22 | 3 | J. Parkhurst & Co. | H | Moulded teapot |
| Nov 22 | 3 | J. Dimmock | H | Moulded teapot |
| Nov 25 | 4 | Keys & Mountford | S | Parian model |
| Dec 16 | 4 | J. Rose & Co. | Cpt | Moulded edge |
| Dec 27 | 1 | Warburton & Britton | Lds | Moulded jug |

### 1853 (Y at top)

| | | | | | |
|---|---|---|---|---|---|
| Jan 3 | 3 | W. T. Copeland | S | Printed designs |
| Jan 12 | 6 | Thomas Goodfellow | T | Plate form |
| Jan 14 | 3 | Davenports & Co. | Lpt | Teawares |
| Jan 14 | 3 | Davenports & Co. | Lpt | Toiletwares |
| Jan 18 | 2 | Davenports & Co. | Lpt | Teawares |
| Jan 18 | 2 | Davenports & Co. | Lpt | Toiletwares |
| Jan 19 | 4 | J. L. Gardner★ | Ln | Ink bottle |
| Feb 4 | 9 | James Parkhurst & Co. | H | Tureen form |
| Feb 10 | 2 | George Wooliscroft | T | Dinnerwares |
| Feb 11 | 6 | Worthington & Green | Sh | Moulded jug |
| Feb 12 | 3 | Minton & Co. | S | Printed borders |
| Feb 17 | 4 | W. S. Kennedy | B | Finger plates |
| Feb 26 | 5 | W. T. Copeland | S | Moulded jug |
| Mar 4 | 12 | Battam & Son★ | L | Finger plates |
| Mar 10 | 2 | J. & M. P. Bell & Co. | G | Printed design |
| Mar 17 | 5 | J. W. Parkhurst & Co. | H | Teapot form |
| Mar 19 | 2 | Minton & Co. | S | Printed design |
| April 2 | 9 | C. Collinson & Co. | B | Water closet |
| April 4 | 6 | J. Rose & Co. | Cpt | Moulded pot |
| April 23 | 2 | W. Adams & Sons | T | Dinnerwares |
| May 7 | 5 | John Alcock | C | Teaware forms |
| May 7 | 5 | John Alcock | C | Dinnerwares |

| Jun 7 | 3 | George Wood & Co. | Sh | Moulded jug |
|---|---|---|---|---|
| Jun 14 | 2 | Livesley, Powell & Co. | H | Moulded jugs |
| Jun 22 | 3 | James Parkhurst & Co. | H | Moulded jug |
| Jun 24 | 3 | G. Wooliscroft | T | Eon print |
| Jun 24 | 11 | Ridgway & Co. | Sh | Dinnerwares |
| July 18 | 4 | John Edwards | L | Teapot form |
| July 20 | 2 | J. H. Baddeley | Sh | Covered jars |
| Aug 8 | 1 | Anthony Shaw | T | Printed design |
| Aug 10 | 2 | Holland & Green | L | Tureen form |
| Sept 3 | 2 | T. & R. Boote | B | Tureen form |
| Sept 6 | 3 | Francis Morley & Co. | Sh | Dinnerwares |
| Sept 21 | 2 | James Edwards | B | Dinnerwares |
| Oct 5 | 2 | Venables, Mann & Co. | B | Teawares |
| Oct 5 | 2 | Venables, Mann & Co. | B | Dinnerwares |
| Oct 6 | 5 | J. Taylor & Son★ | L | Lamp |
| Oct 10 | 3 | Barrow & Co. | F | Covered dish |
| Oct 11 | 5 | Ralph Scragg (modeller) | H | Covered dish |
| Oct 12 | 3 | James Edwards | B | Covered dish |
| Oct 12 | 4 | Livesley, Powell & Co. | H | Dinnerwares |
| Oct 12 | 4 | Livesley, Powell & Co. | H | Teawares |
| Oct 19 | 4 | Minton & Co. | S | Moulded teawares |
| Oct 22 | 1 | T. J. & J. Mayer | B | Dinnerwares |
| Nov 24 | 2 | T. Till & Son | B | Dinnerwares |
| Nov 26 | 2 | W. T. Copeland | S | Panel |
| Nov 30 | 5 | W. Adams & Sons | T | Printed design |
| Dec 6 | 6 | John Alcock | C | Toiletwares |
| Dec 7 | 2 | Ralph Scragg (modeller) | H | Moulded jug |
| Dec 24 | 3 | Samuel Moore & Co. | Su | Aesop prints |
| Dec 24 | 4 | John Alcock | C | Teawares |

**1854 (J at top)**

| Jan 30 | 4 | S. Alcock & Co. | B | Moulded jug |
|---|---|---|---|---|
| Feb 23 | 3 | W. T. Copeland | S | Moulded jug |
| Feb 28 | 2 | Crosse & Blackwell★ | Ln | Moulded jar |
| Mar 3 | 2 | Thomas Jackson★ | M | Bear jar print |
| Mar 11 | 4 | S. Alcock & Co. | B | Printed design |
| Mar 20 | 1 | T. Till & Son | B | Teapot form |
| Mar 22 | 2 | James Edwards & Son | Lpt | Teawares |
| Mar 24 | 3 | Minton & Co. | S | Floral printed design |
| Mar 27 | 3 | George Baguley | H | Moulded jug |
| Mar 27 | 6 | J. Deaville | H | Moulded jug |
| Mar 31 | 1 | Holland & Green | L | Gothic jug |
| Mar 31 | 1 | Holland & Green | L | Teawares |
| Mar 31 | 1 | Holland & Green | L | Toiletwares |
| April 1 | 4 | William Brownfield | C | Moulded jug |
| April 1 | 6 | T. Till & Son | B | Teawares |
| April 4 | 3 | Woolland & Hathesley★ | Cam | Moulded jug |
| April 5 | 3 | Ralph Scragg (modeller) | H | Moulded jug |
| April 6 | 3 | S. Alcock & Co. | B | Toiletwares |
| April 10 | 3 | J. Deaville | H | Moulded jug |
| April 10 | 4 | S. Alcock & Co. | B | Moulded jug |
| April 11 | 5 | Pearson, Farrall & Meakin | Sh | Dinnerwares |

| April 15 | 1 | George Baguley | H | Moulded jug |
| April 21 | 3 | Warburton & Britton | Lds | Moulded jug |
| May 4 | 4 | J. Ridgway & Co. | Sh | Inhibitor |
| May 8 | 3 | William Brownfield | C | Jardinere |
| Jun 3 | 2 | T. Till & Son | B | Moulded jug |
| Jun 9 | 2 | C. Meigh & Son | H | Moulded jug |
| Jun 21 | 5 | T. & R. Boote | B | Toiletwares |
| July 18 | 2 | T. & R. Boote | B | Teawares |
| July 18 | 4 | S. Alcock & Co. | B | Printed design |
| Sept 4 | 2 | J. Tylor & Sons★ | Ln | Lamp |
| Sept 5 | 3 | S. Alcock & Co. | B | Moulded edge |
| Sept 12 | 2 | W. T. Copeland | S | Moulded jug |
| Oct 2 | 3 | William Brownfield | C | Moulded edge |
| Oct 6 | 4 | Davenports & Co. | Lpt | Teawares |
| Oct 9 | 4 | T. J. & J. Mayer | B | Tureen form |
| Oct 31 | 2 | George Ray | L | Moulded jug |
| Nov 10 | 5 | J. Ridgway & Co. | Sh | Printed design |
| Dec 27 | 3 | S. Alcock & Co. | B | Moulded jug |
| Dec 27 | 4 | Parkhurst & Dimmock | H | Moulded jug |
| Dec 29 | 1 | F. & R. Pratt & Co. | F | Printed pot lid |

### 1855 (E at top)

| Jan 4 | 2 | Worthington & Green | Sh | Floral jug |
| Jan 6 | 4 | S. Alcock & Co. | B | Moulded edge |
| Jan 15 | 2 | Pinder, Bourne & Hope | B | Tureen form |
| Jan 15 | 4 | Brougham & Mayer | T | Dinnerwares |
| Jan 15 | 4 | Brougham & Mayer | T | Teawares |
| Jan 15 | 4 | Brougham & Mayer | T | Toiletwares |
| Jan 19 | 3 | Parkhurst & Dimmock | H | Moulded jug |
| Jan 30 | 1 | John Edwards | L | Dinnerwares |
| Feb 3 | 4 | J. & M. P. Bell & Co. | G | Anemone print |
| Feb 5 | 7 | Coombs & Holland | Ws | Printed design |
| Feb 7 | 2 | John Alcock | C | Dinnerwares |
| Feb 17 | 3 | F. & R. Pratt & Co. | F | Moulded jugs |
| Feb 26 | 3 | Lockett, Baguley & Cooper | Sh | Moulded edge |
| Feb 28 | 4 | John Ridgway & Co. | Sh | Water closet |
| Mar 1 | 5 | Minton & Co. | S | Toiletwares |
| Mar 1 | 5 | Minton & Co. | S | Teawares |
| Mar 1 | 5 | Minton & Co. | S | Moulded edge |
| Mar 5 | 3 | Elsmore & Forster | T | Teapot form |
| Mar 13 | 4 | Warburton & Britton | Lds | Moulded jug |
| Mar 17 | 1 | William Baker | F | Tureen form |
| April 7 | 7 | W. T. Copeland | S | Printed design |
| April 17 | 4 | S. Hughes & Son | B | Tureen form |
| April 26 | 1 | W. Brownfield | C | Moulded jugs |
| April 26 | 1 | W. Brownfield | C | Plate form |
| April 28 | 7 | Venables, Mann & Co. | B | Dinnerwares |
| May 10 | 5 | Beech, Hancock & Co. | B | Jug form |
| May 14 | 3 | Minton & Co. | S | Moulded jug |
| Jun 7 | 4 | John Alcock | C | Dinnerwares |
| Jun 11 | 3 | S. Alcock & Co. | B | "British Birds" print |
| July 4 | 5 | Joseph Thompson | Dshire | Moulded jugs |

| July 24 | 1 | C. Meigh & Son | H | Dinnerwares |
|---|---|---|---|---|
| July 24 | 1 | C. Meigh & Son | H | Teawares |
| Aug 6 | 1 | James Dudson | S | Moulded jug |
| Aug 8 | 5 | James Edwards & Son | B | Dinnerwares |
| Aug 11 | 1 | G. Grainger & Co. | W | Moulded edge |
| Aug 20 | 3 | Thomas Ford | Sh | Teawares |
| Aug 27 | 2 | Barrow & Co. | F | Toiletwares |
| Aug 27 | 2 | Barrow & Co. | F | Moulded jug |
| Aug 27 | 2 | Barrow & Co. | F | Teawares |
| Sept 3 | 1 | S. Hughes & Son | B | Moulded jug |
| Sept 27 | 4 | S. Bevington & Son | Sh | Moulded jugs |
| Oct 3 | 2 | George Mayor & Co. | Ln | Covered pot |
| Oct 3 | 3 | Minton & Co. | S | Teawares |
| Oct 17 | 8 | M. Williamson | G | Vase forms |
| Oct 25 | 3 | David Chetwynd (modeller) | C | Tureen form |
| Oct 29 | 6 | G. W. Reade (Designer) | B | Dinnerwares |
| Nov 1 | 3 | Josiah Wedgwood & Sons | E | Toilet jug |
| Nov 22 | 4 | J. & M. P. Bell & Co. | G | Jug form |
| Nov 28 | 3 | W. Brownfield | C | Moulded jug |

**1856 (L at top)**

| Jan 5 | 3 | John Edwards | L | Toiletwares |
|---|---|---|---|---|
| Jan 15 | 4 | James Pankhurst & Co. | H | Moulded jug |
| Jan 23 | 4 | Minton & Co. | S | Moulded jug |
| Jan 31 | 4 | Josiah Wedgwood & Sons | E | Toiletwares |
| Mar 11 | 1 | Davenports & Co. | Lpt | Dessertwares |
| Mar 12 | 3 | F. & R. Pratt & Co. | F | Printed designs |
| April 7 | 2 | Anthony Shaw | T | Dinnerwares |
| April 7 | 2 | Anthony Shaw | T | Teawares |
| April 7 | 3 | J. & M. P. Bell & Co. | G | Printed design |
| April 18 | 2 | William Beech | B | Moulded Jug |
| April 18 | 3 | Ralph Scragg (modeller) | H | Covered dish |
| April 18 | 6 | Edward Walley | C | Moulded jug |
| April 18 | 7 | Ridgway & Abington | H | Moulded jug |
| April 30 | 3 | W. Brownfield | C | Moulded jugs |
| May 8 | 2 | Minton & Co. | S | Covered dish |
| May 22 | 1 | Minton & Co. | S | Covered dish |
| Jun 13 | 3 | C. Meigh & Son | H | Moulded jug |
| Jun 28 | 3 | Worthington & Green | Sh | Moulded jug |
| Jun 30 | 7 | Joseph Clementson | Sh | Printed design |
| July 28 | 3 | Edward Challinor | T | Dora design |
| July 30 | 5 | James Edwards & Son | B | Dinnerwares |
| Aug 12 | 2 | F. & R. Pratt & Co. | F | Pot lid print |
| Aug 19 | 5 | F. & R. Pratt & Co. | F | Hunting print |
| Aug 22 | 4 | T. & R. Boote | B | Dinnerwares |
| Aug 22 | 4 | T. & R. Boote | B | Toiletwares |
| Aug 22 | 4 | T. & R. Boote | B | Teawares |
| Sept 1 | 3 | W. T. Copeland | S | Printed designs |
| Oct 2 | 3 | Henry Baggeley (modeller) | H | Royal Arms |
| Oct 14 | 4 | John Roberts | Kent | Pipe |
| Oct 16 | 2 | Minton & Co. | S | Jug forms |
| Oct 22 | 3 | W. T. Copeland | S | Moulded jug |

| Nov 7 | 6 | F. & R. Pratt & Co. | F | Pot lid print |
|---|---|---|---|---|
| Nov 14 | 9 | Davenports & Co. | Lpt | Dinnerwares |
| Nov 27 | 3 | Davenports & Co. | Lpt | Teawares |
| Nov 27 | 6 | W. Brownfield | C | Tureen form |
| Nov 29 | 1 | Edward Walley | C | Dinnerwares |
| Nov 29 | 1 | Edward Walley | C | Teawares |
| Nov 29 | 1 | Edward Walley | C | Toiletwares |
| Dec 11 | 4 | W. T. Copeland | S | Printed design |
| Dec 18 | 2 | Mayer Brothers & Elliot | Lpt | Oval tureen |
| Dec 23 | 4 | Mayer Brothers & Elliot | Lpt | Circular tureen |

## 1857 (K at top)

| Jan 15 | 5 | F. & R. Pratt & Co. | F | Pot lid print |
|---|---|---|---|---|
| Jan 26 | 7 | James Edwards | B | Coffee pot |
| Feb 4 | 5 | John Meir & Son | T | Dinnerwares |
| Feb 9 | 4 | Minton & Co. | S | Moulded jug |
| Feb 17 | 3 | Minton & Co. | S | Moulded bowl |
| Feb 23 | 9 | Podmore, Walker & Co. | H | Moulded jug |
| Mar 20 | 4 | John Alcock | C | Fluted teawares |
| April 16 | 1 | John Alcock | C | Dinnerwares |
| April 29 | 1 | W. T. Copeland | S | Printed designs |
| Jun 5 | 3 | William Brownfield | C | Moulded shapes |
| Jun 19 | 1 | W. T. Copeland | S | Printed design |
| Jun 19 | 2 | Wilkinson & Rickhuss | H | Moulded jug |
| Jun 25 | 1 | J. & M. P. Bell & Co. | G | Moulded jug |
| July 30 | 2 | J. Ridgway, Bates & Co. | H | Filter |
| Aug 4 | 5 | Taylor, Pears & Co. | F | Fluted dinner ware |
| Aug 11 | 3 | Kerr & Binns | W | Dinnerwares |
| Sept 7 | 2 | W. T. Copeland | S | Printed design |
| Oct 3 | 3 | Doulton & Watts | Ln | Scent jars |
| Oct 14 | 1 | Ridgway & Abington | H | Moulded jug |
| Oct 17 | 1 | Mayer, Brothers & Elliot | B | Tureen form |
| Oct 17 | 2 | T. & R. Boote | B | Teawares |
| Oct 22 | 1 | Pratt & Co. | F | Printed figures |
| Nov 3 | 3 | Maw & Co. | Br | Tiles |
| Nov 6 | 3 | B. Richardson | Wy | Handle form |
| Nov 28 | 2 | Kerr & Binns | W | Flower holder |
| Dec 4 | 4 | Minton & Co. | S | Border form |
| Dec 9 | 2 | William Brownfield | C | Moulded jug |

## 1858 (B at top)

| Jan 29 | 3 | Cockson & Harding | H | Moulded jug |
|---|---|---|---|---|
| Jan 29 | 4 | E. & W. Walley | C | Moulded jug |
| Feb 16 | 2 | Crosse & Blackwell★ | Ln | Moulded jar |
| Mar 25 | 2 | Kerr & Binns | W | Candle holder |
| April 9 | 2 | Kerr & Binns | W | Flower vase |
| April 17 | 4 | Ridgway & Abington | H | Moulded border |
| April 22 | 5 | T. & R. Boote | B | Dinnerwares |
| April 30 | 5 | Minton & Co. | S | Vase form |
| May 6 | 4 | John Edwards | L | Teawares |
| May 25 | 4 | Anthony Shaw | T | Printed design |
| May 31 | 1 | Holland & Green | L | Dinnerwares |

| May 31 | 1 | Holland & Green | L | Teawares |
|---|---|---|---|---|
| May 31 | 1 | Holland & Green | L | Toiletwares |
| May 31 | 4 | William Adams (junior) | T | Dinnerwares |
| Jun 2 | 1 | William Brownfield | C | Dinnerwares |
| Jun 23 | 6 | S. Alcock & Co. | B | Fluted teawares |
| July 13 | 2 | Mayer (&) Elliot | B | Tureen form |
| July 29 | 4 | S. Alcock & Co. | B | Moulded jug |
| Aug 24 | 2 | William Brownfield | C | Jug form |
| Sept 3 | 2 | Sharpe Brothers & Co. | Sw | Moulded jug |
| Sept 6 | 5 | James Edwards | L | Dinnerwares |
| Sept 10 | 3 | John Edwards | L | Teapot form |
| Sept 10 | 6 | Bridgwood & Clarke | B | Dinnerwares |
| Oct 5 | 2 | Minton & Co. | S | Moulded jug |
| Oct 5 | 3 | William Brownfield | C | Moulded jug |
| Oct 7 | 1 | Ridgway & Abington | H | Moulded jug |
| Oct 18 | 3 | Minton & Co. | S | Printed design |
| Oct 29 | 2 | Benjamin Green | F | Moulded jug |
| Nov 3 | 8 | James Stiff | Ln | Moulded form |
| Nov 5 | 5 | William Savage★ | Win | Jug form |
| Nov 11 | | E. & W. Walley | C | Moulded jug |
| Dec 8 | 11 | T. & R. Boote | B | Teawares |
| Dec 8 | 11 | T. & R. Boote | B | Toiletwares |
| Dec 17 | 6 | W. T. Copeland | S | Printed design |
| Dec 23 | 2 | Joseph Clementson | Sh | Toiletwares |
| Dec 23 | 9 | W. T. Copeland | S | Toiletwares |
| Dec 27 | 4 | Joseph Clementson | Sh | Dinnerwares |

**1859 (M at top)**

| Jan 25 | 4 | W. T. Copeland | S | Printed border |
|---|---|---|---|---|
| Feb 2 | 3 | T. & R. Boote | B | Oval tureen |
| Feb 3 | 2 | Davenports & Co. | Lpt | Teawares |
| Feb 3 | 2 | Davenports & Co. | Lpt | Toiletwares |
| Feb 8 | 6 | Levison Hill | S | Moulded jug |
| Mar 19 | 1 | Alsop, Downes, Spilsbury & Co. | Ln | Button |
| Mar 21 | 7 | T. & R. Boote | B | "Atlantic" jug |
| Mar 29 | 7 | T. & R. Boote | B | Teapot form |
| May 7 | 1 | E. & W. Walley | C | Moulded jugs |
| May 10 | 2 | S. Alcock & Co. | B | Saxon print |
| May 20 | 1 | W. Brownfield | C | Moulded jug |
| May 26 | 1 | Lockett, Baguley & Cooper | H | Moulded jug |
| July 2 | 2 | W. T. Copeland | S | Plate design |
| Aug 6 | 7 | F. & R. Pratt & Co. | F | Printed design |
| Aug 27 | 6 | S. Alcock & Co. | B | Moulded jug |
| Sept 1 | 3 | James Edwards & Son | Lpt | Dinnerwares |
| Oct 12 | 4 | W. Adams, junior | T | Dinnerwares |
| Oct 14 | 4 | W. T. Copeland | S | Printed border |
| Oct 25 | 1 | Minton & Co. | S | Moulded jug |
| Oct 25 | 1 | Minton & Co. | S | Ribbon edgings |
| Oct 28 | 1 | Davenports & Co. | Lpt | Dinnerwares |
| Nov 2 | 3 | Elsmore & Forster | T | Teawares |
| Nov 2 | 3 | Elsmore & Forster | T | Toiletwares |
| Nov 2 | 3 | Elsmore & Forster | T | Dinnerwares |

| Nov 5 | 4 | W. Brownfield | C | Moulded jug |
|---|---|---|---|---|
| Nov 17 | 4 | Minton & Co. | S | Printed designs |
| Nov 23 | 4 | Minton & Co. | S | Printed design |
| Dec 10 | 5 | J. Wedgwood & Sons | E | Jeddo design |
| Dec 14 | 2 | E. & W. Walley | C | Moulded jug |
| Dec 15 | 3 | Minton & Co. | S | Moulded design |

**1860 (Z at top)**

| Jan 10 | 4 | W. T. Copeland | S | Printed border |
|---|---|---|---|---|
| Jan 23 | 7 | Mayer & Elliot | Lpt | Tureen form |
| Feb 14 | 9 | W. T. Copeland | S | Moulded vases |
| Mar 1 | 2 | Bates, Brown-Westhead & Moore | Sh | Jug form |
| Mar 27 | 1 | Bates, Brown-Westhead & Moore | Sh | Jug form |
| April 5 | 1 | G. Grainger & Co. | W | Plate form |
| April 12 | 4 | Minton & Co. | S | Moulded plate |
| May 2 | 2 | John Meir & Son | T | Printed design |
| May 19 | 9 | Lockett, Baguley & Cooper | H | Moulded jug |
| May 30 | 10 | Edward Corn | B | Printed design |
| Jun 6 | 4 | W. Brownfield | C | Moulded jug |
| Jun 6 | 4 | W. Brownfield | C | Tureen form |
| Jun 6 | 4 | W. Brownfield | C | Plate edging |
| Jun 19 | 4 | John Phillpot★ | Ln | Ham stand |
| Jun 22 | 2 | Minton & Co. | S | Printed design |
| Jun 23 | 4 | Sandford Estate Pottery Clay Co. | Wm | Moulded jug |
| Jun 23 | 4 | Sandford Estate Pottery Clay Co. | Wm | Jardinere |
| Jun 28 | 2 | Minton & Co. | S | Printed design |
| July 6 | 5 | Sandford Estate Pottery Clay Co. | Wm | Moulded jugs |
| July 7 | 9 | Sandford Estate Pottery Clay Co. | Wm | Moulded jugs |
| Aug 1 | 5 | Sandford Estate Pottery Clay Co. | Wm | Moulded jugs |
| Aug 3 | 2 | Sandford Estate Pottery Clay Co. | Wm | Moulded jug |
| Aug 21 | 2 | John Wedge Wood | T | Printed design |
| Aug 23 | 9 | Sandford Estate Pottery Clay Co. | Wm | Moulded jugs |
| Aug 28 | 5 | Sandford Estate Pottery Clay Co. | Wm | Moulded jugs |
| Aug 28 | 5 | Sandford Estate Pottery Clay Co. | Wm | Covered dish |
| Sept 24 | 3 | Minton & Co. | S | Printed design |
| Sept 28 | 7 | Sandford Estate Pottery Clay Co. | Wm | Jardinere |
| Sept 28 | 7 | Sandford Estate Pottery Clay Co. | Wm | Moulded jug |
| Sept 29 | 7 | Minton & Co. | S | Printed border |
| Oct 4 | 4 | Sandford Estate Pottery Clay Co. | Wm | Moulded vase |
| Oct 13 | 5 | Benjamin Green | F | Fluted teawares |
| Oct 18 | 4 | Bates, Brown-Westhead & Moore | Sh | Toiletwares |
| Oct 18 | 4 | Bates, Brown-Westhead & Moore | Sh | Dinnerwares |
| Oct 19 | 4 | Joseph Clementson | Sh | Dinnerwares |
| Oct 19 | 4 | Joseph Clementson | Sh | Teawares |
| Oct 19 | 4 | Joseph Clementson | Sh | Toiletwares |
| Oct 19 | 5 | Holland & Green | L | Dinnerwares |
| Oct 19 | 5 | Holland & Green | L | Teawares |
| Oct 19 | 5 | Holland & Green | L | Toiletwares |
| Oct 29 | 3 | Minton & Co. | S | Moulded jug |
| Oct 29 | 9 | W. Brownfield | C | Moulded jug |
| Nov 23 | 9 | T. & R. Boote | B | Toiletwares |
| Nov 29 | 4 | Sandford Estate Pottery Clay Co. | Wm | Moulded vases |

| Nov 29 | 4 | Sandford Estate Pottery Clay Co. | Wm | Finger plate |
|---|---|---|---|---|
| Dec 3 | 3 | Bates, Brown-Westhead & Moore | Sh | Printed designs |
| Dec 12 | 3 | Bates & Co. | Sh | Moulded jug |

**1861 (R at top)**

| Jan 8 | 6 | T. & R. Boote | B | Garibaldi jug |
|---|---|---|---|---|
| Jan 21 | 7 | Wedgwood & Co. | T | Moulded jug |
| Feb 12 | 5 | Sandford Estate Pottery Clay Co. | Wm | Flower holders |
| Feb 15 | 3 | J. Furnival & Co. | C | Tureen form |
| Feb 27 | 5 | James Edwards & Sons | Lpt | Dinnerwares |
| Mar 7 | 7 | Turner & Tomkinson | T | Printed borders |
| Mar 19 | 3 | W. T. Copeland | S | Printed design |
| Mar 19 | 4 | W. H. Kerr & Co. | W | Ink & perfume pots |
| April 5 | 3 | Pinder, Bourne & Hope | B | Moulded jug |
| April 6 | 1 | Minton, Hollins & Co. | S | Tiles |
| April 12 | 3 | Davenports & Co. | Lpt | Dinnerwares "Erie" |
| April 12 | 3 | Davenports & Co. | Lpt | Teawares "Erie" |
| April 18 | 5 | T. & R. Boote | B | Plate form |
| April 20 | 6 | F. & R. Pratt & Co. | F | Printed designs |
| April 25 | 2 | James Dudson | H | Moulded jug |
| May 1 | 5 | Silicated Carbon Filter Co.★ | S | Printed design |
| May 3 | 8 | W. T. Copeland | S | Printed design |
| May 6 | 3 | Hill Pottery Co. | B | Printed design |
| May 6 | 5 | Old Hall Earthenware Co. Ltd. | H | Moulded jugs |
| May 9 | 3 | Bates, Brown-Westhead & Moore | Sh | Printed design |
| May 9 | 3 | Bates, Brown-Westhead & Moore | Sh | Jug form |
| May 13 | 7 | Minton & Co. | S | Printed border |
| May 14 | 2 | W. H. Kerr & Co. | W | Moulded bottle |
| May 25 | 2 | W. H. Kerr & Co. | W | Dinnerwares |
| May 31 | 3 | Cork, Edge & Malkin | B | Moulded jug |
| Jun 4 | 1 | Bates, Brown-Westhead & Moore | Sh | Moulded jug |
| Jun 7 | 5 | Hill Pottery Co. | B | Plate shape |
| Jun 11 | 2 | W. T. Copeland | S | Printed design |
| Jun 11 | 2 | W. T. Copeland | S | Jug form |
| Jun 13 | 6 | Minton & Co. | S | Printed design |
| July 4 | 2 | Lockett & Cooper | H | Moulded jug |
| July 5 | 2 | Beech & Hancock | T | Moulded jug |
| July 6 | 2 | William Brownfield | C | Moulded jug |
| July 18 | 4 | J. Wedgwood & Sons | E | Printed designs |
| Aug 19 | 7 | T. & R. Boote | B | Tureen form |
| Aug 22 | 7 | Wedgwood & Co. | T | Moulded jug |
| Aug 23 | 2 | G. W. Brade | C | Moulded jug |
| Sept 6 | 6 | W. Brownfield | C | Printed design |
| Sept 12 | 6 | J. & J. Peake | N | Printed design |
| Sept 17 | 2 | W. T. Copeland | S | Printed design |
| Sept 18 | 7 | William Beech | B | Jug form |
| Sept 26 | 7 | John Cliff & Co. | Ln | Stoneware jar |
| Oct 10 | 5 | W. H. Kerr | W | Teawares |
| Oct 11 | 3 | Mountford & Scarratt | F | Jug forms |
| Oct 11 | 4 | T. & R. Boote | B | Dinnerwares |
| Oct 15 | 3 | Executors of Levison Hill | S | Moulded jug |
| Oct 18 | 3 | W. T. Copeland | S | Printed design |

| Oct 24 | 5 | Hulse, Nixon & Adderley | L | Coffee pot form |
| Oct 28 | 7 | Bates, Brown-Westhead & Moore | Sh | Dinnerwares |
| Nov 18 | 3 | Joseph Clementson | Sh | Dinnerwares |
| Nov 18 | 3 | Joseph Clementson | Sh | Teawares |
| Nov 18 | 3 | Joseph Clementson | Sh | Toiletwares |
| Nov 29 | 5 | J. Wedgwood & Sons | E | "Doric" jug |
| Dec 4 | 7 | W. Brownfield | C | Moulded jug |
| Dec 4 | 7 | W. Brownfield | C | Jardinere |
| Dec 5 | 5 | Till, Bullock & Smith | H | Moulded jug |
| Dec 20 | 7 | Lockett & Cooper | H | Printed design |
| Dec 20 | 9 | Wedgwood & Co. | T | Printed design |

**1862 (O at top)**

| Jan 11 | 5 | W. Brownfield | C | Printed border |
| Jan 25 | 3 | W. Brownfield | C | Moulded jug |
| Feb 1 | 4 | Elliot Brothers | Lpt | Moulded jug |
| Feb 10 | 6 | W. H. Kerr & Co. | W | Flower holder |
| Feb 10 | 8 | Minton & Co. | S | Printed design |
| Feb 27 | 4 | James Dudson | H | Moulded jugs |
| Mar 1 | 6 | T. & R. Boote | B | Teapot |
| Mar 13 | 6 | W. T. Copeland | S | Printed design |
| Mar 13 | 7 | William Adams, junior | T | Dinnerwares |
| Mar 13 | 7 | William Adams, junior | T | Teawares |
| Mar 14 | 8 | Joseph Knight | F | Splash ornamentation |
| Mar 14 | 9 | Wedgwood & Co. | T | Printed design |
| Mar 14 | 10 | W. Brownfield | C | Printed design |
| Mar 14 | 10 | W. Brownfield | C | Dinnerwares |
| Mar 21 | 6 | Thompson Brothers | Dshire | Teapot form |
| Mar 22 | 9 | T. & R. Boote | B | Toiletwares |
| Mar 27 | 5 | J. & M. P. Bell & Co. | G | Printed design |
| Mar 27 | 5 | J. & M. P. Bell & Co. | G | Tureen form |
| Mar 27 | 5 | J. & M. P. Bell & Co. | G | Jug & candlestick |
| Mar 29 | 3 | Minton & Co. | S | Toiletwares |
| April 1 | 5 | J. Wedgwood & Sons | E | Tureen forms |
| April 4 | 2 | Minton & Co. | S | Honey pot |
| April 4 | 5 | J. & T. Furnival | C | Printed design |
| April 7 | 12 | G. Grainger & Co. | W | Dinnerwares |
| April 9 | 3 | Old Hall Earthenware Co. Ltd | H | Moulded jug |
| April 16 | 9 | H. A. Abrahams | L | 1862 Exhibition print |
| April 17 | 5 | Thompson Brothers | Dshire | Fluted dish |
| April 24 | 2 | Turner & Tomkinson | T | Printed design |
| May 1 | 7 | Eardley & Hammersley | T | Printed design |
| May 3 | 3 | G. L. Ashworth Bros | Sh | Dinnerwares |
| May 5 | 5 | John Cliff | Ln | Water container |
| May 9 | 9 | Brown-Westhead, Moore & Co. | Sh | Dinnerwares |
| May 9 | 9 | Brown-Westhead, Moore & Co. | Sh | Toiletwares |
| May 14 | 3 | George Jones & Co. | S | Printed designs |
| May 27 | 3 | Edward Challinor | T | Printed design |
| May 29 | 5 | J. Furnival & Co. | C | Moulded jug |
| Jun 24 | 5 | Brown-Westhead, Moore & Co. | Sh | Printed design |
| July 2 | 4 | Minton & Co. | S | Printed border |
| July 4 | 8 | Joseph Clementson | Sh | Toiletwares |

| July 12 | 4 | Joseph Clementson | Sh | Teawares |
|---|---|---|---|---|
| July 14 | 2 | Beech & Hancock | T | Moulded jug |
| July 19 | 6 | Joseph Clementson | Sh | Tureen form |
| July 31 | 3 | Jones & Ellis | L | Printed design |
| July 31 | 4 | Minton & Co. | S | Jug form |
| Aug 16 | 5 | Richard Edwards | Lpt | Dinnerwares |
| Aug 16 | 7 | J. H. Baddeley | H | Cheese dish |
| Aug 18 | 4 | Hulse, Nixon & Adderley | L | Moulded jug |
| Aug 19 | 4 | G. L. Ashworth & Bros. | Sh | Moulded jug |
| Aug 25 | 3 | E. F. Bodley & Co. | B | Printed designs |
| Aug 25 | 8 | F. Button & Sons | Notts | Printed border |
| Aug 30 | 3 | Thomas Fell & Co. | NT | Printed design |
| Aug 30 | 4 | T. & R. Boote | B | Moulded teapot |
| Sept 6 | 2 | Malkin, Walker & Hulse | L | Printed design |
| Sept 11 | 3 | Minton & Co. | S | Printed design |
| Sept 12 | 2 | Thomas Cooper | L | Fluted jug |
| Sept 17 | 6 | Hope & Carter | B | Tureen forms |
| Sept 22 | 7 | Minton & Co. | S | Printed design |
| Sept 26 | 1 | Hope & Carter | B | Dinnerwares |
| Sept 26 | 1 | Hope & Carter | B | Toiletwares |
| Sept 26 | 1 | Hope & Carter | B | Teawares |
| Oct 1 | 7 | Thomas Fell & Co. | NT | Printed designs |
| Oct 9 | 3 | Owners of Hill Pottery | B | Tureen form |
| Oct 15 | 2 | Turner & Tomkinson | T | Printed design "Star" |
| Oct 23 | 8 | William Baker & Co. | F | Toiletwares |
| Oct 23 | 8 | William Baker & Co. | F | Teawares |
| Oct 23 | 8 | William Baker & Co. | F | Dinnerwares |
| Nov 11 | 3 | E. F. Bodley & Co. | B | Tureen form |
| Nov 19 | 5 | George Woolliscroft | T | Tureen form |
| Nov 28 | 4 | Minton & Co. | S | Vase form |
| Dec 3 | 5 | Brown-Westhead, Moore & Co. | Sh | Tureen forms |
| Dec 5 | 2 | W. Brownfield | C | Printed design |
| Dec 9 | 5 | Thomas Cooper | H | Moulded jug |
| Dec 17 | 5 | Old Hall Earthenware Co. Ltd | H | Tureen forms |
| Dec 18 | 3 | George Jones | S | Printed design |

**1863 (G at top)**

| Jan 12 | 6 | Davenport, Banks & Co. | E | Jug form |
|---|---|---|---|---|
| Jan 16 | 2 | Minton & Co. | S | Moulded jug |
| Jan 16 | 8 | Liddle Elliot & Sons | Lpt | Moulded jug |
| Jan 29 | 1 | J. Wedgwood & Sons | E | Printed design |
| Jan 30 | 3 | T. & R. Boote | B | Dinnerwares |
| Feb 2 | 3 | Minton & Co. | S | Plate form |
| Feb 17 | 1 | T. & R. Boote | B | Toiletwares |
| Feb 24 | 5 | J. Stiff & Sons | Ln | Tile |
| Mar 6 | 2 | G. L. Ashworth & Bros. | Sh | Teawares |
| Mar 13 | 2 | Hope & Carter | B | Tureen forms |
| Mar 13 | 3 | Wilkinson & Son | H | Moulded jug |
| Mar 20 | 8 | Worthington & Green | H | Moulded jug |
| Mar 20 | 9 | John Pratt & Co. | F | Moulded jug |
| Mar 20 | 9 | John Pratt & Co. | F | Moulded cup or vase |
| Mar 21 | 2 | Beech & Hancock | T | Moulded jug |

| Mar 21 | 4 | Hulse, Nixon & Adderley | L | Moulded jug |
| Mar 21 | 5 | J. Edwards & Son | B | Tureen form |
| Mar 23 | 2 | Bodley & Harrold | B | Moulded jug |
| Mar 23 | 2 | Bodley & Harrold | B | Printed design |
| Mar 27 | 4 | J. Hinks & Son★ | Bir | Lamp bases |
| April 11 | 1 | James Macintyre | B | Moulded jug |
| April 15 | 5 | F. A. Wint★ | B | Vase form |
| April 23 | 4 | Brown-Westhead, Moore & Co. | Sh | Toiletwares |
| April 25 | 1 | Beech & Hancock | T | Moulded jug |
| April 30 | 3 | Wilkinson & Son | H | Moulded jug |
| May 4 | 6 | Harding & Cotterill | BT | Teapot form |
| May 11 | 3 | Edward Pearson | C | Dinnerwares |
| May 11 | 3 | Edward Pearson | C | Teawares |
| May 12 | 1 | Bodley & Harrold | B | Printed design |
| May 15 | 10 | Harding & Cotterill | BT | Moulded jug |
| May 22 | 4 | W. T. Copeland | S | Printed design |
| May 22 | 4 | W. T. Copeland | S | Jug form |
| May 26 | 9 | Brown-Westhead, Moore & Co. | Sh | Dinnerwares |
| Jun 4 | 5 | Old Hall Earthenware Co. Ltd | H | Printed design |
| Jun 8 | 15 | Minton & Co. | S | Basket form |
| Jun 8 | 16 | W. Brownfield | C | Jardinere |
| Jun 20 | 7 | Edmund Ratcliff★ | Bir | Lamp base |
| July 11 | 6 | F. A. Wint★ | B | Vase form |
| July 14 | 2 | Turner & Tomkinson | T | Tureen form |
| July 15 | 3 | Henry Venables | H | Printed design |
| July 20 | 3 | W. Brownfield | C | Tureen form |
| July 24 | 3 | W. T. Copeland | S | Printed designs |
| July 27 | 7 | Architectural Pottery Co. | Poole | Mosaics |
| July 28 | 6 | Minton & Co. | S | Printed design |
| Aug 1 | 2 | Architectural Pottery Co. | Poole | Mosaics |
| Aug 11 | 3 | Turner & Tomkinson | T | Printed designs |
| Aug 12 | 4 | Hancock, Whittingham & Co. | B | Moulded jug |
| Aug 21 | 1 | J. Clementson | H | Tureen form |
| Aug 28 | 5 | Henry Venables | H | Printed design |
| Sept 7 | 6 | T. & R. Boote | B | Toiletwares |
| Sept 28 | 4 | Henry Venables | H | Vase form |
| Sept 28 | 6 | J. Edwards & Son | B | Moulded plate |
| Sept 28 | 6 | J. Edwards & Son | B | Teawares |
| Oct 2 | 5 | Henry Venables | H | Vase form |
| Oct 6 | 5 | Thompson Brothers | BT | Toiletwares |
| Oct 14 | 7 | W. Brownfield | C | Moulded jug |
| Oct 15 | 2 | F. Brewer & Son | L | Moulded plate |
| Oct 17 | 1 | T. & R. Boote | B | Teapot form |
| Oct 22 | 5 | Eardley & Hammersley | T | Printed design |
| Oct 24 | 5 | J. Wedgwood & Sons | E | Dessertwares |
| Oct 26 | 7 | Old Hall Earthenware Co. Ltd | H | Dinnerwares |
| Oct 26 | 7 | Old Hall Earthenware Co. Ltd | H | Printed design |
| Oct 28 | 8 | George Jones & Co. | S | Printed design |
| Oct 31 | 3 | Edmund T. Wood | T | Dinnerwares |
| Oct 31 | 3 | Edmund T. Wood | T | Toiletwares |
| Oct 31 | 3 | Edmund T. Wood | T | Teawares |
| Nov 3 | 5 | John Meir & Son | T | Printed design |

| Nov 4 | 7 | T. & R. Boote | B | Dinnerwares |
|---|---|---|---|---|
| Nov 6 | 1 | George Jones & Co. | S | Printed designs |
| Nov 16 | 10 | William Kirkham | S | Moulded jug |
| Nov 26 | 12 | W. Brownfield | C | Dinnerwares |
| Nov 27 | 3 | Bodley & Harrold | B | Printed design |
| Dec 2 | 5 | J. W. Pankhurst & Co. | H | Dinnerwares |
| Dec 2 | 6 | T. & R. Boote | B | Plate form |
| Dec 18 | 4 | F. & R. Pratt & Co. | F | Moulded jug |
| Dec 23 | 2 | W. Brownfield | C | Jug form |
| Dec 30 | 1 | Brown-Westhead, Moore & Co. | Sh | Tureen forms |

**1864 (N at top)**

| Jan 5 | 2 | W. Brownfield | C | Dinnerwares |
|---|---|---|---|---|
| Jan 11 | 5 | Malkin, Walker & Hulse | L | Printed design |
| Feb 2 | 5 | J. Wedgwood & Sons | E | Flower vase |
| Feb 5 | 5 | Hope & Carter | B | Plate edging |
| Feb 6 | 3 | Thomas Goode & Co.★ | Ln | Toiletwares |
| Feb 13 | 6 | W. T. Copeland | S | Moulded jug |
| Feb 22 | 7 | Cork, Edge & Malkin | B | Teapot form |
| Feb 25 | 6 | Liddle Elliot & Son | L | Moulded jug |
| Feb 29 | 6 | J. & D. Hampson | L | Fluted jug |
| Mar 1 | 1 | Coalbrookdale Company | Cpt | Terracotta box |
| Mar 3 | 4 | G. L. Ashworth & Bros. | H | Tureen form |
| Mar 5 | 3 | F. A. Wint★ | B | Candlesticks |
| Mar 12 | 5 | Cork, Edge & Malkin | B | Jug form |
| Mar 18 | 1 | Brown-Westhead, Moore & Co. | Sh | Tureen forms |
| Mar 22 | 3 | Minton & Co. | S | Plate borders |
| Mar 23 | 4 | Burgess & Leigh | B | Moulded jug |
| April 2 | 4 | Coalbrookdale Company | Cpt | Wall bracket |
| April 9 | 4 | J. Wedgwood & Sons | E | Tureen forms |
| April 15 | 4 | George Jones | S | Printed design |
| April 18 | 5 | Minton & Co. | S | Jardinere form |
| April 21 | 4 | Brown-Westhead, Moore & Co. | Sh | Moulded jug |
| April 21 | 8 | Liddle Elliot & Son | L | Tureen form |
| April 23 | 11 | G. L. Ashworth & Bros. | H | Printed design |
| April 25 | 8 | W. H. Ward★ | Ln | Covered pot |
| April 26 | 3 | Bodley & Harrold | B | Printed design |
| April 27 | 4 | Hope & Carter | B | Printed design |
| April 29 | 2 | W. Brownfield | C | "Argos" jug |
| May 9 | 3 | R. T. Boughton & Co. | B | Shakespeare jug |
| May 10 | 5 | George Jones & Co. | S | Printed designs |
| May 11 | 3 | R. H. Grove | H | Printed design |
| May 12 | 5 | Naylor & Co. | Ln | Centrepiece |
| May 18 | 5 | George Ray | L | Teapot form |
| May 19 | 4 | J. L. Lloyd | Bir | Moulded jug |
| May 21 | 1 | J. & D. Hampson | L | Printed designs |
| Jun 9 | 7 | Minton & Co. | S | Jug form |
| Jun 16 | 3 | Hope & Carter | B | Jardinere forms |
| Jun 24 | 1 | Johnston Fraser & Co. | G | Toiletwares |
| Jun 30 | 4 | W. Brownfield | C | Printed design |
| Jun 30 | 10 | Worcester Royal Porcelain Co. Ltd | W | Vase form |
| July 2 | 3 | Wood & Sale | H | Moulded jug |

| July 9 | 5 | Pinder, Bourne & Co. | B | Printed design |
| July 11 | 8 | Pinder, Bourne & Co. | B | Tureen forms |
| July 18 | 6 | Bodley & Harrold | B | Tray shape |
| July 18 | 7 | Evans & Booth | B | Printed design |
| July 19 | 4 | Hope & Carter | B | Tureen forms |
| July 22 | 5 | J. Hinks★ | Bir | Door furniture |
| July 28 | 4 | Holland & Green | L | Dinnerwares |
| July 28 | 4 | Holland & Green | L | Toiletwares |
| July 28 | 4 | Holland & Green | L | Teawares |
| Aug 20 | 10 | George Jones & Co. | S | Tureen form |
| Aug 26 | 5 | Brown-Westhead, Moore & Co. | Sh | Toiletwares |
| Sept 6 | 5 | W. T. Copeland | S | Printed designs |
| Sept 10 | 1 | Minton & Co. | S | Toiletwares |
| Sept 12 | 2 | Minton & Co. | S | Printed design |
| Sept 14 | 4 | Bodley & Harrold | B | Tray form |
| Sept 16 | 6 | G. L. Ashworth & Bros | H | Tureen forms |
| Sept 19 | 1 | J. Wedgwood & Sons | E | Teawares |
| Sept 21 | 1 | Minton & Co. | S | Printed borders |
| Sept 22 | 1 | J. Hinks★ | Bir | Lamp base |
| Sept 22 | 6 | J. Wedgwood & Sons | E | Comport forms |
| Sept 22 | 6 | J. Wedgwood & Sons | E | Flower vase |
| Sept 22 | 6 | J. Wedgwood & Sons | E | Jug jardinere |
| Oct 4 | 2 | George Jones & Co. | S | Printed border |
| Oct 12 | 4 | W. Brownfield | C | Moulded jug |
| Oct 27 | 4 | Evans & Booth | B | Oval tureen |
| Oct 28 | 2 | Worcester Royal Porcelain Co. | W | Vase, hand form |
| Oct 28 | 4 | Bodley & Harrold | B | Moulded jug |
| Oct 28 | 9 | Minton & Co. | S | Cup form |
| Oct 29 | 2 | C. Collinson & Co. | B | Moulded jug |
| Oct 31 | 3 | Cork, Edge & Malkin | B | Moulded jug |
| Nov 1 | 7 | W. T. Copeland | S | Circular container |
| Nov 4 | 3 | Livesley Powell & Co. | H | Moulded jug |
| Nov 10 | 2 | Elsmore & Foster | T | Dinnerwares |
| Nov 10 | 2 | Elsmore & Foster | T | Teawares |
| Nov 10 | 3 | Hope & Carter | B | Print "Dancers" |
| Nov 10 | 10 | George Jones & Co. | S | Printed design |
| Nov 24 | 5 | Brown-Westhead, Moore & Co. | Sh | Dinnerwares |
| Nov 29 | 1 | Hope & Carter | B | Teapot form |
| Dec 9 | 1 | William Kirkham | S | Moulded jug |
| Dec 10 | 8 | Hope & Carter | B | Tureen forms |
| Dec 21 | 2 | Coalbrookdale Company | Cpt | Vases, etc |
| Dec 31 | 6 | George Jones & Co. | S | Printed design |

### 1865 (W at top)

| Jan 6 | 3 | Hope & Carter | B | Printed design |
| Jan 6 | 4 | Minton & Co. | S | Moulded jug |
| Jan 14 | 4 | George Jones & Co. | S | Moulded dish |
| Feb 1 | 1 | Minton & Co. | S | Printed designs |
| Feb 1 | 1 | Minton & Co. | S | Light fitting |
| Feb 2 | 4 | G. L. Ashworth & Bros. | H | Circular ornaments |
| Feb 13 | 7 | F. & R. Pratt & Co. | F | Teapot form |
| Feb 14 | 4 | Liddle Elliot & Son | Lpt | Tureen form |

| Feb 27 | 4 | Livesley Powell & Co. | H | Fluted jug |
|---|---|---|---|---|
| Mar 31 | 3 | Hope & Carter | B | "Odessa" print |
| April 1 | 4 | W. Brownfield | C | Fluted jug |
| April 4 | 4 | Minton & Co. | S | Printed design |
| April 22 | 5 | T. Till & Sons | B | Printed design |
| April 22 | 7 | J. Edwards & Sons | B | Moulded jug |
| April 26 | 5 | J. Edwards & Sons | B | Tureen form |
| April 28 | 4 | Hope & Carter | B | Tureen forms |
| April 28 | 7 | Henry Alcock & Co. | C | Tureen forms |
| April 29 | 3 | Worcester Royal Porcelain Co. | W | Vase, hand form |
| May 2 | 8 | Livesley Powell & Co. | H | Jardinere |
| May 15 | 2 | J. T. Hudden | L | "Toulon" print |
| May 17 | 2 | Minton & Co. | S | Comport shape |
| Jun 6 | 6 | J. T. Hudden | L | Printed designs |
| Jun 9 | 4 | Worcester Royal Porcelain Co. | W | Basket centrepiece |
| Jun 13 | 5 | Worcester Royal Porcelain Co. | W | Basket shape |
| Jun 14 | 6 | Hill Pottery Co. Ltd. | B | Printed design |
| Jun 15 | 2 | J. T. Hudden | L | "Choice" print |
| Jun 16 | 1 | Evans & Booth | B | Printed border |
| Jun 17 | 5 | Worcester Royal Porcelain Co. | W | Centrepiece-bust |
| Jun 29 | 2 | Edward F. Bodley & Co. | B | Cobden print |
| Jun 29 | 2 | Edward F. Bodley & Co. | B | Moulded jug |
| Jun 29 | 3 | G. R. Ward★ | Ln | Hand ornament |
| Jun 30 | 1 | Hill Pottery Co. Ltd. | B | Teawares |
| July 3 | 7 | Brown-Westhead, Moore & Co. | Sh | Openwork edgings |
| July 7 | 3 | J. H. Battam★ | Ln | Shell vase |
| July 12 | 3 | J. Edwards & Son | B | Moulded jug |
| Aug 21 | 6 | J. Furnival & Co. | C | Tureen form |
| Aug 23 | 5 | J. Wedgwood & Sons | E | Moulded dish |
| Aug 24 | 5 | Virgoe, Son & Co. | L | Paste pot |
| Aug 25 | 8 | A. J. Claddo | Bir | Printed plate |
| Sept 11 | 4 | R. T. Boughton & Co. | B | Tureen form |
| Sept 11 | 5 | Thomas Cooper, executors of | H | Tureen form |
| Sept 14 | 2 | Brown-Westhead, Moore & Co. | Sh | Centrepiece |
| Sept 18 | 6 | Liddle Elliot & Son | Lpt | Tureen form |
| Sept 28 | 4 | Minton & Co. | S | Printed border |
| Sept 30 | 4 | S. Barker & Son | Sn | "York" print |
| Oct 13 | 8 | Brown-Westhead, Moore & Co. | Sh | Dinnerwares |
| Oct 30 | 4 | W. Brownfield | C | Tureen forms |
| Oct 30 | 4 | W. Brownfield | C | Moulded jug |
| Nov 10 | 4 | Pinder Bourne & Co with Anthony Shaw | B | Moulded edging |
| Nov 23 | 10 | Old Hall Earthenware Co. Ltd | H | Vase form |
| Nov 29 | 8 | J. Edwards & Son | B | Tureen forms |
| Dec 2 | 3 | Worcester Royal Porcelain Co. | W | Ornament |
| Dec 23 | 3 | James Dudson | H | Moulded jug |

## 1866 (Q at top)

| Jan 2 | 4 | Pratt & Co. | F | Printed hunting design |
|---|---|---|---|---|
| Jan 3 | 6 | J. T. Close & Co. | S | Dinnerwares |
| Jan 13 | 2 | Edward F. Bodley & Co. | B | Coffee pot form |
| Jan 17 | 4 | Burgess & Leigh | B | Printed design |

| | | | | |
|---|---|---|---|---|
| Jan 24 | 1 | Minton & Co. | S | Tureen forms |
| Jan 31 | 5 | J. Edwards & Son | B | Jug form |
| Feb 2 | 7 | W. T. Copeland | S | Covered box |
| Mar 1 | 9 | Coalbrookdale Company | Cpt | Chimney pots |
| Mar 2 | 2 | Ford, Challinor & Co. | T | Printed design |
| Mar 3 | 8 | J. Robbins & Co. | Ln | Vase form |
| Mar 10 | 1 | Old Hall Earthenware Co. Ltd | H | Plate form |
| April 14 | 6 | Walker & Carter | L | Printed design |
| April 14 | 7 | G. L. Ashworth & Bros. | H | Dinnerwares |
| April 14 | 7 | G. L. Ashworth & Bros. | H | Teawares |
| April 14 | 7 | G. L. Ashworth & Bros. | H | Toiletwares |
| April 16 | 8 | Old Hall Earthenware Co. Ltd | H | Tureen form |
| April 18 | 4 | J. Edwards & Son | B | Moulded jug |
| April 20 | 7 | W. Brownfield | C | Tureen forms |
| April 20 | 7 | W. Brownfield | C | Moulded jug |
| May 1 | 4 | J. Furnival & Co. | C | Tureen forms |
| May 25 | 1 | Hope & Carter | B | Moulded jug |
| May 25 | 1 | Hope & Carter | B | Jardinere |
| Jun 4 | 4 | J. Broadhurst | L | Printed design |
| Jun 12 | 1 | J. Edwards | F | Dinnerwares |
| Jun 12 | 1 | J. Edwards | F | Toiletwares |
| Jun 12 | 1 | J. Edwards | F | Teawares |
| Jun 13 | 8 | T. W. Cowan | Ws | Vases & brackets |
| Jun 21 | 4 | Pinder Bourne & Co. | B | Tureen forms |
| Jun 30 | 4 | Thomas Minshall | S | Printed design |
| July 19 | 5 | J. T. Hudden | L | Printed design |
| July 25 | 3 | George Jones | S | Tureen form |
| Aug 17 | 3 | Morgan, Wood & Co. | B | Printed design |
| Aug 29 | 4 | Edward F. Bodley & Co. | B | "Sydney" print |
| Sept 6 | 4 | F. & R. Pratt & Co. | F | Moulded jug |
| Sept 13 | 9 | T. & C. Ford | H | Dinnerwares |
| Sept 15 | 8 | G. L. Ashworth & Bros | H | Printed design |
| Sept 20 | 8 | Anthony Keeling | T | "Kew" print |
| Oct 8 | 3 | Minton & Co. | S | Printed designs |
| Oct 8 | 3 | Minton & Co. | S | Openwork edging |
| Oct 13 | 3 | Thomas Furnival | C | Printed design |
| Nov 3 | 6 | Minton & Co. | S | Moulded ewer |
| Nov 12 | 3 | W. T. Copeland | S | Printed design |
| Nov 14 | 8 | Brown–Westhead, Moore & Co. | Sh | Tureen & plate |
| Nov 15 | 4 | G. Grainger & Co. | W | Moulded jug |
| Dec 13 | 4 | Liddle Elliot & Son | B | Jug form |
| Dec 14 | 8 | Samuel Barker & Son | Sn | Floral print |
| Dec 15 | 5 | Brown–Westhead, Moore & Co. | Sh | Tureen form |
| Dec 19 | 5 | J. Meir & Co. | T | Moulded jug |
| Dec 22 | 6 | Pellatt & Co.★ | Ln | Vase form |
| Dec 24 | 2 | J. T. Hudden | L | "Oxford" print |
| Dec 29 | 2 | Pellatt & Co.★ | Ln | Teawares |

**1867 (T at top)**

| | | | | |
|---|---|---|---|---|
| Jan 8 | 5 | J. Edwards & Son | B | Moulded jug |
| Jan 17 | 3 | Edward F. Bodley & Co. | B | Tureen form |
| Jan 23 | 2 | Worcester Royal Porcelain Co. | W | Dove vase |

| Feb 9 | 1 | Edward F. Bodley & Co. | B | Tureen form |
|---|---|---|---|---|
| Feb 23 | 5 | Worthington & Harrop | H | Vase form |
| Mar 2 | 7 | J. Wedgwood & Sons | E | Tureen form |
| Mar 4 | 4 | Brown-Westhead, Moore & Co. | Sh | Dessert shapes |
| Mar 5 | 6 | Powell & Bishop | H | Cheese dish |
| Mar 6 | 4 | Old Hall Earthenware Co. | H | Oval tureen |
| Mar 9 | 3 | John Edwards | F | Teawares |
| Mar 11 | 2 | J. Wedgwood & Sons | E | Ornamental form |
| Mar 14 | 1 | Davenport, Banks & Co. | E | Printed design |
| Mar 15 | 7 | W. Brownfield | C | Jardinere |
| Mar 15 | 7 | W. Brownfield | C | Vases & jug |
| Mar 15 | 7 | W. Brownfield | C | Dessertwares |
| Mar 15 | 7 | W. Brownfield | C | Tureen forms |
| Mar 18 | 5 | Cockson, Chetwynd & Co. | C | Toiletwares |
| Mar 18 | 5 | Cockson, Chetwynd & Co. | C | Teawares |
| Mar 19 | 5 | James Edwards & Son | B | Plate design |
| Mar 20 | 2 | J. Wedgwood & Sons | E | Printed design |
| Mar 21 | 10 | James Edwards & Son | B | Tureen forms |
| Mar 25 | 3 | J. Wedgwood & Sons | E | Jug form |
| Mar 26 | 4 | Minton & Co. | S | Oyster plates |
| April 3 | 5 | Minton & Co. | S | Strawberry dish |
| April 4 | 2 | J. Wedgwood & Sons | E | Moulded edge |
| April 4 | 9 | Elsmore & Foster | T | Dinnerwares |
| April 4 | 9 | Elsmore & Foster | T | Teawares |
| April 17 | 1 | Charles Hobson | B | Printed design |
| April 23 | 3 | Adams, Scrivener & Co. | L | Dessertwares |
| April 24 | 2 | W. T. Copeland & Sons | S | Teapot form |
| May 6 | 3 | J. & M. P. Bell & Co. | G | Moulded jug |
| May 7 | 4 | J. Meir & Son | T | Tureen form |
| May 8 | 6 | Brown-Westhead, Moore & Co. | H | Dessertwares |
| May 18 | 7 | William McAdam | G | Royal Arms jar |
| May 22 | 6 | Clementson Brothers | H | Dinnerwares |
| May 22 | 6 | Clementson Brothers | H | Jug form |
| Jun 6 | 3 | J. Wedgwood & Sons | E | Moulded jug |
| Jun 11 | 6 | Clementson Brothers | H | Teawares |
| Jun 11 | 7 | Cockson, Chetwynd & Co. | C | Tureen forms |
| Jun 13 | 3 | W. & J. A. Bailey | Alloa | Teawares |
| Jun 15 | 5 | J. Cartland & Son★ | Bir | Door handle |
| Jun 21 | 4 | W. Brownfield | C | Moulded jug |
| Jun 21 | 8 | E. & D. Chetwynd (modeller) | H | Tureen forms |
| Jun 24 | 4 | E. & D. Chetwynd (modeller) | H | Tureen form |
| Jun 24 | 4 | E. & D. Chetwynd (modeller) | H | Teapot form |
| Jun 28 | 1 | J. G. Hughes★ | Ln | Moulded edging |
| July 1 | 7 | J. Ball, junior | L | Printed border |
| July 4 | 5 | E. J. Ridgway | H | Fluted jug |
| July 8 | 3 | G. L. Ashworth & Bros | H | Printed design |
| July 11 | 6 | J. Johnson & Sons | Ln | Printed design |
| July 12 | 5 | George Jones | S | Tureen form |
| July 15 | 2 | J. Wedgwood & Sons | E | Printed design |
| July 17 | 2 | E. & D. Chetwynd (modeller) | H | Oval tureen |
| July 17 | 2 | E. & D. Chetwynd (modeller) | H | Teawares |
| July 25 | 3 | Hope & Carter | B | Printed design |

| Aug 28 | 10 | Worcester Royal Porcelain Co. | W | Vase form |
|--------|----|-------------------------------|-----|-----------|
| Aug 29 | 3 | James Miller | G | Water filter |
| Sept 16 | 7 | Thomas Goode & Co.★ | Ln | Toiletwares |
| Sept 17 | 3 | Wedgwood & Co. | T | Printed design |
| Sept 21 | 1 | G. L. Ashworth & Bros | Sh | Moulded jug |
| Sept 23 | 8 | J. H. Battam★ | Ln | Ornament |
| Sept 25 | 9 | Powell & Bishop | H | Tureen form |
| Sept 25 | 9 | Powell & Bishop | H | Teawares |
| Oct 2 | 1 | Minton & Co | S | Printed design |
| Oct 3 | 5 | Thompson Brothers | BoT | Teapot form |
| Oct 3 | 6 | Minton & Co | S | Printed design |
| Oct 7 | 4 | Minton & Co | S | Printed design |
| Oct 10 | 1 | Thomas Booth | H | Moulded jug |
| Oct 24 | 5 | Ford, Challinor & Co | T | Printed design |
| Oct 26 | 1 | W. T. Copeland & Sons | T | Printed Xmas design |
| Oct 28 | 4 | W. T. Copeland & Sons | T | Printed design |
| Oct 29 | 3 | J. Wedgwood & Sons | E | Dessertwares |
| Oct 29 | 3 | J. Wedgwood & Sons | E | Butter dish |
| Oct 30 | 3 | J. T. Hudden | L | "Jewell" print |
| Oct 31 | 7 | Powell & Bishop | H | Moulded jug |
| Nov 6 | 7 | W. & J. A. Bailey | Alloa | Teapot form |
| Nov 7 | 4 | J. Edwards & Son | B | Dinnerwares |
| Nov 18 | 9 | Ford, Challinor & Co | T | Printed design |
| Nov 27 | 7 | J. G. Hughes & Co★ | L | Printed design |
| Dec 3 | 3 | W. T. Copeland & Sons | S | Moulded jug |
| Dec 12 | 6 | F. & R. Pratt & Co | F | Printed design |
| Dec 20 | 3 | J. Wedgwood & Sons | E | Moulded jug |
| Dec 27 | 1 | J. & J. B. Bebbington | H | Moulded jug |

## 1868 (X at right)

| Jan 3 | 1 | Minton & Co | S | Egg cup stand |
|-------|----|-------------|-----|---------------|
| Jan 7 | 8 | Thompson Brothers | BT | Moulded jug |
| Jan 7 | 11 | Cockson, Chetwynd & Co | C | Dinnerwares |
| Jan 7 | 11 | Cockson, Chetwynd & Co | C | Teawares |
| Jan 7 | 11 | Cockson, Chetwynd & Co | C | Toiletwares |
| Jan 8 | 5 | T. & R. Boote | B | Teawares |
| Jan 9 | 7 | Taylor, Tunnicliffe & Co | H | Door fittings |
| Jan 10 | 2 | Cork, Edge & Malkin | B | Printed design |
| Jan 11 | 2 | W. Brownfield | C | Sardine dish |
| Jan 13 | 2 | G. L. Ashworth & Bros | H | "Daisy" punt |
| Jan 16 | 13 | Old Hall Earthenware Co Ltd | H | Printed border |
| Jan 18 | 7 | Pellatt & Co★ | Ln | Jug form |
| Jan 25 | 3 | Hope & Carter | B | Scenic print |
| Jan 30 | 6 | Jacob Furnival & Co | C | Moulded jug |
| Jan 31 | 8 | J. Wedgwood & Sons | E | Centrepiece |
| Jan 31 | 14 | T. & R. Boote | B | Tureen form |
| Feb 5 | 3 | Carpi, Loly & Co★ | Liv | Printed design |
| Feb 5 | 4 | Adams, Scrivener & Co | L | Moulded jug |
| Feb 5 | 8 | Elijah Hodgkinson | H | Moulded jug |
| Feb 10 | 8 | Minton & Co | S | Openwork baskets |
| Feb 12 | 1 | J. Wedgwood & Sons | E | Partridge pie dish |
| Feb 14 | 10 | John Mortlock★ | Ln | Moulded jug |

| Feb 18 | 1 | J. Wedgwood & Sons | E | Jardinere |
|--------|---|--------------------|---|-----------|
| Feb 18 | 2 | Brown-Westhead, Moore & Co | Sh | Moulded jug |
| Feb 18 | 2 | Brown-Westhead, Moore & Co | Sh | Plate form |
| Feb 20 | 9 | Minton & Co | S | Dish stand |
| Feb 25 | 6 | J. Rose & Co | Cpt | Teawares |
| Feb 27 | 5 | Alcock & Diggory | B | Dessertwares |
| Feb 28 | 7 | W. & J. A. Bailey | Alloa | Teapot form |
| Mar 5 | 12 | Thomas Goode & Co★ | Ln | Dinnerwares |
| Mar 5 | 15 | Minton & Co | S | Moulded jug |
| Mar 7 | 11 | Battam & Son★ | Ln | Finger plate |
| Mar 7 | 12 | Frankham & Wilson★ | Ln | China slides |
| Mar 16 | 4 | Carpi, Loly & Co★ | Liv | Printed design |
| Mar 25 | 7 | W. T. Copeland & Sons | S | Acorn print |
| Mar 25 | 8 | Worcester Royal Porcelain Co | W | Basket form |
| Mar 25 | 8 | Worcester Royal Porcelain Co | W | Vase form |
| Mar 26 | 3 | Walker & Carter | L | Moulded jug |
| April 1 | 6 | Minton & Co | S | Teawares |
| April 6 | 5 | Mary White | Fife | Wall brackets |
| April 6 | 6 | Pinder, Bourne & Co | B | Printed designs |
| April 16 | 7 | G. L. Ashworth & Bros | H | Printed design |
| April 21 | 6 | Beech & Hancock | T | Printed border |
| April 23 | 8 | R. Hammersley | T | "Gem" print |
| April 28 | 7 | T. G. Green | BT | Teapot form |
| May 6 | 5 | Pellatt & Co★ | Ln | Jug form |
| May 13 | 1 | Adams, Scrivener & Co | L | Moulded jug |
| May 14 | 2 | Hope & Carter | B | Printed design |
| May 26 | 5 | Brown-Westhead, Moore & Co | Sh | Printed design |
| May 26 | 6 | Pinder, Bourne & Co | B | "Bird" prints |
| May 28 | 3 | Holdcroft & Wood | T | Printed design |
| May 28 | 5 | Minton & Co | S | Dinnerwares |
| May 28 | 5 | Minton & Co | S | Divided dish |
| May 28 | 7 | J. & T. Bevington | H | Cupid & shell |
| May 30 | 4 | T. & R. Boote | B | Jug forms |
| Jun 8 | 4 | Burgess & Leigh | B | "Oak" print |
| Jun 12 | 5 | W. Brownfield | C | Teapot form |
| Jun 12 | 5 | W. Brownfield | C | Jug form |
| Jun 16 | 4 | W. P. & G. Phillips★ | Ln | Fruit dish |
| Jun 18 | 6 | Mary White★ | Fife | Wall brackets |
| Jun 22 | 5 | H. Minton & Co | S | Printed design |
| July 10 | 3 | J. Wedgwood & Sons | E | Flower holder |
| July 16 | 3 | Hackney & Co | L | Moulded jug |
| July 20 | 2 | Hope & Carter | B | Printed borders |
| July 24 | 4 | W. T. Copeland | S | Moulded jug |
| July 30 | 6 | Adams, Scrivener & Co | L | Moulded jug |
| Aug 1 | 5 | T. & R. Boote | B | Dinnerwares |
| Aug 1 | 5 | T. & R. Boote | B | Teawares |
| Aug 13 | 1 | J. Wedgwood & Sons | E | Printed design |
| Aug 15 | 8 | J. Edwards & Son | B | Toiletwares |
| Aug 15 | 8 | J. Edwards & Son | B | Dinnerwares |
| Aug 15 | 8 | J. Edwards & Son | B | Teawares |
| Aug 17 | 2 | Edward F. Bodley | B | Printed design |
| Aug 21 | 2 | Ralph Malkin | F | Printed design |

| Aug 31 | 3 | Ralph Malkin | F | Moulded jug |
| Aug 31 | 7 | T. & R. Boote | B | Printed border |
| Sept 1 | 1 | James Wardle | H | Vase forms |
| Sept 4 | 6 | Gelson Brothers | H | Jug form |
| Sept 4 | 6 | Gelson Brothers | H | Printed design |
| Sept 5 | 3 | Brown-Westhead, Moore & Co | Sh | Plate form |
| Sept 5 | 6 | D. McBinney | Bel | Moulded plate |
| Sept 5 | 6 | D. McBinney | Bel | Vase forms |
| Sept 9 | 4 | Hope & Carter | H | "Thames" print |
| Sept 9 | 5 | Frederick Jones & Co | L | Moulded jug |
| Sept 9 | 6 | Wedgwood & Co | T | Printed design |
| Sept 9 | 9 | J. & T. Bevington | H | Eagle vase |
| Sept 12 | 3 | Minton & Co | S | Printed border |
| Sept 12 | 3 | Minton & Co | S | Plate form |
| Sept 14 | 4 | Thomas Booth & Co | B | Printed design |
| Sept 17 | 4 | T. C. Sambrook & Co | B | Printed design |
| Sept 21 | 4 | George Ash | H | Vase forms |
| Sept 25 | 4 | Minton & Co | S | Printed designs |
| Sept 25 | 13 | Brown-Westhead, Moore & Co | Sh | Plate form |
| Sept 25 | 13 | Brown-Westhead, Moore & Co | Sh | Cup form |
| Oct 8 | 7 | Minton & Co | S | Printed design |
| Oct 9 | 2 | Joseph Holdcroft | S | Vase form |
| Oct 9 | 3 | Hope & Carter | B | Moulded jug |
| Oct 9 | 5 | Davenports & Co | Lpt | Dinnerwares |
| Oct 9 | 5 | Davenports & Co | Lpt | Toiletwares |
| Oct 9 | 5 | Davenports & Co | Lpt | Teawares |
| Oct 14 | 8 | George Jones | S | Moulded jug |
| Oct 17 | 4 | Minton & Co | S | Jardinere |
| Oct 21 | 8 | W. P. & G. Phillips★ (produced by W. Brownfield) | Ln | Jug form |
| Oct 22 | 1 | D. McBinney | Bel | Teawares |
| Oct 22 | 5 | James Edwards & Son | B | Jug forms |
| Nov 3 | 5 | Minton & Co | S | Printed design |
| Nov 3 | 5 | Minton & Co | S | Shaped dish |
| Nov 3 | 6 | Brown-Westhead, Moore & Co | Sh | Plate form |
| Nov 6 | 13 | Powell & Bishop | H | Butter pot |
| Nov 9 | 5 | J. Wedgwood & Sons | E | Divided dish |
| Nov 16 | 3 | Knapper & Blackhurst | T | Printed design |
| Nov 17 | 1 | Moore Brothers | C | Dinnerwares |
| Nov 17 | 1 | Moore Brothers | C | Teawares |
| Nov 21 | 5 | Minton & Co | S | Moulded jug |
| Nov 24 | 5 | Brown-Westhead, Moore & Co | Sh | Plate form |
| Nov 25 | 4 | Cork, Edge & Malkin | B | "Ruth" jug form |
| Nov 25 | 6 | D. Hulett & Co | Ln | Stove |
| Dec 1 | 4 | Brown-Westhead, Moore & Co | Sh | Tureen forms |
| Dec 3 | 5 | Worcester Royal Porcelain Co | W | Comport-vase |
| Dec 11 | 5 | Edward F. Bodley & Co | B | Printed design |
| Dec 12 | 4 | W. Brownfield | C | Dish form |
| Dec 14 | 7 | Cockson, Chetwynd & Co | C | Teaware forms |
| Dec 23 | 5 | Minton & Co | S | Shell dish |
| Dec 23 | 6 | Worcester Royal Porcelain Co | W | Vase |

| Dec 31 | 6 | G. L. Ashworth & Bros | H | Moulded jug |
|--------|---|----------------------|---|-------------|
| Dec 31 | 7 | Ralph Hammersley | T | Printed design |

## 1869 (H at right)

| Jan 1 | 8 | George Jones | S | Oval tureen |
|-------|---|--------------|---|-------------|
| Jan 4 | 4 | Minton & Co | S | Dove vase |
| Jan 7 | 6 | T. Goode & Co | Ln | Bird ornament |
| Jan 21 | 6 | Minton & Co | S | Toiletwares |
| Jan 21 | 6 | Minton & Co | S | Plate form |
| Jan 22 | 5 | Gelson Bros | H | Plate form |
| Jan 22 | 13 | Brown-Westhead, Moore & Co | Sh | Tureen forms |
| Jan 25 | 3 | Worthington & Son | H | Printed design |
| Jan 28 | 5 | Minton & Co | S | Printed design |
| Jan 28 | 10 | George Ash | H | Vase forms |
| Feb 1 | 7 | Brown-Westhead, Moore & Co | Sh | Teaware forms |
| Feb 2 | 4 | George Yearsley | L | Parian figure |
| Feb 9 | 5 | Minton & Co | S | Ornament – boots |
| Feb 11 | 10 | George Jones | S | "Grecian" print |
| Feb 15 | 1 | Thomas Booth & Co | B | Printed design |
| Feb 19 | 2 | J. Wedgwood & Sons | E | Printed border |
| Feb 22 | 6 | J. Wedgwood & Sons | E | Tobacco jar |
| Feb 22 | 11 | D. McBirney | Bel | Teawares |
| Feb 22 | 13 | Pinder, Bourne & Co | B | Printed design |
| Feb 27 | 5 | J. Wedgwood & Sons | E | Cigar ash tray |
| Mar 1 | 8 | Worthington & Son | H | Teapot form |
| Mar 1 | 8 | Worthington & Son | H | Jug form |
| Mar 1 | 8 | Worthington & Son | H | Printed design |
| Mar 3 | 8 | T. Till & Son | H | Printed design |
| Mar 4 | 6 | J. Lawton | Bir | Knob form |
| Mar 6 | 8 | F. Primavesi & Sons★ | Cf | Printed design |
| Mar 8 | 6 | F. & R. Pratt & Co | F | Cruet shape |
| Mar 9 | 1 | George Jones | S | Dessertwares |
| Mar 9 | 1 | George Jones | S | "Crete" print |
| Mar 9 | 3 | George Jones | I | Ornamental tray |
| Mar 10 | 10 | F. Primavesi & Sons★ | Cf | Printed design |
| Mar 18 | 12 | R. H. Grove | L | Printed design |
| Mar 18 | 12 | R. H. Grove | L | Knife sharpener |
| Mar 24 | 1 | James F. Wileman | F | Moulded jug |
| April 1 | 1 | Wood & Pigott | T | Printed design |
| April 2 | 6 | W. Brownfield | C | Jardinere |
| April 2 | 7 | Minton & Co | S | Flower holder – dove |
| April 6 | 3 | Baker & Chetwynd | B | Teawares |
| April 6 | 3 | Baker & Chetwynd | B | Jug forms |
| April 7 | 2 | Minton & Co | S | Butterfly handle |
| April 7 | 4 | Worcester Royal Porcelain Co | W | Birds nest vase |
| April 12 | 4 | Taylor, Tunnicliffe & Co | H | Door furniture |
| April 12 | 5 | Liddle Elliot & Son | B | Dinnerwares |
| April 12 | 5 | Liddle Elliot & Son | B | Toiletwares |
| April 12 | 5 | Liddle Elliot & Son | B | Teawares |
| April 20 | 5 | Liddle Elliot & Son | B | Tureen forms |
| April 28 | 13 | J. & T. Bevington | H | Cupid centrepiece |
| May 4 | 3 | Trachtenberg & Pantes★ | Odessa | Printed design |

| | | | | |
|---|---|---|---|---|
| May 11 | 1 | Adams, Scrivener & Co | L | Teawares |
| May 13 | 16 | J. Edwards & Son | B | Tureen forms |
| May 21 | 1 | Worthington & Son | H | Printed design |
| May 26 | 4 | Thomas Booth | H | Moulded jug |
| May 27 | 8 | Davenports & Co | Lpt | Dinnerwares – vine |
| May 27 | 8 | Davenports & Co | Lpt | Toiletwares – vine |
| May 27 | 8 | Davenports & Co | Lpt | Teawares – vine |
| Jun 3 | 6 | D. McBirney | Bel | Dish form |
| Jun 8 | 7 | Phillip & Pearce★ | Ln | Flower trough |
| Jun 19 | 5 | W. Brownfield | C | Moulded teapot |
| Jun 19 | 5 | W. Brownfield | C | "Severn" jug |
| Jun 25 | 4 | J. Edwards & Son | B | Jug form |
| Jun 26 | 9 | Minton & Co | S | Swan vase |
| July 3 | 9 | J. Wedgwood & Sons | E | Strawberry dish |
| July 3 | 9 | J. Wedgwood & Sons | E | Supper set |
| July 6 | 3 | J. Meir & Son | T | "Talbot" print |
| July 16 | 8 | Charles Stanley | Sn | Printed design |
| July 19 | 8 | J. Wardle | H | Vase form |
| July 20 | 2 | J. Wedgwood & Sons | E | Printed border |
| July 21 | 6 | George Ash | H | Bird vases |
| July 23 | 6 | Minton & Co | S | Nut dish |
| July 24 | 4 | W. T. Copeland & Sons | S | Cup & stand |
| July 26 | 4 | Levison Hill, executors of | S | Cupid vase |
| July 27 | 4 | J. T. Hudden | L | "Regent" print |
| Aug 2 | 6 | W. T. Copeland & Sons | S | Shell ornament |
| Aug 3 | 5 | John Edwards | F | Teawares |
| Aug 4 | 4 | Tomkinson Bros & Co | H | Dinnerwares |
| Aug 11 | 13 | Phillip & Pearce★ | Ln | Flower trough |
| | | (produced by Royal Worcester) | | |
| Aug 19 | 6 | W. T. Copeland & Sons | S | Teawares |
| Aug 26 | 6 | W. T. Copeland & Sons | S | Covered box |
| Aug 31 | 6 | John Pratt & Co | F | Printed designs |
| Aug 31 | 12 | W. T. Copeland & Sons | S | Teawares |
| Sept 4 | 3 | Minton & Co | S | Tureen – lobster |
| Sept 8 | 5 | W. T. Copeland & Sons | S | Teawares |
| Sept 8 | 6 | Pinder, Bourne & Co | B | Printed design |
| Sept 9 | 3 | John Pratt & Co | F | Printed design |
| Sept 10 | 4 | Minton & Co | S | Printed design |
| Sept 15 | 1 | J. Cartland & Son | Bir | Door furniture |
| Sept 21 | 7 | Gelson Bros | H | Dinnerwares |
| Sept 22 | 10 | W. & J. A. Bailey | Alloa | Teapot form |
| Sept 30 | 8 | Brown-Westhead, Moore & Co | Sh | Jug forms |
| Sept 30 | 8 | Brown-Westhead, Moore & Co | Sh | Jardinere |
| Sept 30 | 9 | F. Lloyd & Co★ | Ln | Cigar holder |
| Oct 1 | 3 | Minton & Co | S | Bird dish |
| Oct 1 | 3 | Minton & Co | S | Printed design |
| Oct 4 | 6 | Minton & Co | S | Pineapple pot |
| Oct 14 | 3 | D. McBirney & Co | Bel | Spill vase |
| Oct 15 | 6 | George Jones | S | Cake stand |
| Oct 23 | 4 | George Jones | S | Cigar ash tray |
| Oct 26 | 2 | James Ellis & Son | H | Moulded jug |
| Oct 27 | 4 | Smith & Chamberlain★ | Bir | Screen base |

| Oct 27 | 5 | D. McBirney & Co | Bel | Egg holder |
|---|---|---|---|---|
| Oct 29 | 3 | Minton & Co | S | Tray – birds |
| Oct 29 | 3 | Minton & Co | S | Tray – rabbit |
| Oct 29 | 4 | Powell & Bishop | H | Dinnerwares |
| Oct 29 | 4 | Powell & Bishop | H | Teawares |
| Nov 2 | 12 | Edward Clarke | T | Teawares |
| Nov 2 | 12 | Edward Clarke | T | Toiletwares |
| Nov 3 | 12 | Brown-Westhead, Moore & Co | Sh | Plate form |
| Nov 8 | 1 | D. McBirney & Co | Bel | Vase forms |
| Nov 8 | 2 | Brown-Westhead, Moore & Co | Sh | Spill vase |
| Nov 9 | 11 | Tams & Lowe | L | "Tonia" print |
| Nov 10 | 3 | W. Brownfield | C | Dinnerwares |
| Nov 13 | 5 | D. McBirney & Co | Bel | Sailor-boy boxes |
| Nov 15 | 8 | Liddle Elliot & Son | B | Printed designs |
| Nov 18 | 5 | Alcock & Diggory | B | Teawares |
| Nov 18 | 6 | J. S. Crapper★ | H | Spittoon |
| Nov 19 | 12 | Worcester Royal Porcelain Co | W | Elephant vase |
| Nov 20 | 8 | T. Goode & Co★ | Ln | Teapot form |
| Nov 20 | 9 | J. Mortlock★ | Ln | Swan jug |
| Nov 23 | 1 | D. McBirney & Co | Bel | Cheese stand |
| Nov 24 | 4 | Minton & Co | S | Cat ornament |
| Nov 26 | 3 | Minton & Co | S | Printed border |
| Dec 1 | 3 | George Jones | S | Printed design |
| Dec 3 | 9 | W. Brownfield | C | Covered dish |
| Dec 14 | 4 | J. S. Crapper★ | H | Spittoon |
| Dec 17 | 7 | Minton & Co | S | Printed border |
| Dec 18 | 2 | Powell & Bishop | H | Toiletwares |
| Dec 18 | 2 | Powell & Bishop | H | Teawares |
| Dec 20 | 8 | George Ash | H | Bird vase |
| Dec 22 | 7 | George Jones | S | Nut tray |
| Dec 24 | 1 | Gelson Bros | H | Tureen form |
| Dec 28 | 2 | John Pratt & Co | F | Printed design |
| Dec 31 | 2 | Minton & Co | S | Printed design |

**1870 (C at right)**

| Jan 1 | 5 | Brown-Westhead, Moore & Co | Sh | Jardinere |
|---|---|---|---|---|
| Jan 3 | 4 | George Jones | S | Tureen form |
| Jan 7 | 9 | Pellatt & Co★ | Ln | Swan vase |
| Jan 15 | 12 | Liddle Elliot & Son | B | Printed borders |
| Jan 27 | 8 | C. Hobson | S | Teapot & jug |
| Jan 29 | 3 | Minton & Co | S | Butterfly plate |
| Feb 1 | 6 | Brown-Westhead, Moore & Co | Sh | Dessertwares |
| Feb 3 | 13 | Brown-Westhead, Moore & Co | Sh | Jug forms |
| Feb 3 | 13 | Brown-Westhead, Moore & Co | Sh | Toilet wares |
| Feb 3 | 13 | Brown-Westhead, Moore & Co | Sh | Dressing table set |
| Feb 4 | 7 | Powell & Bishop | H | Moulded teapot |
| Feb 7 | 5 | Wiltshaw, Wood & Co | B | Covered pot |
| Feb 7 | 6 | W. & J. A. Bailey | Alloa | Moulded teapot |
| Feb 9 | 2 | J. Wedgwood & Sons | E | Printed design |
| Feb 10 | 8 | Minton & Co | S | Flower trough |
| Feb 11 | 12 | Phillip & Pearce★ (produced by Royal Worcester) | Ln | Flower troughs |

| | | | | |
|---|---|---|---|---|
| Feb 15 | 6 | Brown-Westhead, Moore & Co | Sh | Dessertwares |
| Feb 25 | 2 | Minton & Co | S | Asparagus dish |
| Feb 28 | 6 | Minton & Co | S | Printed design |
| Mar 2 | 4 | Minton & Co | S | Bird ornament |
| Mar 7 | 6 | C. Hobson | B | Printed design |
| Mar 8 | 1 | George Jones | S | Bird trays |
| Mar 10 | 1 | George Jones | S | Toilet jug |
| Mar 10 | 9 | Powell & Bishop | H | Dinnerwares |
| Mar 11 | 8 | Levison Hill, executors of | S | Figure vase |
| Mar 14 | 4 | Brown-Westhead, Moore & Co | Sh | Dessert edging |
| Mar 15 | 6 | T. Till & Sons | B | Tureen forms |
| Mar 16 | 2 | Minton & Co | S | Flower trough |
| Mar 16 | 2 | Minton & Co | S | Bird dish |
| Mar 17 | 4 | D. McBirney & Co | Bel | Vases |
| Mar 17 | 7 | Worcester Royal Porcelain Co | W | Vase |
| Mar 17 | 9 | J. Mortlock★ | Ln | Butterfly vase |
| Mar 18 | 1 | W. Cadman★ | Ln | Lobster dish |
| Mar 18 | 6 | Minton & Co | S | Printed design |
| Mar 23 | 9 | J. Blackshaw & Co | S | Vase & Jug |
| Mar 25 | 4 | Hope & Carter | B | Dinnerwares |
| Mar 25 | 5 | Minton & Co | S | Circular stand |
| Mar 25 | 5 | Minton & Co | S | Scuttle ornament |
| Mar 26 | 1 | Minton & Co | S | Leaf dish |
| Mar 26 | 1 | Minton & Co | S | Figure centrepiece |
| Mar 26 | 2 | Worthington & Son | H | Teapot form |
| Mar 28 | 9 | Old Hall Earthenware Co Ltd | H | Tureen form |
| April 7 | 9 | Cork, Edge & Malkin | B | Printed design |
| April 7 | 10 | Baker & Co | F | Printed designs |
| April 7 | 11 | Harvey Adams & Co | L | Moulded jug |
| April 9 | 1 | Minton & Co | S | Printed design |
| April 11 | 3 | Worcester Royal Porcelain Co Ltd | W | Dove basket |
| April 13 | 4 | T. Goode & Co★ | Ln | Breakfastwares |
| April 14 | 7 | Minton & Co | S | Ribbon edge |
| May 5 | 1 | James Oldham & Co | H | Moulded jug |
| May 6 | 5 | D. McBirney & Co | Bel | Ribbon motif |
| May 6 | 5 | D. McBirney & Co | Bel | Fern ornament |
| May 10 | 4 | George Ash | H | Bird vases |
| May 11 | 9 | J. S. Crapper★ | H | Condenser |
| May 13 | 8 | Brown-Westhead, Moore & Co | Sh | Toiletwares |
| May 17 | 7 | Brown-Westhead, Moore & Co | Sh | Shell salt |
| May 18 | 6 | Bates Elliot & Co | B | Printed borders |
| May 21 | 6 | Old Hall Earthenwares Co Ltd | H | Tureen forms |
| May 21 | 12 | J. Edwards & Son | B | Toiletwares |
| May 25 | 7 | J. Edwards & Son | B | Jug form |
| May 26 | 5 | Minton | S | Toiletwares |
| May 27 | 11 | C. Christodulo | Liv | Printed design |
| May 30 | 15 | George Jones | S | Tureen form |
| Jun 3 | 8 | F. & R. Pratt & Co | F | Jug form |
| Jun 7 | 15 | Hope & Carter | B | Printed border |
| Jun 7 | 16 | Thomas Booth | H | Teapot form |
| Jun 9 | 3 | Brown-Westhead, Moore & Co | Sh | Flower trough |
| Jun 10 | 1 | W. Brownfield | C | Toiletwares |

| Jun 10 | 1 | W. Brownfield | C | Teapot & jug |
|--------|-----|-------------------------------|-----|---------------------|
| Jun 11 | 3 | J. Edwards & Son | B | Fluted jug |
| Jun 17 | 7 | Minton Hollins & Co | S | Printed tiles |
| Jun 22 | 1 | Harvey Adams & Co | L | Teawares |
| Jun 22 | 1 | Harvey Adams & Co | L | Dessertwares |
| Jun 22 | 3 | Minton Hollins & Co | S | Printed tiles |
| Jun 22 | 4 | Worcester Royal Porcelain Co | W | Flower holder |
| Jun 27 | 1 | George Jones | S | Pineapple teapot |
| July 5 | 5 | Baker & Co | F | Printed design |
| July 8 | 7 | James Wardle | H | Vase designs |
| July 12 | 6 | Joseph Parkes★ | Ln | Moulded jug |
| July 13 | 8 | J. Edwards & Son | B | Moulded jug |
| July 14 | 9 | Minton Hollins & Co | S | Printed tiles |
| July 14 | 10 | Worcester Royal Porcelain Co | W | Printed design |
| July 15 | 1 | W. T. Copeland & Sons | S | Moulded jug |
| July 16 | 2 | J. Wardle | H | Vase |
| July 19 | 6 | F. & R. Pratt & Co | F | Printed border |
| July 20 | 5 | T. Booth | H | Moulded jug |
| July 21 | 1 | T. Booth | H | Moulded teapot |
| July 22 | 1 | Cork, Edge & Malkin | B | Moulded jug |
| July 27 | 1 | Beech, Unwin & Co | L | Band print |
| Aug 1 | 2 | R. G. Scrivener & Co | H | Cup forms |
| Aug 4 | 4 | J. Wardle | H | Elephant vase |
| Aug 4 | 5 | James Broadhurst | S | Crest motifs |
| Aug 9 | 2 | W. Brownfield | C | Dessertwares |
| Aug 22 | 4 | T. & R. Boote | B | Dinnerwares |
| Aug 22 | 4 | T. & R. Boote | B | Toiletwares |
| Aug 23 | 6 | George Jones | S | Figure dish |
| Aug 25 | 5 | T. & R. Boote | B | Teawares |
| Sept 7 | 7 | Bailey & Cooke | H | Basket ornament |
| Sept 10 | 9 | Minton & Co | S | Plate form |
| Sept 16 | 5 | Minton & Co | S | Printed design |
| Sept 19 | 2 | W. Brownfield | C | Jug form |
| Sept 27 | 4 | Elsmore Foster & Co | T | Dinnerwares |
| Sept 27 | 6 | Phillips & Pearce★ | Ln | Jardinere |
| Sept 28 | 11 | Gelson Bros | H | Moulded jug |
| Oct 4 | 7 | Joseph Holdcroft | L | Bird dish |
| Oct 4 | 8 | Minton & Co | S | Toiletwares |
| Oct 6 | 4 | Minton & Co | S | Printed design |
| Oct 6 | 5 | James Broadhurst | L | Printed border |
| Oct 7 | 3 | Minton & Co | S | Plate form |
| Oct 8 | 9 | Powell & Bishop | H | Printed design |
| Oct 19 | 2 | George Jones | S | Divided dish |
| Oct 19 | 2 | George Jones | S | Biscuit barrel |
| Oct 22 | 2 | W. Brownfield | C | Teawares |
| Oct 25 | 6 | Brown-Westhead, Moore & Co | Sh | Teawares |
| Nov 4 | 9 | Brown-Westhead, Moore & Co | Sh | Dinnerwares |
| Nov 9 | 7 | Blumberg & Co★ | Ln | Dressing table set |
| Nov 9 | 8 | J. Meir & Son | T | Printed design |
| Nov 9 | 9 | Pellatt & Co★ | Ln | Divided dish |
| Nov 10 | 5 | Minton & Co | S | Covered box – log |
| Nov 10 | 5 | Minton & Co | S | Condiment |
| Nov 10 | 5 | Minton & Co | S | Teawares |

| Nov 10 | 10 | W. Brownfield | C | Dinnerwares |
|---|---|---|---|---|
| Nov 10 | 10 | W. Brownfield | C | Moulded jug |
| Nov 12 | 3 | D. McBirney & Co | Bel | Teawares |
| Nov 12 | 8 | Minton Hollins & Co | S | Printed tiles |
| Nov 21 | 5 | Joseph Partners★ | Ln | Jug designs |
| Nov 22 | 3 | George Jones | S | Dinnerwares |
| Nov 24 | 3 | Minton & Co | S | Ornamental basket |
| Nov 24 | 8 | Bates Elliot & Co | B | Printed design |
| Nov 25 | 1 | Minton & Co | S | Bamboo vase |
| Nov 25 | 2 | Turner Goddard & Co | T | Jug form |
| Nov 26 | 9 | T. & R. Boote | B | Dinnerwares |
| Nov 26 | 9 | T. & R. Boote | B | Toiletwares |
| Nov 26 | 9 | T. & R. Boote | B | Teawares |
| Dec 1 | 7 | W. Brownfield | C | Cheese stand |
| Dec 2 | 11 | Brown-Westhead, Moore & Co | Sh | Tureen form |
| Dec 5 | 4 | Minton Hollins & Co | S | Printed tiles |
| Dec 8 | 4 | Blumberg & Co★ | Ln | Teawares |
| Dec 16 | 5 | Bates Elliot & Co | B | Printed border |
| Dec 17 | 11 | Bates Elliot & Co | B | Bird print |
| Dec 19 | 9 | Harvey Adams & Co | L | Moulded plate |
| Dec 27 | 4 | J. Edwards & Son | B | Moulded jug |

## 1871 (A at right)

| Jan 2 | 2 | Gelson Bros | H | Tureen form |
|---|---|---|---|---|
| Jan 6 | 3 | Minton & Co | S | Jardinere |
| Jan 7 | 8 | Bates, Elliot & Co | B | Printed design |
| Jan 9 | 4 | D. McBirney & Co | Bel | Shell teawares |
| Jan 10 | 7 | George Jones | S | Dog covered box |
| Jan 11 | 4 | J. Mortlock★ | Ln | Water can ornament |
| Jan 12 | 7 | D. McBirney & Co | Bel | Jug form |
| Jan 12 | 12 | Soane & Smith★ | Ln | Dressing set |
| Jan 24 | 4 | Soane & Smith★ | Ln | Teawares |
| Jan 26 | 8 | Minton, Hollins & Co | S | Tile designs |
| Jan 27 | 9 | Worcester Royal Porcelain Co | W | Pierced edging |
| Jan 30 | 2 | Gelson Bros | H | Tureen form |
| Jan 30 | 7 | R. Minton Taylor & Co | S | Tile design |
| Feb 2 | 3 | J. Edwards & Son | B | Tureen form |
| Feb 6 | 5 | D. McBirney | Bel | Tureen & dish |
| Feb 6 | 5 | D. McBirney | Bel | Honey pot |
| Feb 6 | 5 | D. McBirney | Bel | Border design |
| Feb 8 | 9 | J. Macintyre & Co | B | Door furniture |
| Feb 11 | 9 | Brown-Westhead, Moore & Co | Sh | Dessertwares |
| Feb 13 | 6 | Edge, Malkin & Co | B | Teapot form |
| Feb 13 | 7 | Worthington & Son | H | Candleholder |
| Feb 13 | 9 | Powell & Bishop | H | Dinnerwares |
| Feb 13 | 10 | Edward F. Bodley & Co | B | Candleholder |
| Feb 15 | 7 | Powell & Bishop | H | Teawares |
| Feb 17 | 7 | Thomas Peake | T | Tile designs |
| Feb 20 | 2 | Elsmore & Forster | T | Dinnerwares |
| Feb 20 | 2 | Elsmore & Forster | T | Toiletwares |
| Feb 28 | 8 | Watcombe Terra Cotta Clay Co Ltd | Wat | Jar |
| Mar 9 | 4 | J. & T. Bevington | H | Flower vase |

| Mar 14 | 4 | John Pratt & Co | F | Printed border |
|---|---|---|---|---|
| Mar 15 | 10 | Bates, Elliot & Co | B | Printed border |
| Mar 16 | 5 | George Skey | Tm | Gas stoves |
| Mar 27 | 1 | W. Brownfield | C | Teapot |
| Mar 29 | 1 | T. Furnival & Son | C | Jug & decoration |
| April 4 | 4 | D. McBirney & Co | Bel | Printed shell border |
| April 22 | 4 | J. Pratt & Co | F | Printed border |
| April 24 | 4 | J. Wedgwood & Sons | E | Bambo teapot |
| April 26 | 12 | Minton, Hollins & Co | S | Tile design |
| April 27 | 7 | Wood & Clarke | B | Printed designs |
| April 27 | 8 | Phillip & Pearce★ | Ln | Comport |
| April 27 | 8 | Phillip & Pearce★ | Ln | Candelabra |
| April 28 | 1 | Wood & Clarke | B | Printed design |
| April 29 | 6 | Wood & Clarke | B | Printed design |
| April 29 | 7 | J. Edwards & Son | B | Covered dish |
| May 1 | 9 | Brown-Westhead, Moore & Co | Sh | Flower troughs |
| May 2 | 3 | Ambrose Bevington | H | Vase |
| May 2 | 4 | W. Brownfield & Son | C | Dessertwares |
| May 2 | 4 | W. Brownfield & Son | C | Toiletwares |
| May 2 | 4 | W. Brownfield & Son | C | Jug and pot |
| May 3 | 4 | J. Jackson & Co | Y | Printed design |
| May 6 | 1 | Phillips & Pearce★ | Ln | Jug forms |
| May 9 | 9 | Liddle Elliot & Co | B | Printed border |
| May 11 | 13 | Powell & Bishop | H | Toiletwares |
| May 13 | 6 | Elsmore, Forster & Co | T | Teawares |
| May 22 | 8 | J. Lawton | Bir | Bedstead unit |
| May 22 | 9 | D. McBirney & Co | Bel | Flower trough |
| May 24 | 10 | J. Meir & Son | T | Dinnerwares |
| Jun 2 | 4 | Brown-Westhead, Moore & Co | Sh | Teawares |
| Jun 7 | 7 | Grove & Stark | L | Flower vase |
| Jun 16 | 9 | John Twigg | Y | Printed designs |
| Jun 17 | 3 | Minton & Co | S | Toiletwares |
| Jun 17 | 3 | Minton & Co | S | Printed border |
| Jun 19 | 9 | Pinder, Bourne & Co | B | Fish print |
| Jun 19 | 9 | Pinder, Bourne & Co | B | Washstand |
| Jun 22 | 1 | T. Till & Sons | B | Printed border |
| Jun 23 | 9 | Bates, Elliot & Co | B | Printed design |
| July 4 | 8 | W. T. Copeland & Sons | S | Teawares |
| July 14 | 6 | Taylor, Tunnicliffe & Co | H | Door furniture |
| July 15 | 2 | Thomas Booth | H | Moulded jug |
| July 19 | 2 | Ambrose Bevington | H | Printed border |
| July 22 | 8 | Haviland & Co | Fr | Tureen form |
| July 22 | 8 | Haviland & Co | Fr | Teapot forms |
| July 25 | 12 | Bates, Elliot & Co | B | Printed border |
| July 29 | 6 | Hope & Carter | B | Dinnerwares |
| Aug 2 | 3 | Robinson & Leadbeater | S | Owl ornament |
| Aug 9 | 7 | Bates, Elliot & Co | B | Printed design |
| Aug 18 | 10 | Pratt & Co | F | Meat pot |
| Aug 28 | 5 | James Wardle | H | Leaf dish |
| Aug 29 | 2 | George Jones | S | Fish dish |
| Aug 30 | 4 | Thomas Barlow | L | Jug form |
| Aug 31 | 9 | J. H. & J. Davis | H | Printed design |

| Sept 15 | 7 | J. Bevington & Co | H | Jug form |
|---|---|---|---|---|
| Sept 15 | 10 | Thomas Barlow | L | Moustache cup |
| Sept 19 | 2 | Minton & Co | S | "Delft" print |
| Sept 25 | 8 | Brown-Westhead, Moore & Co | Sh | Jug form |
| Sept 28 | 5 | Thomas Booth & Co | T | Printed design |
| Oct 4 | 7 | Minton & Co | S | Tile designs |
| Oct 4 | 9 | Pinder, Bourne & Co | B | Printed design |
| Oct 6 | 6 | Moore & Son | L | Teapot |
| Oct 6 | 6 | Moore & Son | L | Mirror frame |
| Oct 6 | 6 | Moore & Son | L | Floral bowl |
| Oct 9 | 8 | E. J. Ridgway & Son | H | Dinnerwares |
| Oct 10 | 3 | J. T. Hudden | L | "Tichborne" print |
| Oct 10 | 6 | Brown-Westhead, Moore & Co | Sh | Toiletwares |
| Oct 11 | 4 | D. McBirney & Co | Bel | Vase |
| Oct 14 | 6 | Thomas Booth & Co | T | Printed ribbon design |
| Oct 14 | 7 | J. Wedgwood & Sons | E | Dinnerwares |
| Oct 18 | 4 | Moore & Son | L | Teapot form |
| Oct 19 | 6 | W. T. Copeland & Sons | S | Moulded jug |
| Oct 24 | 3 | Robert Cooke | H | Boat ornament |
| Oct 31 | 5 | Minton & Co | S | "Danish" print |
| Oct 31 | 6 | Edge, Hill & Palmer | L | Match holder |
| Nov 3 | 4 | R. G. Scrivener | H | Dish form |
| Nov 3 | 4 | R. G. Scrivener | H | Teawares |
| Nov 3 | 5 | J. F. Wileman | F | Printed design |
| Nov 15 | 4 | J. Thomson & Son | G | "Birds" print |
| Nov 23 | 6 | Thomas Ford | H | Dessertwares |
| Dec 1 | 6 | George Jones | S | Bird tray |
| Dec 15 | 5 | Robinson & Leadbeater | S | Monkey vase |
| Dec 16 | 7 | D. McBirney & Co | Bel | Centrepiece |
| Dec 22 | 6 | F. & R. Pratt | F | Fluted jar |
| Dec 23 | 3 | George Jones | S | Camel box |
| Dec 23 | 3 | George Jones | S | Comfort |
| Dec 23 | 5 | Robert Cooke | H | Moulded teapot |
| Dec 29 | 10 | Brown-Westhead, Moore & Co | Sh | Basket – dish |

**1872 (I at right)**

| Jan 1 | 5 | Moore & Son | L | Teapot |
|---|---|---|---|---|
| Jan 1 | 6 | Edge, Malkin & Co | B | Moulded jug |
| Jan 5 | 3 | D. McBirney & Co | Bel | Centrepiece |
| Jan 6 | 1 | Minton & Co | S | Fancy dish |
| Jan 18 | 6 | Worcester Royal Porcelain Co Ltd | W | Teapot |
| Jan 20 | 6 | George Jones | S | Comport |
| Jan 30 | 7 | W. T. Copeland | S | Teawares |
| Feb 2 | 2 | Moore & Son | L | Fan – dish |
| Feb 2 | 11 | Turner & Tomkinson | T | Printed border |
| Feb 3 | 4 | George Jones | S | Comport |
| Feb 3 | 4 | George Jones | S | Flower container |
| Feb 7 | 3 | Ambrose Bevington | H | Patterned plate |
| Feb 15 | 3 | Powell & Bishop | H | Moulded jug |
| Feb 16 | 6 | D. McBirney & Co | Bel | Teapot |
| Feb 16 | 7 | George Jones | S | Strawberry dish |
| Feb 16 | 7 | George Jones | S | Comports |

| | | | | |
|---|---|---|---|---|
| Feb 19 | 6 | W. H. Goss | S | Brooch |
| Feb 20 | 4 | Worcester Royal Porcelain Co Ltd | W | Squirrel vase |
| Feb 22 | 3 | Minton & Co | S | Lily bowl |
| Feb 26 | 6 | E. Wood★ | Ln | Tobacco jar |
| Mar 4 | 3 | George Jones | S | Elephant vase |
| Mar 4 | 4 | Minton & Co | S | Tile design |
| Mar 4 | 4 | Minton & Co | S | Floral print |
| Mar 4 | 6 | Minton, Hollins & Co | S | Printed tile |
| Mar 7 | 7 | Harvey Adams & Co | L | Teawares |
| Mar 7 | 10 | Bates, Elliot & Co | B | Floral jug |
| Mar 8 | 5 | Minton, Hollins & Co | S | Printed tiles |
| Mar 9 | 1 | D. McBirney & Co | Bel | Dragon teapot |
| Mar 13 | 8 | Minton, Hollins & Co | S | Printed tile |
| Mar 16 | 6 | Minton & Co | S | Printed tile |
| Mar 18 | 6 | Minton & Co | S | Openwork edge |
| Mar 20 | 10 | Worcester Royal Porcelain Co Ltd | W | Candle snuffer |
| Mar 21 | 14 | R. Minton Taylor & Co | F | Printed design |
| Mar 22 | 5 | Joseph Holdcroft | L | Fancy dish |
| Mar 22 | 8 | Brown-Westhead, Moore & Co | Sh | Dinnerwares |
| Mar 26 | 3 | Robinson & Leadbeater | S | Parian ornament |
| Mar 26 | 3 | Robinson & Leadbeater | S | Parian cow |
| Mar 26 | 6 | Phillips & Pearce★ | Ln | Basket |
| April 5 | 4 | Wedgwood & Co | T | Printed border |
| April 5 | 5 | Minton & Co | S | Teawares |
| April 6 | 1 | Joseph Holdcroft | L | Bird dishes |
| April 9 | 6 | Brown-Westhead, Moore & Co | Sh | Ship's jug |
| April 10 | 11 | T. Furnival & Son | C | Jug |
| April 17 | 13 | E. J. Ridgway & Son | H | Toiletwares |
| April 19 | 5 | Minton, Hollins & Co | S | Printed tile |
| April 24 | 5 | J. Pratt & Co Ltd | F | Printed border |
| April 27 | 9 | Moore & Son | L | Boy in canoe |
| May 2 | 9 | Harvey Adams & Co | L | Teawares |
| May 2 | 9 | Harvey Adams & Co | L | Floral vase |
| May 2 | 11 | T. Furnival & Son | C | Prints for jugs |
| May 3 | 9 | Minton & Co | S | Monkey vase |
| May 3 | 9 | Minton & Co | S | Pineapple tureen |
| May 3 | 11 | Bates, Elliot & Co | B | Toiletwares |
| May 6 | 3 | Moore & Son | L | Jardinere |
| May 6 | 3 | Moore & Son | L | Fan vase |
| May 6 | 3 | Moore & Son | L | Bird wall-pocket |
| May 6 | 8 | Bates, Elliot & Co | B | Printed border |
| May 6 | 9 | Minton Hollins & Co | S | Printed tiles |
| May 10 | 1 | Moore & Son | L | Wall vase |
| May 11 | 4 | T. Booth & Sons | H | Punch prints |
| May 14 | 6 | Thomson & Kelley★ | Ln | Pot lid designs |
| May 27 | 1 | George Jones | S | Jug – foxes |
| May 27 | 3 | Minton Hollins & Co | S | Printed tile |
| May 29 | 2 | George Jones | S | Match box |
| May 29 | 5 | G. Grainger & Co | W | Teapot designs |
| May 29 | 5 | G. Grainger & Co | W | Plate edging |
| May 30 | 1 | Minton & Co | S | Vase |
| May 30 | 1 | Minton & Co | S | Divisional dish |

| Jun 3 | 6 | Watcombe Terra Cotta Clay Co | Wat | Jug |
|---|---|---|---|---|
| Jun 5 | 3 | Hope & Carter | B | Printed border |
| Jun 6 | 6 | W. Brownfield & Son | C | Dinnerwares |
| Jun 7 | 4 | Minton, Hollins & Co | S | Tile design |
| Jun 11 | 5 | J. Wedgwood & Sons | E | Tureen form |
| Jun 11 | 12 | W. T. Copeland & Sons | S | Jug form |
| Jun 18 | 3 | G. L. Ashworth & Bros | Sh | Fluted kettle |
| Jun 18 | 3 | G. L. Ashworth & Bros | Sh | Teapot |
| Jun 18 | 4 | Minton, Hollins & Co | S | Tile design |
| Jun 21 | 7 | Minton, Hollins & Co | S | Tile designs |
| Jun 22 | 5 | Minton & Co | S | Tile design |
| Jun 22 | 8 | W. Brownfield & Son | C | Fancy dishes |
| Jun 27 | 1 | Brown-Westhead, Moore & Co | Sh | Dinnerwares |
| July 2 | 2 | Robinson & Leadbeater | S | Dog match holders |
| July 2 | 3 | J. Wedgwood & Sons | E | Mask match pot |
| July 13 | 5 | Gelson Bros | H | Gravy dish |
| July 15 | 4 | Robinson & Leadbeater | S | Parian group |
| July 16 | 5 | Minton, Hollins & Co | S | Tile design |
| July 19 | 5 | R. Minton Taylor | F | Tile designs |
| July 20 | 3 | George Jones | S | Flower-holder |
| July 20 | 3 | George Jones | S | Lily dish |
| July 24 | 2 | W. & T. Adams | T | Printed armorials |
| July 29 | 7 | J. Dimmock & Co | H | Dinnerwares |
| July 31 | 3 | Minton & Co | S | Designs for tiles |
| Aug 2 | 1 | E. J. Ridgway & Son | H | Printed designs |
| Aug 14 | 4 | T. Booth & Co | T | Printed design |
| Aug 16 | 1 | W. Brownfield & Son | C | Comports |
| Aug 16 | 1 | W. Brownfield & Son | C | Divided dish |
| Aug 19 | 4 | W. E. Cartlidge | H | Low bowl |
| Aug 19 | 5 | W. & J.A. Bailey | Alloa | Teapot |
| Sept 2 | 3 | D. McBirney & Co | Bel | Vase |
| Sept 2 | 8 | Bates, Elliot & Co | B | Jug |
| Sept 7 | 14 | George Skey | Tam | Stoves |
| Sept 12 | 6 | Minton Hollins & Co | S | Tile design |
| Sept 25 | 9 | Minton Hollins & Co | S | Tile designs |
| Sept 26 | 2 | Frederick Jones | L | Fluted teawares |
| Sept 26 | 5 | W. E. Cartlidge | H | Jug |
| Oct 7 | 7 | Brown-Westhead, Moore & Co | Sh | Jardinere |
| Oct 11 | 5 | J. Wedgwood & Sons | E | Jardineres |
| Oct 11 | 5 | J. Wedgwood & Sons | E | Toiletwares |
| Oct 11 | 5 | J. Wedgwood & Sons | E | Match holder |
| Oct 11 | 5 | J. Wedgwood & Sons | E | Vase |
| Oct 12 | 10 | Bates, Elliot & Co | B | Teapot |
| Oct 12 | 10 | Bates, Elliot & Co | B | Jug |
| Oct 14 | 4 | Minton Hollins & Co | S | Tile design |
| Oct 17 | 8 | J. Wedgwood & Sons | E | Match holders |
| Oct 18 | 5 | G. Jones | S | Jug |
| Oct 18 | 5 | G. Jones | S | Basket |
| Oct 18 | 5 | G. Jones | S | Honey pot |
| Oct 18 | 7 | Masbro Stove Co | Y | Tiles |
| Oct 30 | 2 | J. F. Wileman | F | Printed design |
| Oct 30 | 5 | Brownhills Pottery Co | T | Toiletwares |

| Oct 30 | 9 | Maw & Co | Br | Fireplace |
|---|---|---|---|---|
| Nov 2 | 6 | Worcester Royal Porcelain Co | W | Teawares |
| Nov 2 | 6 | Worcester Royal Porcelain Co | W | Flower trough |
| Nov 4 | 3 | G. Grainger & Co | W | Swan ornament |
| Nov 11 | 2 | W. E. Cartlidge | H | Teapot |
| Nov 12 | 4 | Minton & Co | S | Printed design |
| Nov 14 | 13 | W. Brownfield & Son | C | Centrepiece |
| Nov 14 | 13 | W. Brownfield & Son | C | Teapot |
| Nov 14 | 13 | W. Brownfield & Son | C | Candlelabra |
| Nov 14 | 14 | Moore Brothers | L | Cupid vase |
| Nov 18 | 3 | Holland & Green | L | Printed design |
| Nov 30 | 8 | Belfield & Co | Sc | Teapot |
| Dec 2 | 5 | Brown-Westhead, Moore & Co | Sh | Teawares |
| Dec 4 | 3 | John Pratt & Co Ltd | F | Printed border |
| Dec 10 | 2 | Minton & Co | S | Printed designs |
| Dec 11 | 8 | Old Hall Earthenware Co Ltd | H | Tureen forms |
| Dec 11 | 8 | Old Hall Earthenware Co Ltd | H | Jug |
| Dec 14 | 5 | W. Brownfield & Son | C | Jug |
| Dec 14 | 5 | W. Brownfield & Son | C | Tureen forms |
| Dec 24 | 1 | Cockson & Chetwynd | C | Jug |
| Dec 27 | 4 | John Adams – executors of | L | Teawares |
| Dec 27 | 5 | R.G. Scrivener & Co | H | Jug |
| Dec 27 | 8 | Meir & Son | T | Printed design |
| Dec 28 | 1 | Charles Ellis | L | Bottle form |
| | | (manufactured by Doultons, Lambeth) | | |

### 1873 (F at right)

| Jan 10 | 1 | G. Jones | S | Plate shape |
|---|---|---|---|---|
| Jan 13 | 4 | W.T. Copeland & Sons | S | Toiletwares |
| Jan 14 | 8 | J. Defries & Sons* | Ln | Printed design |
| Jan 15 | 2 | Worthington & Son | H | Jug form |
| Jan 29 | 1 | Minton, Hollins & Co | S | Tile designs |
| Jan 29 | 2 | Moore Brothers | L | Leaf teawares |
| Jan 29 | 2 | Moore Brothers | L | Fan dishes |
| Feb 1 | 1 | Minton, Hollins & Co | S | Tile designs |
| Feb 10 | 2 | W. & J. A. Bailey | Alloa | Teapot |
| Feb 12 | 4 | Bates, Elliot & Co | B | Plate shape |
| Feb 15 | 1 | Minton & Co | S | Tile design |
| Feb 19 | 14 | J. & T. Bevington | H | Jug |
| Feb 19 | 14 | J. & T. Bevington | H | Swan ornament |
| Feb 25 | 6 | G. Jones | S | Jug |
| Feb 27 | 4 | T. Till & Sons | B | Printed border |
| Feb 27 | 8 | Minton, Hollins & Co | S | Tile design |
| Mar 6 | 1 | Minton & Co | S | Tile designs |
| Mar 6 | 9 | Brownhills Pottery Co | T | Covered jar |
| Mar 15 | 10 | J. Lawton & Sons | Bir | Bedstead units |
| Mar 26 | 6 | G. Jones | S | Tureen |
| Mar 26 | 6 | G. Jones | S | Leaf dish |
| April 3 | 6 | Minton & Co | S | Openwork edge |
| April 15 | 4 | Taylor, Tunnicliffe & Co | H | Bedstead knob |
| April 19 | 1 | T. Davidson, junior & Co | G | Teapot forms |
| April 19 | 2 | Minton & Co | S | Teapot forms |

| April 23 | 6 | Gelson Brothers | H | Toiletwares |
|---|---|---|---|---|
| April 28 | 5 | Powell & Bishop | H | Printed designs |
| April 29 | 3 | G. Jones | S | Strawberry set |
| April 29 | 3 | G. Jones | S | Teawares |
| April 29 | 3 | G. Jones | S | Breakfastwares |
| May 2 | 8 | W. Whiteley★ | Ln | Teapot |
| | | (manufactured by A. Bevington) | | |
| May 3 | 2 | T. Till & Sons | B | Tureen forms |
| May 3 | 7 | W. Brownfield & Son | C | Footbath |
| May 3 | 7 | W. Brownfield & Son | C | Pail |
| May 3 | 7 | W. Brownfield & Son | C | Centrepiece |
| May 3 | 7 | W. Brownfield & Son | C | Cupid dish |
| May 3 | 8 | Minton & Co | S | Tile designs |
| May 6 | 2 | Minton & Co | S | Moulded plate |
| May 12 | 8 | Brown-Westhead, Moore & Co | Sh | Jug |
| May 14 | 2 | F. Atkins & Co | Ln | Filter |
| May 14 | 7 | Moore Brothers | L | Dessertwares |
| May 16 | 6 | Minton, Hollins & Co | S | Tile design |
| May 22 | 5 | Worthington & Co | H | Oval dish |
| May 26 | 7 | Moore Brothers | L | Jardinere |
| May 26 | 7 | Moore Brothers | L | Basket dish |
| May 26 | 8 | Soane & Smith★ | Ln | Tea kettle |
| May 29 | 4 | Worthington & Son | H | Printed design |
| May 29 | 8 | T. Ford | H | Teawares |
| May 30 | 15 | Brown-Westhead, Moore & Co | Sh | Jug |
| Jun 11 | 4 | Bates, Elliot & Co | B | Pot lid prints |
| Jun 17 | 3 | Taylor, Tunnicliffe & Co | H | Castor |
| Jun 19 | 3 | Pinder, Bourne & Co | B | Jug |
| Jun 28 | 4 | T. Goode & Co★ | Ln | Plate border |
| Jun 30 | 3 | Minton, Hollins & Co | S | Tile designs |
| July 3 | 9 | Minton, Hollins & Co | S | Tile designs |
| July 4 | 7 | Brown-Westhead, Moore & Co | Sh | Welled plate |
| July 28 | 2 | Charles Hobson | B | Printed design |
| July 28 | 8 | J. Meir & Sons | T | Printed design |
| July 29 | 3 | D. McBirney & Co | Bel | Lighthouse ornament |
| July 31 | 1 | Mintons | S | Menu holders |
| Aug 5 | 2 | Baker & Chetwynd | B | Basket dish |
| Aug 5 | 3 | George Skey | Tam | Gas stove |
| Aug 14 | 10 | Brown-Westhead, Moore & Co | Sh | Teawares |
| Aug 25 | 1 | G. Jones | S | Castle box |
| Aug 25 | 1 | G. Jones | S | Tortoise box |
| Aug 27 | 1 | Worcester Royal Porcelain Co Ltd | W | Bird ornament |
| Aug 30 | 2 | Brown-Westhead, Moore & Co | Sh | Fluted jug |
| Sept 2 | 8 | Edge, Malkin & Co | B | "Tiger" print |
| Sept 4 | 3 | Mintons | S | Recessed plate |
| Sept 10 | 7 | Powell & Bishop | H | Dinnerwares |
| Sept 15 | 3 | Brown-Westhead, Moore & Co | Sh | Toiletwares |
| Sept 16 | 4 | Brown-Westhead, Moore & Co | Sh | Toiletwares |
| Sept 17 | 8 | Worcester Royal Porcelain Co Ltd | W | Bird ornament |
| Sept 19 | 4 | Brown-Westhead, Moore & Co | Sh | Teawares |
| Sept 25 | 8 | Harvey Adams & Co | L | Trinket set |
| Sept 25 | 10 | Jane Beech | B | Washington jug |

| Sept 29 | 2 | W. Brownfield & Son | C | Teapot |
|---|---|---|---|---|
| Oct 4 | 3 | Moore Brothers | L | Cupid centrepiece |
| Oct 4 | 3 | Moore Brothers | L | Wall pocket |
| Oct 4 | 3 | Moore Brothers | L | Swan ornament |
| Oct 4 | 4 | Heath & Blackhurst | B | "Rustic" print |
| Oct 6 | 6 | Brown–Westhead, Moore & Co | Sh | Teawares |
| Oct 11 | 6 | Mintons | S | Printed design |
| Oct 13 | 3 | G. Jones | S | Printed designs |
| Oct 22 | 6 | Mintons | S | Printed design |
| Nov 3 | 3 | Hope & Carter | B | Printed design |
| Nov 3 | 4 | G. Jones | S | Bird dish |
| Nov 3 | 4 | G. Jones | S | Dish – birds |
| Nov 3 | 4 | G. Jones | S | Bird honey pot |
| Nov 6 | 6 | Wedgwood & Co | T | Printed design |
| Nov 10 | 7 | Brown–Westhead, Moore & Co | Sh | Toiletwares |
| Nov 12 | 3 | Worthington & Son | H | Jug |
| Dec 2 | 6 | Taylor, Tunnicliffe & Co | H | Inkstand |
| Dec 2 | 6 | Taylor, Tunnicliffe & Co | H | Elephant lamp |
| Dec 2 | 6 | Taylor, Tunnicliffe & Co | H | Flower centrepiece |
| Dec 2 | 6 | Taylor, Tunnicliffe & Co | H | Flower holder |
| Dec 4 | 6 | Old Hall Earthenware Co Ltd | H | Printed design |
| Dec 5 | 1 | Harvey Adams & Co | L | Teawares |
| Dec 5 | 8 | W. Brownfield & Son | C | Cupid flower holder |
| Dec 10 | 12 | G. Jones | S | Bird dish |
| Dec 22 | 7 | J. Blashfield | Lincs | Chimney pot |
| Dec 27 | 7 | G. Jones & Sons | S | Game pie dish |

## 1874 (U at right)

| Jan 1 | 3 | Bates, Elliot & Co | B | 4-seasons prints |
|---|---|---|---|---|
| Jan 10 | 15 | Davenports & Co | Lpt | Menu tablets |
| Jan 20 | 3 | Powell & Bishop | H | Printed design |
| Jan 21 | 7 | W. T. Copeland & Sons | S | Teapot |
| Jan 23 | 2 | Charles Southwell* | Ln | Fluted teawares |
| Jan 23 | 5 | J. Meir & Son | T | Tureen forms |
| Jan 30 | 4 | Haviland & Co | Fr | Tureen forms |
| Jan 30 | 4 | Haviland & Co | Fr | Dish forms |
| Feb 9 | 4 | Worcester Royal Porcelain Co Ltd | W | "Terrier" jug |
| Feb 9 | 5 | Bodley & Co | B | Jug |
| Feb 11 | 2 | T. Booth & Sons | H | Teapot |
| Feb 14 | 9 | Worthington & Son | H | Jug |
| Feb 19 | 1 | G. Jones & Sons | S | Jug |
| Feb 25 | 6 | Robinson & Leadbeater | S | Dove basket |
| Feb 25 | 7 | G. Jones & Sons | S | Bird dish |
| Feb 26 | 7 | Minton, Hollins & Co | S | Tile designs |
| Mar 2 | 1 | D. McBirney & Co | Bel | Egg cup basket |
| Mar 3 | 4 | G. Jones & Sons | S | Printed design |
| Mar 4 | 3 | Mintons | S | Printed design |
| Mar 4 | 8 | Worcester Royal Porcelain Co Ltd | W | Dessert comports |
| Mar 13 | 6 | J. Dimmock & Co | H | Dinnerwares |
| Mar 14 | 2 | Mintons | S | Printed menu tablet |
| Mar 17 | 5 | Powell & Bishop | H | "Autumn" print |
| Mar 21 | 5 | Powell & Bishop | H | Bird printed designs |

| Mar 24 | 4 | Mintons | S | Menu tablet |
|---|---|---|---|---|
| Mar 27 | 2 | Worthington & Son | H | Jug |
| Mar 28 | 3 | G. Jones & Sons | S | Sardine box |
| Mar 28 | 3 | G. Jones & Sons | S | Flower & card holder |
| Mar 30 | 1 | Worthington & Son | H | Teapot |
| April 7 | 4 | Worcester Royal Porcelain Co Ltd | W | Egg cup stand |
| April 14 | 4 | Ambrose Bevington | H | Teawares |
| April 15 | 7 | Mintons | S | Vase |
| April 20 | 7 | Minton, Hollins & Co | S | Tile designs |
| April 21 | 8 | G. Jones & Sons | S | Printed design |
| April 22 | 1 | W. Brownfield & Son | C | Sauceboat |
| April 23 | 8 | Brown-Westhead, Moore & Co | Sh | Fluted teapot |
| April 25 | 2 | G. Jones & Sons | S | Jug |
| April 29 | 7 | Ridgway, Sparks & Ridgway | H | Printed border |
| April 29 | 9 | T. Furnival & Son | C | Printed design |
| April 30 | 2 | T. Booth & Sons | H | Jug |
| May 5 | 3 | Bates, Elliot & Co | B | Printed design |
| May 7 | 7 | Crosse & Blackwell★ | Ln | Covered pot |
| May 9 | 3 | G. Jones & Sons | S | Centrepiece |
| May 9 | 3 | G. Jones & Sons | S | Garden seat |
| May 11 | 2 | Moore Brothers | L | Camel teapot |
| May 11 | 2 | Moore Brothers | L | Flower bowl |
| May 11 | 2 | Moore Brothers | L | Squirrel jug |
| May 11 | 3 | J. Thomson & Sons | G | "Oaknut" print |
| May 11 | 4 | Holland & Green | L | Jug |
| May 20 | 11 | Bates, Elliot & Co | B | Printed design |
| May 21 | 5 | Mintons | S | Figure menu |
| May 22 | 8 | Mintons | S | Figure menu |
| May 23 | 4 | G. Jones & Sons | S | Flower centrepiece |
| May 23 | 4 | G. Jones & Sons | S | Wall vase |
| Jun 1 | 7 | Worcester Royal Porcelain Co Ltd | W | Hanging ornament |
| Jun 6 | 2 | W. Brownfield & Son | C | Menu holder |
| Jun 6 | 2 | W. Brownfield & Son | C | Dog flower holder |
| Jun 6 | 2 | W. Brownfield & Son | C | Teapot |
| Jun 6 | 2 | W. Brownfield & Son | C | Lamp holder |
| Jun 6 | 5 | Charles Ford | H | Teacup |
| Jun 10 | 8 | Daniel Pearce★ | Ln | Menu holder |
| Jun 16 | 6 | Cockson & Chetwynd | C | Tureen form |
| Jun 17 | 7 | Edge, Malkin & Co | B | Jug |
| Jun 18 | 1 | Mintons | S | Pierced edging |
| Jun 23 | 3 | Williamson & Son | L | Printed design |
| Jun 23 | 7 | Worcester Royal Porcelain Co Ltd | W | Nest wall pocket |
| Jun 25 | 5 | Thomas Ford | H | Wall pockets |
| Jun 25 | 5 | Thomas Ford | H | Menu stands |
| Jun 26 | 4 | Pinder, Bourne & Co | B | Jug |
| July 10 | 2 | Mintons | S | Leaf dish |
| July 13 | 6 | Brown-Westhead, Moore & Co | Sh | Tea kettle |
| July 13 | 6 | Brown-Westhead, Moore & Co | Sh | Printed border |
| July 25 | 7 | J. Curling Hope★ | Hgs | Fisherman match holder |
| July 27 | 1 | Hulse & Adderley | L | Printed border |
| July 30 | 5 | Minton, Hollins & Co | S | Tile design |
| Aug 1 | 8 | Mintons | S | Tile designs |

| Aug 1 | 9 | Cockson & Chetwynd | C | Teawares |
|---|---|---|---|---|
| Aug 6 | 7 | Brown-Westhead, Moore & Co | Sh | Toilet jug |
| Aug 8 | 2 | W. Brownfield & Son | C | Jardinere |
| Aug 8 | 2 | W. Brownfield & Son | C | Vase - boot |
| Aug 10 | 7 | John Moir & Son★ | Ln | Jar form |
| Aug 15 | 4 | Bates, Elliot & Co | B | Teawares |
| Aug 22 | 6 | J. T. Hudden | L | Printed design |
| Aug 28 | 4 | G. Jones & Sons | S | Jardinere |
| Aug 28 | 4 | G. Jones & Sons | S | Tray form |
| Aug 31 | 6 | T. J. & J. Emberton | T | Vine print |
| Sept 1 | 3 | T. Till & Sons | B | Jug |
| Sept 3 | 12 | Cockson & Chetwynd | C | Jugs |
| Sept 4 | 3 | Mintons | S | Teawares |
| Sept 5 | 4 | Worcester Royal Porcelain Co Ltd | W | Figure menu card |
| Sept 5 | 4 | Worcester Royal Porcelain Co Ltd | W | Dove flower holder |
| Sept 5 | 7 | T. Furnival & Son | C | Printed border |
| Sept 7 | 3 | T. Booth & Sons | H | Jugs |
| Sept 10 | 3 | W. Brownfield & Son | C | Toiletwares |
| Sept 12 | 1 | Mintons | S | Printed border |
| Sept 15 | 2 | G. Jones & Sons | S | Oyster plate |
| Sept 17 | 4 | R. Britton & Sons | Lds | Printed design |
| Sept 19 | 8 | James McKee★ | Ln | Washstand |
| Sept 30 | 4 | W. Brownfield & Son | C | Pair figures |
| Oct 2 | 5 | G. Grainger & Co | W | Wall pocket |
| Oct 2 | 5 | G. Grainger & Co | W | Baskets |
| Oct 3 | 4 | Moore Brothers | L | Cat ornaments |
| Oct 3 | 4 | Moore Brothers | L | Centrepiece - bowl |
| Oct 3 | 4 | Moore Brothers | L | Frame |
| Oct 6 | 3 | Mintons | S | Printed design |
| Oct 6 | 4 | Grove & Stark | L | Jug form |
| Oct 10 | 4 | Mintons | S | Cat jug |
| Oct 12 | 2 | Powell & Bishop | H | Toiletwares |
| Oct 17 | 8 | Bates, Elliot & Co | B | Printed design |
| Oct 21 | 8 | G. Jones & Sons | S | Menu holder |
| Oct 21 | 8 | G. Jones & Sons | S | Napkin holder |
| Oct 24 | 3 | Robinson & Leadbeater | S | Shell matchbox |
| Oct 24 | 3 | Robinson & Leadbeater | S | Butler matchbox |
| Oct 27 | 1 | George Ash | H | Flower vase |
| Oct 28 | 9 | Pinder, Bourne & Co | B | Printed border |
| Oct 30 | 5 | Benjamin Green | F | Printed design |
| Nov 2 | 3 | J. Edwards & Son | B | Tureen form |
| Nov 3 | 4 | W. & E. Corn | B | Dinnerwares |
| Nov 3 | 4 | W. & E. Corn | B | Teawares |
| Nov 3 | 4 | W. & E. Corn | B | Jug forms |
| Nov 6 | 3 | W. Brownfield & Son | C | Dessertwares |
| Nov 7 | 4 | Thomas Ford | H | Wall pockets |
| Nov 7 | 4 | Thomas Ford | H | Shell dishes |
| Nov 7 | 4 | Thomas Ford | H | Shell condiment |
| Nov 10 | 3 | G. Jones & Sons | S | Flower vase |
| Nov 12 | 3 | Mintons | S | Printed design |
| Nov 12 | 12 | Bates, Elliot & Co | B | Printed design |
| Nov 20 | 12 | F. & R. Pratt & Co | F | Jug |

| Nov 25 | 7 | Minton, Hollins & Co | S | Tile designs |
| Dec 1 | 5 | W. T. Copeland & Sons | S | Candlestick |
| Dec 4 | 6 | Thomas Barlow | L | Teawares |
| Dec 5 | 4 | Holmes & Plant | B | Knob form |
| Dec 7 | 8 | Brown-Westhead, Moore & Co | Sh | Baskets |
| Dec 7 | 8 | Brown-Westhead, Moore & Co | Sh | Spittoon |
| Dec 7 | 8 | Brown-Westhead, Moore & Co | Sh | Brush stand |
| Dec 8 | 2 | G. Jones & Sons | S | Jug |
| Dec 10 | 4 | Pinder, Bourne & Co | B | Jug |
| Dec 10 | 11 | Worcester Royal Porcelain Co Ltd | W | Menu holders |
| Dec 12 | 3 | G. Jones & Sons | S | Cheese stand |
| Dec 12 | 5 | Port Dundas Pottery Co | G | Teapot |
| Dec 18 | 4 | T. Barlow | L | Teawares |
| Dec 18 | 6 | G. Jones & Sons | S | Trinket set |
| Dec 18 | 7 | Ambrose Bevington | H | Plate form |
| Dec 18 | 9 | G. Grainger & Co | W | Menu holder |
| Dec 18 | 11 | Minton, Hollins & Co | S | Tile designs |

### 1875 (S at right)

| Jan 2 | 4 | Brown-Westhead, Moore & Co | Sh | Dinnerwares |
| Jan 2 | 4 | Brown-Westhead, Moore & Co | Sh | Teawares |
| Jan 6 | 3 | Minton, Hollins & Co | S | Tile designs |
| Jan 11 | 11 | W. Toogood★ | Ln | Animal ornaments |
| Jan 12 | 3 | Worcester Royal Porcelain Co Ltd | W | Menu card |
| Jan 16 | 9 | Brownhills Pottery Co | T | Jug |
| Jan 18 | 8 | Brown-Westhead, Moore & Co | Sh | Dog ornament |
| Jan 20 | 3 | Robinson & Leadbeater | S | Flower holder |
| Jan 20 | 4 | W. Brownfield & Son | C | Teawares |
| Jan 20 | 4 | W. Brownfield & Son | C | Leaf dishes |
| Jan 20 | 4 | W. Brownfield & Son | C | Menu holder |
| Jan 20 | 4 | W. Brownfield & Son | C | Cruet |
| Jan 21 | 2 | G. Jones & Sons | S | Dinnerwares |
| Jan 23 | 9 | Brown-Westhead, Moore & Co | Sh | Dinnerwares |
| Jan 23 | 9 | Brown-Westhead, Moore & Co | Sh | Toiletwares |
| Jan 28 | 4 | C. Denham★ | Ln | Spoonwarmer |
| Jan 28 | 5 | Mintons | S | Teawares |
| Jan 29 | 1 | Worthington & Son | H | Teapot |
| Jan 29 | 1 | Worthington & Son | H | Jug |
| Feb 3 | 7 | Charles Ford | H | Menu holder |
| Feb 5 | 5 | T. & R. Boote | B | Tureen form |
| Feb 6 | 2 | Moore Brothers | L | Cat ornament |
| Feb 9 | 1 | Pinder, Bourne & Co | B | Printed designs |
| Feb 9 | 2 | G. Jones & Sons | S | Strawberry set |
| Feb 12 | 6 | J. Maddock & Sons | B | Dinnerwares |
| Feb 15 | 2 | Moore Brothers | L | Kitten & basket |
| Feb 17 | 7 | Mintons | S | Bird comports |
| Feb 23 | 5 | J. Maddock & Sons | B | Dinnerwares |
| Feb 23 | 6 | G. Jones & Sons | S | Spill vase |
| Feb 23 | 8 | George Ash | H | Small vases |
| Feb 24 | 3 | Stephen Clive | T | Printed design |
| Mar 5 | 2 | W. Brownfield & Son | C | Cat ornament |
| Mar 12 | 5 | G. Jones & Sons | S | Jugs |

| Mar 12 | 5 | G. Jones & Sons | S | Sardine dish |
|---|---|---|---|---|
| Mar 24 | 13 | Minton, Hollins & Co | S | Tile design |
| Mar 24 | 14 | Brown-Westhead, Moore & Co | Sh | Teawares |
| Mar 30 | 1 | T. Booth & Sons | H | Jug |
| Mar 31 | 5 | W. Brownfield & Sons | C | Fan dish |
| Mar 31 | 5 | W. Brownfield & Sons | C | Cat flower stand |
| Mar 31 | 8 | James McKee★ | Ln | Jug |
| April 3 | 7 | J. Dimmock & Co | H | Covered dish |
| April 3 | 9 | Edward F. Bodley & Son | B | Teawares |
| April 7 | 3 | Mintons | S | Jug – oak leaf |
| April 9 | 6 | W. Brownfield & Son | C | Candlelabra |
| April 9 | 6 | W. Brownfield & Son | C | Menu tablet |
| April 9 | 6 | W. Brownfield & Son | C | Name tablet |
| April 10 | 7 | Powell & Bishop | H | Teawares |
| April 10 | 7 | Powell & Bishop | H | Printed design |
| April 15 | 5 | Ralph Malkin | F | Printed design |
| April 17 | 1 | Pinder, Bourne & Co | B | Vase |
| April 20 | 1 | J. Dimmock & Co | H | Slipper ornament |
| April 20 | 2 | Mintons | S | Ornamental stand |
| April 21 | 5 | Stephen Clive | T | Printed design |
| April 22 | 3 | W. P. & G. Phillips★ | Ln | Flower troughs |
| April 22 | 4 | Minton, Hollins & Co | S | Tile designs |
| May 7 | 7 | G. Jones & Sons | S | Trinket stand |
| May 7 | 8 | Burgess & Leigh | B | Jug |
| May 11 | 5 | J. Jeckyle★ | Ln | Tile design |
| May 11 | 6 | T. Goode & Co★ | Ln | Bear ornament |
| May 20 | 1 | Bates, Elliot & Co | B | Printed design |
| May 20 | 3 | J. Dimmock & Co | H | Oval dish |
| May 22 | 1 | Holland & Green | L | Printed design |
| May 26 | 6 | Brown-Westhead, Moore & Co | Sh | Jugs |
| May 26 | 6 | Brown-Westhead, Moore & Co | Sh | Tureen form |
| May 28 | 10 | Campbellfield Pottery Co | G | Teapot |
| May 31 | 8 | G. Jones & Sons | S | Flower pot |
| May 31 | 18 | Ridgway, Sparks & Ridgway | H | "Chelsea" print |
| Jun 2 | 9 | Minton, Hollins & Co | S | Tile designs |
| Jun 5 | 7 | W. P. & G. Phillips★ (manufactured by Brownfields) | Ln | Figures with baskets |
| Jun 7 | 3 | W. & T. Adams | T | Printed border |
| Jun 8 | 4 | Worcester Royal Porcelain Co Ltd | W | Flower holder |
| Jun 10 | 6 | W. Brownfield & Son | C | Printed designs |
| Jun 12 | 6 | Maddock & Gates | B | Tureens |
| Jun 12 | 10 | T. Furnival & Sons | C | Printed designs |
| Jun 15 | 5 | J. Wedgwood & Sons | E | Beer set |
| Jun 19 | 6 | T. Till & Sons | B | Printed border |
| Jun 26 | 2 | G. Jones & Sons | S | Tea & dessertwares |
| July 5 | 1 | W. Brownfield & Son | C | Fruit basket |
| July 7 | 8 | Moore Brothers | L | Cupid centrepiece |
| July 7 | 8 | Moore Brothers | L | Swan centrepiece |
| July 8 | 5 | Moore Brothers | L | Lily vase |
| July 20 | 4 | Edwin J. D. Bodley | B | Basket |
| July 23 | 10 | Brown-Westhead, Moore & Co | Sh | Garden seat |
| July 27 | 5 | Grove & Stark | L | Printed design |

| July 28 | 7 | Minton, Hollins & Co | S | Tile design |
|---|---|---|---|---|
| Aug 19 | 7 | Grove & Stark | L | Printed design |
| Aug 28 | 6 | W. P. & G. Phillips★ | Ln | Figures |
| Sept 2 | 3 | Thomas Elsmore & Son | T | Tureen form |
| Sept 13 | 2 | G. Jones & Sons | S | Punch centrepiece |
| Sept 13 | 2 | G. Jones & Sons | S | Jug |
| Sept 14 | 9 | Minton, Hollins & Co | S | Tile design |
| Sept 18 | 2 | G. Jones & Sons | S | Flower holders |
| Sept 21 | 1 | R. Cockran & Co | G | Printed border |
| Sept 22 | 9 | J. Graham & Co | G | Brackets |
| Sept 24 | 2 | H. Aynsley & Co | L | Printed design |
| Sept 25 | 3 | Grove & Stark | L | Printed design |
| Sept 25 | 4 | W. Toogood★ | Ln | Cupid vase |
| Sept 25 | 4 | W. Toogood★ | Ln | Ornamental basket |
| Sept 28 | 6 | Brown-Westhead, Moore & Co | Sh | Tureen forms |
| Sept 30 | 4 | John Edwards | F | Dinnerwares |
| Sept 30 | 4 | John Edwards | F | Jug |
| Oct 2 | 6 | J. Wedgwood & Sons | E | Tureen forms |
| Oct 6 | 4 | Robert Cooke | H | Teawares |
| Oct 11 | 4 | Powell & Bishop | H | Toilet jug |
| Oct 11 | 10 | Brownhills Pottery Co | T | Jug |
| Oct 11 | 10 | Brownhills Pottery Co | T | Vase form |
| Oct 16 | 8 | Burgess & Leigh & Co | B | Printed border |
| Oct 28 | 3 | Minton, Hollins & Co | S | Printed tile |
| Oct 30 | 9 | W. P. & G. Phillips★ | Ln | Child figures |
| Nov 5 | 3 | G. Jones & Sons | S | Ornamental trays |
| Nov 8 | 4 | Minton, Hollins & Co | S | Tile designs |
| Nov 8 | 8 | W. T. Copeland & Sons | S | Jug |
| Nov 12 | 1 | G. Jones & Sons | S | Centrepiece |
| Nov 12 | 2 | Burgess, Leigh & Co | B | Cheese dish |
| Nov 13 | 8 | Worcester Royal Porcelain Co Ltd | W | Figure menu holder |
| Dec 1 | 2 | W. Brownfield & Sons | C | Vase |
| Dec 1 | 9 | Gelson Brothers | H | Dinnerwares |
| Dec 3 | 4 | G. Jones & Sons | S | Fruit tray |
| Dec 6 | 8 | J. Meir & Son | T | Toiletwares |
| Dec 10 | 3 | Mintons | S | Teapot |
| Dec 10 | 8 | A. Care & Co★ | Ln | Fancy baskets |
| Dec 11 | 5 | Grove & Stark | L | Printed border |
| Dec 11 | 8 | Soane & Smith★ | Ln | Vase |
| Dec 13 | 8 | Minton, Hollins & Co | S | Tile designs |
| Dec 15 | 2 | Mintons | S | Teawares |
| Dec 15 | 3 | Mintons | S | Printed designs |
| Dec 24 | 4 | Charles Ford | H | Wall pockets |
| Dec 24 | 6 | Bates, Walker & Co | B | Printed design |
| Dec 29 | 5 | Edge, Malkin & Co | B | Teapot |
| Dec 29 | 6 | Brown-Westhead, Moore & Co | Sh | Jug |
| Dec 29 | 6 | Brown-Westhead, Moore & Co | Sh | Spoon warmer |
| Dec 30 | 2 | Mintons | S | Figure |
| Dec 30 | 6 | William Toogood★ | Ln | Figure menu – holder |
| Dec 30 | 8 | Minton, Hollins & Co | S | Tile design |

## 1876 (V at right)

| | | | | |
|---|---|---|---|---|
| Jan 4 | 4 | Mintons | S | Japanese style vase |
| Jan 6 | 2 | Moore Brothers | L | Cupid centrepiece |
| Jan 11 | 7 | Edwin J. D. Bodley | B | Cup form |
| Jan 21 | 13 | Bale & Co | E | Printed designs |
| Jan 22 | 6 | George Jones & Sons | S | Strainer dish |
| Jan 22 | 6 | George Jones & Sons | S | Ornamental dishes |
| Jan 22 | 8 | Charles Ford | H | Menu tablet |
| Jan 24 | 1 | Mintons | S | Teapot |
| Jan 24 | 6 | Bates, Walker & Co | B | Printed design |
| Jan 24 | 6 | Bates, Walker & Co | B | Jug |
| Jan 26 | 2 | Edge, Malkin & Co | B | Covered bowl |
| Jan 26 | 3 | Powell & Bishop | H | Jug |
| Jan 28 | 8 | J. Edwards & Son | B | Jug |
| Jan 29 | 3 | W. Brownfield & Son | C | Flower holder |
| Jan 29 | 3 | W. Brownfield & Son | C | "Yeddo" jug |
| Jan 29 | 3 | W. Brownfield & Son | C | Flower trough |
| Feb 1 | 2 | W. Brownfield & Son | C | Figures with baskets |
| Feb 2 | 7 | J. Wedgwood & Sons | E | Canoe dishes |
| Feb 2 | 12 | Ridgway, Sparks & Ridgway | H | Print – shells |
| Feb 3 | 5 | Powell & Bishop | H | Jug |
| Feb 4 | 6 | Mintons | S | Eagle vase |
| Feb 4 | 12 | Worcester Royal Porcelain Co Ltd | W | Jardinere |
| Feb 4 | 12 | Worcester Royal Porcelain Co Ltd | W | Swan flower vase |
| Feb 8 | 9 | Bates, Walker & Co | B | Printed design |
| Feb 15 | 5 | G. Curling Hope★ | Hgs | Fisherman match holder |
| Feb 19 | 5 | G. Jones & Sons | S | Strawberry dish |
| Feb 21 | 4 | Worcester Royal Porcelain Co Ltd | W | Nest wall pocket |
| Feb 22 | 3 | Minton, Hollins & Co | S | Tile designs |
| Feb 29 | 9 | J. Dimmock & Co | H | Toiletwares |
| Feb 29 | 11 | W. Toogood★ | Ln | Wall pocket |
| Mar 2 | 8 | T. Gelson & Co | H | Jug forms |
| Mar 2 | 8 | T. Gelson & Co | H | Tureen form |
| Mar 2 | 11 | Brownhills Pottery Co | T | Tureen form |
| Mar 10 | 8 | Minton, Hollins & Co | S | Tile designs |
| Mar 14 | 5 | Brown–Westhead, Moore & Co | Sh | Jug |
| Mar 17 | 5 | Mintons | S | Figure group |
| Mar 18 | 3 | Robinson & Chapman | L | Printed design |
| Mar 23 | 8 | Edwin J. D. Bodley | B | Jug |
| Mar 24 | 7 | Bates, Walker & Co | B | Tureen form |
| Mar 28 | 8 | W.E. Withinshaw | B | Toilet jug |
| Mar 30 | 4 | G. Jones & Sons | S | Jardinere |
| Mar 30 | 4 | G. Jones & Sons | S | Wall pocket |
| Mar 30 | 4 | G. Jones & Sons | S | Teapot |
| April 8 | 6 | Bates, Walker & Co | B | Printed border |
| April 11 | 4 | T. Gelson & Co | H | Jug |
| April 12 | 4 | Powell & Bishop | H | Printed design |
| April 12 | 11 | J. Dimmock & Co | H | Teapot |
| April 21 | 7 | Minton, Hollins & Co | S | Tile design |
| April 21 | 10 | T. Furnival & Son | C | Printed designs |
| April 22 | 5 | Worcester Royal Porcelain Co Ltd | W | Flower holder |
| April 27 | 3 | Mintons | S | Jug |

| May 8 | 7 | Brown-Westhead, Moore & Co | Sh | Strawberry dish |
|---|---|---|---|---|
| May 8 | 7 | Brown-Westhead, Moore & Co | Sh | Baskets |
| May 10 | 3 | G. Jones & Sons | S | Bird tray |
| May 11 | 9 | F. & R. Pratt & Co | F | Cold cream print |
| May 16 | 7 | Mintons | S | Menu stands |
| May 16 | 7 | Mintons | S | Pair figures |
| May 22 | 3 | Moore Brothers | L | Bird dish |
| May 22 | 4 | J. Wedgwood & Sons | E | Teapot |
| May 22 | 4 | J. Wedgwood & Sons | E | Jug forms |
| May 23 | 7 | Haviland & Co | Fr | Tureen forms |
| May 24 | 3 | Mintons | S | Monkey ornament |
| May 25 | 6 | Moore Brothers | L | Owl ornament |
| May 29 | 8 | G. Jones & Sons | S | Teawares |
| Jun 3 | 2 | Mintons | S | Fan-shape box |
| Jun 3 | 7 | J. S. Crapper | H | Swan, spittoon |
| Jun 3 | 5 | Edwin J. D. Bodley | B | Teawares |
| Jun 3 | 5 | Edwin J. D. Bodley | B | Dinnerwares |
| Jun 3 | 5 | Edwin J. D. Bodley | B | Cruet |
| Jun 7 | 1 | T. Gelson & Co | H | Tureen |
| Jun 8 | 4 | Mintons | S | Candlestick |
| Jun 9 | 6 | W. T. Copeland & Sons | S | Toilet forms |
| Jun 15 | 1 | H. Meir & Son | T | "Indian Star" print |
| Jun 15 | 9 | Minton, Hollins & Co | S | Tile designs |
| Jun 19 | 2 | J. Wedgwood & Sons | E | Jug |
| Jun 19 | 7 | T. Whetstone★ | Ln | Welsh tea party print |
| Jun 19 | 9 | J. Holdcroft | L | Wall pocket |
| Jun 20 | 3 | T. Whetstone★ | Ln | Plate ornamentation |
| Jun 21 | 4 | Mintons | S | Figure menu holder |
| Jun 22 | 4 | T. Gelson & Co | H | Tureen form |
| Jun 23 | 5 | Mintons | S | Jardinere |
| Jun 26 | 6 | Minton, Hollins & Co | S | Tile designs |
| Jun 28 | 8 | J. Aynsley | L | Pierced edging |
| July 1 | 3 | Mintons | S | Monkey ornament |
| July 1 | 3 | Mintons | S | Pillar ornament |
| July 1 | 4 | John Tams | L | "Shamrock" print |
| July 3 | 2 | Ford & Challinor | T | Teapot |
| July 5 | 1 | T. Till & Sons | B | Jug |
| July 5 | 7 | W. T. Copeland & Sons | S | Hanging parrot |
| July 10 | 3 | T. Gelson & Co | H | Ashtray |
| July 12 | 2 | Edwin J. D. Bodley | B | Comport |
| July 18 | 3 | Soane & Smith★ | Ln | Water ewer |
| July 26 | 3 | G. Jones & Sons | S | Hat flower holder |
| July 28 | 10 | T. Gelson & Co | H | Tureen form |
| July 28 | 11 | Powell & Bishop | H | Tureen form |
| July 31 | 8 | G. Grainger & Co | W | Eagle vase |
| Aug 8 | 1 | Robinson & Chapman | L | Printed design |
| Aug 25 | 8 | F. & R. Pratt & Co | F | Swan print |
| Sept 5 | 5 | Bates, Walker & Co | B | Printed designs |
| Sept 6 | 9 | Pinder, Bourne & Co | B | Jug |
| Sept 6 | 10 | W. Brownfield & Sons | C | Jug |
| Sept 9 | 8 | Worthington & Son | H | Printed design |
| Sept 9 | 9 | Brown-Westhead, Moore & Co | Sh | Jug |

| Sept 11 | 1 | Edwin J. D. Bodley | B | Teawares |
|---|---|---|---|---|
| Sept 12 | 6 | G. Jones & Sons | S | Fish & lobster tureens |
| Sept 18 | 10 | G. L. Ashworth & Bros | H | Printed design |
| Sept 20 | 3 | Hollinshead & Kirkham | B | Toiletwares |
| Sept 22 | 3 | Powell & Bishop | H | Toiletwares |
| Sept 25 | 4 | W. Toogood★ | Ln | Monkey & cat basket |
| Sept 26 | 5 | Hope & Carter | B | Printed design |
| Sept 26 | 10 | Brown–Westhead, Moore & Co | Sh | Bread tray |
| Sept 28 | 2 | Moore Brothers | L | Rustic flower holder |
| Sept 28 | 2 | Moore Brothers | L | Cupid flower holder |
| Sept 28 | 10 | Hope & Carter | B | Jug |
| Oct 3 | 2 | W. B. Simpson & Sons | Ln | Tile design |
| Oct 7 | 2 | W. Harrop | H | Embossed jug |
| Oct 7 | 3 | W. Brownfield & Sons | C | Table ornaments |
| Oct 7 | 4 | J. Wedgwood & Sons | E | Dinnerwares |
| Oct 7 | 6 | W. Adams | T | Jug |
| Oct 7 | 6 | W. Adams | T | Teapot |
| Oct 9 | 1 | G. Jones & Sons | S | Egg basket |
| Oct 9 | 1 | G. Jones & Sons | S | Sardine box |
| Oct 12 | 8 | Ambrose Bevington | H | Oval tureen |
| Oct 17 | 4 | Brown–Westhead, Moore & Co | Sh | Toilet jug |
| Oct 17 | 9 | Wardle & Co | H | Jug |
| Oct 19 | 3 | Burgess, Leigh & Co | B | Jug |
| Oct 20 | 2 | Mintons | S | Printed designs |
| Oct 21 | 1 | Edge, Malkin & Co | B | Jug |
| Oct 23 | 2 | Mintons | S | Printed designs |
| Oct 31 | 2 | W. Brownfield & Sons | C | Teapot forms |
| Oct 31 | 2 | W. Brownfield & Sons | C | Spittoon |
| Oct 31 | 2 | W. Brownfield & Sons | C | Leaf dish |
| Nov 1 | 2 | Moore Brothers | L | Candlelabra |
| Nov 4 | 16 | W. Stokes & Co | Du | Battle form |
| Nov 7 | 3 | Robert Jones | H | Toilet mirror |
| Nov 8 | 3 | G. Jones & Sons | S | Jug |
| Nov 8 | 9 | W. Brownfield & Sons | C | Elephant vase |
| Nov 9 | 10 | Belfield & Co | Sc | Leaf dessertware |
| Nov 11 | 9 | Moore Brothers | L | Chicken teapot |
| Nov 13 | 3 | Mintons | S | Printed border |
| Nov 14 | 2 | J. Wedgwood & Sons | E | Candlestick |
| Nov 14 | 8 | Clementson Brothers | H | Teawares |
| Nov 17 | 3 | Banks & Thorley | H | Jug |
| Nov 18 | 3 | Minton, Hollins & Co | S | Tile design |
| Nov 18 | 7 | Minton, Hollins & Co | S | Tile design |
| Nov 18 | 9 | Worcester Royal Porcelain Co Ltd | W | Flower holder |
| Nov 23 | 5 | W. Adams | T | Printed design "Pearl" |
| Nov 24 | 15 | T. Furnival & Sons | C | Printed borders |
| Nov 28 | 2 | W. Hudson & Son | L | Flower prints |
| Nov 29 | 11 | T. Furnival & Sons | C | Jug |
| Dec 5 | 2 | Wedgwood & Co | T | Printed design |
| Dec 8 | 2 | Wittman & Roth★ | Ln | Gladstone figure |
| Dec 8 | 2 | Wittman & Roth★ | Ln | Disraeli figure |
| Dec 11 | 2 | J. Tams | L | Printed design |
| Dec 12 | 11 | Campbell Brick & Tile Co | S | Tile design |

| | | | | |
|---|---|---|---|---|
| Dec 14 | 1 | Harvey Adams & Co | L | Masonic menu |
| Dec 14 | 11 | J. Dimmock & Co | H | Jug |
| Dec 18 | 9 | James Beech | L | Oak print |
| Dec 20 | 7 | J. & T. Bevington | H | Napkin ring |
| Dec 21 | 2 | Grove & Stark | L | Jug |
| Dec 23 | 5 | Charles Ford | H | Handle form |
| Dec 27 | 15 | Campbell Brick & Tile Co | S | Tile design |
| Dec 28 | 6 | Harvey Adams & Co | L | Cup form |

## 1877 (P at right)

| | | | | |
|---|---|---|---|---|
| Jan 4 | 10 | Campbellfield Pottery Co | G | Teapot form |
| Jan 17 | 5 | Worcester Royal Porcelain Co Ltd | W | Wall pocket |
| Jan 20 | 2 | Grove & Stark | L | Printed design – birds |
| Jan 24 | 10 | W. Brownfield & Sons | C | Printed design – Puck |
| Jan 25 | 6 | Wood & Co | B | Jug |
| Jan 25 | 7 | G. Jones & Sons | S | Wall pocket |
| Jan 25 | 7 | G. Jones & Sons | S | Teawares |
| Jan 25 | 7 | G. Jones & Sons | S | Basket |
| Jan 26 | 3 | Mintons | S | Tile design |
| Jan 26 | 4 | Powell & Bishop | H | Teapot |
| Feb 1 | 6 | J. Edwards & Son | B | Teapot |
| Feb 2 | 7 | Worcester Royal Porcelain Co Ltd | W | Water carrier figure |
| Feb 2 | 7 | Worcester Royal Porcelain Co Ltd | W | Jug |
| Feb 2 | 7 | Worcester Royal Porcelain Co Ltd | W | Flower holder |
| Feb 3 | 4 | Minton, Hollins & Co | S | Tile designs |
| Feb 5 | 2 | D. McBirney & Co | Bel | Cupid print |
| Feb 5 | 2 | D. McBirney & Co | Bel | Toiletwares |
| Feb 7 | 3 | Holland & Green | L | Toiletwares |
| Feb 7 | 7 | W. Brownfield & Sons | C | Printed designs |
| Feb 7 | 7 | W. Brownfield & Sons | C | Cheese dish |
| Feb 7 | 7 | W. Brownfield & Sons | C | Dessertwares |
| Feb 9 | 7 | Robinson & Co | L | Floral print |
| Feb 9 | 11 | Brown-Westhead, Moore & Co | Sh | Animal prints |
| Feb 12 | 3 | James Beech | L | Orchid design |
| Feb 14 | 16 | Worcester Royal Porcelain Co Ltd | W | Figures with baskets |
| Feb 15 | 10 | Minton, Hollins & Co | S | Tile design |
| Feb 16 | 9 | J. Rose & Co | Cpt | Tureen forms |
| Feb 19 | 2 | W. Brownfield & Sons | C | Toiletwares |
| Feb 20 | 8 | G. Grainger & Co | W | Wall pocket |
| Feb 21 | 6 | Mintons | S | Plate edging |
| Feb 21 | 9 | W. T. Copeland & Sons | S | Parrot |
| Feb 24 | 3 | Thomas Hughes | B | Printed design |
| Feb 27 | 2 | Mintons | S | Cup form |
| Mar 1 | 4 | Hallam, Johnson & Co | L | Biblical prints |
| Mar 8 | 14 | W. T. Copeland & Sons | S | Lamp |
| Mar 10 | 7 | G. Jones & Sons | S | Strawberry basket |
| Mar 14 | 9 | Campbell Brick & Tile Co | S | Tile design |
| Mar 20 | 3 | Clementson Brothers | H | Dinnerwares |
| Mar 20 | 3 | Clementson Brothers | H | Teawares |
| Mar 20 | 3 | Clementson Brothers | H | Toiletwares |
| Mar 20 | 8 | J. Dimmock & Co | H | Tureen form |
| Mar 20 | 9 | W. B. Simpson & Sons | Ln | Tile design |

| Mar 22 | 14 | Edwin J. D. Bodley | B | Dessertwares |
|---|---|---|---|---|
| Mar 24 | 1 | Powell & Bishop | H | Printed designs |
| Mar 31 | 7 | E.F. Bodley & Co | B | Vine print |
| April 3 | 1 | Powell & Bishop | H | Jug |
| April 4 | 5 | John Mortlock★ | Ln | Pie dish |
| April 5 | 2 | Ford, Challinor & Co | T | Jug |
| April 12 | 11 | John Dimmock & Co | H | Printed design – Moses |
| April 12 | 12 | T. S. Bale | H | Candlestick |
| April 21 | 11 | Silber & Fleming★ | Ln | Printed design |
| April 23 | 4 | J. Tams | L | Jug |
| April 26 | 2 | J. & T. Bevington | H | Basket form |
| April 26 | 7 | Worcester Royal Porcelain Co Ltd | W | Teawares |
| April 27 | 10 | J. Rose & Co | Cpl | Teawares |
| May 2 | 2 | G. Jones & Sons | S | Flower trough |
| May 2 | 2 | G. Jones & Sons | S | Flower basket |
| May 2 | 2 | G. Jones & Sons | S | Wall pocket |
| May 2 | 2 | G. Jones & Sons | S | Caviare set |
| May 4 | 13 | Old Hall Earthenware Co Ltd | H | Jug |
| May 5 | 4 | J. Wedgwood & Sons | E | Printed border |
| May 12 | 7 | T. Furnival & Sons | C | Jug |
| May 16 | 5 | W. Brownfield & Sons | C | Flower basket |
| May 18 | 6 | J. Wedgwood & Sons | E | Jug |
| May 22 | 5 | W. Brownfield & Sons | C | Bear ornament |
| May 22 | 5 | W. Brownfield & Sons | C | Sack biscuit box |
| May 22 | 5 | W. Brownfield & Sons | C | Monkey ornament |
| May 24 | 8 | Brown-Westhead, Moore & Co | Sh | Centrepiece |
| May 30 | 13 | T. Furnival & Sons | C | Tureen |
| Jun 1 | 2 | J. & R. Hammersley | H | Jug form |
| Jun 5 | 6 | Edwin J. D. Bodley | B | Dinnerwares |
| Jun 7 | 1 | Edwin J. D. Bodley | B | Cat ornament |
| Jun 7 | 2 | J. Holdcroft | L | Jug |
| Jun 8 | 7 | Minton, Hollins & Co | S | Tile designs |
| Jun 9 | 3 | Baker & Co | F | Dinnerwares |
| Jun 9 | 3 | Baker & Co | F | Teawares |
| Jun 13 | 2 | Baker & Co | F | Animal ornament |
| Jun 15 | 7 | Ridgway, Sparks & Ridgway | H | "Indus" print |
| Jun 19 | 4 | Ford & Challinor | T | Printed design |
| Jun 19 | 6 | Murray & Co | G | Teapot |
| Jun 22 | 3 | Walker & Carter | S | Printed design |
| Jun 22 | 13 | Steele & Wood | S | Tile designs |
| Jun 22 | 14 | Edward F. Bodley & Co | B | Printed shell design |
| Jun 26 | 11 | T. Furnival & Sons | C | Printed designs |
| Jun 28 | 9 | T. Furnival & Sons | C | Printed design |
| Jun 29 | 10 | Sherwin & Cotton | H | Tile designs |
| July 2 | 3 | W. T. Copeland & Sons | S | Jug |
| July 6 | 2 | Mintons | S | Pierced border |
| July 7 | 4 | Ridge, Meigh & Co | L | Printed design |
| July 9 | 2 | Minton, Hollins & Co | S | Tile design |
| July 14 | 2 | J. Tams | L | Printed designs |
| July 17 | 9 | J. Edwards & Son | B | Plate design |
| July 17 | 9 | J. Edwards & Son | B | Finger plates |
| July 17 | 9 | J. Edwards & Son | B | Jug |

| July 20 | 7 | Haviland & Co | Fr | Tureen forms |
|---|---|---|---|---|
| July 20 | 7 | Haviland & Co | Fr | Jug |
| July 20 | 15 | Taylor, Tunnicliffe & Co | H | Water bottle |
| July 20 | 15 | Taylor, Tunnicliffe & Co | H | Jug & spittoon |
| July 23 | 2 | J. Edwards | F | Dinnerwares |
| July 23 | 2 | J. Edwards | F | Teawares |
| July 25 | 5 | Ford, Challinor & Co | T | Jug |
| July 26 | 6 | Minton, Hollins & Co | S | Tile designs |
| July 31 | 1 | D. McBirney & Co | Bel | Printed design |
| July 31 | 2 | Minton, Hollins & Co | S | Tile design |
| Aug 1 | 4 | Holmes, Stonier & Hollinshead | H | Printed design |
| Aug 1 | 12 | J. Vernon | Sc | Toilet jug |
| Aug 3 | 14 | Campbell Brick & Tile Co | S | Tile design |
| Aug 13 | 5 | Haviland & Co | Fr | Jug |
| Aug 15 | 7 | Campbell Brick & Tile Co | S | Tile design |
| Aug 15 | 10 | G. Picket★ | Ln | Water filter |
| Aug 17 | 11 | Ridgway, Sparks & Ridgway | H | Dinnerwares |
| Aug 18 | 6 | Minton, Hollins & Co | S | Tile designs |
| Aug 18 | 7 | Furnival & Son | C | Printed border |
| Aug 23 | 6 | W. Hudson & Son | L | Printed design |
| Aug 25 | 2 | W. Wood & Co | B | Finger plate |
| Aug 25 | 2 | W. Wood & Co | B | Printed design |
| Aug 25 | 3 | Minton, Hollins & Co | S | Tile designs |
| Aug 28 | 9 | Brown-Westhead, Moore & Co | Sh | Printed design |
| Sept 11 | 3 | G. W. Turner & Sons | T | Printed design |
| Sept 19 | 5 | Minton, Hollins & Co | S | Tile design |
| Sept 20 | 3 | J. Wedgwood & Sons | E | Toiletwares |
| Sept 22 | 7 | Mintons | S | Printed design |
| Sept 22 | 7 | Mintons | S | Teawares |
| Sept 22 | 13 | Minton, Hollins & Co | S | Tile - squirrel |
| Sept 25 | 5 | Mintons | S | Basket |
| Sept 28 | 9 | J. Holdcroft | L | Jug |
| Oct 2 | 7 | Bates, Walker & Co | B | Printed design |
| Oct 3 | 2 | Robinson & Leadbeater | S | Flower holder |
| Oct 4 | 4 | J. & T. Bevington | H | Dog ornament |
| Oct 4 | 4 | J. & T. Bevington | H | Cat ornament |
| Oct 10 | 3 | John Edwards | F | Lion ornament |
| Oct 10 | 5 | W. Brownfield & Sons | C | Toiletwares |
| Oct 15 | 2 | G. Jones & Sons | S | Jardinere - lily |
| Oct 15 | 2 | G. Jones & Sons | S | Jardinere - swan |
| Oct 16 | 6 | Powell & Bishop | H | Teawares |
| Oct 19 | 8 | Minton, Hollins & Co | S | Tile design |
| Oct 19 | 13 | Brown-Westhead, Moore & Co | Sh | Fruit box |
| Oct 24 | 10 | Grove & Stark | L | Printed design |
| Oct 24 | 14 | F. & R. Pratt & Co | F | Jug |
| Oct 30 | 7 | Wedgwood & Co | T | Tureen form |
| Oct 31 | 6 | G. Jones & Sons | S | Jardinere |
| Nov 5 | 4 | Powell & Bishop | H | Cleopatra's Needle |
| Nov 6 | 11 | W. Brownfield & Sons | C | Jug |
| Nov 6 | 11 | W. Brownfield & Sons | C | Flower holder |
| Nov 6 | 11 | W. Brownfield & Sons | C | Cat, basket |
| Nov 6 | 11 | W. Brownfield & Sons | C | Dog, basket |

| Nov 7 | 1 | Edwin J. D. Bodley | B | Flower holder |
|---|---|---|---|---|
| Nov 7 | 1 | Edwin J. D. Bodley | B | Ewer & basin |
| Nov 7 | 1 | Edwin J. D. Bodley | B | Wall pocket |
| Nov 7 | 2 | Mintons | S | Tile design |
| Nov 7 | 10 | Pinder, Bourne & Co | B | Jug |
| Nov 9 | 8 | Taylor, Tunnicliffe & Co | H | Knob form |
| Nov 15 | 12 | Brown-Westhead, Moore & Co | Sh | Vase |
| Nov 20 | 9 | J. Edwards & Son | B | Tureen form |
| Nov 21 | 8 | Davenports & Co | Lpt | Lily toiletware |
| Nov 22 | 1 | Old Hall Earthenware Co Ltd | H | Tureen forms |
| Nov 22 | 13 | B. & S. Hancock | S | Printed design |
| Nov 24 | 7 | J. Dimmock & Co | H | Printed design |
| Nov 29 | 3 | J. Holdcroft | L | Teaset on tray |
| Dec 1 | 5 | J. Holdcroft | L | Bird cruet |
| Dec 1 | 6 | Oakes, Clare & Chadwick | B | Jug |
| Dec 5 | 2 | Edwin J. D. Bodley | B | Cat and basket |
| Dec 6 | 4 | Mintons | S | Dinnerwares |
| Dec 7 | 14 | Joseph Unwin | L | Printed design |
| Dec 14 | 1 | J. Dimmock & Co | H | Tureen form |
| Dec 15 | 10 | Worcester Royal Porcelain Co Ltd | W | Dessert forms |
| Dec 15 | 10 | Worcester Royal Porcelain Co Ltd | W | Pierced edging |
| Dec 21 | 6 | Mintons | S | Boar's head tureen |
| Dec 21 | 10 | T. Furnival & Son | C | Dinnerwares |
| Dec 22 | 5 | W. Brownfield & Sons | C | Bear honey-pot |
| Dec 22 | 5 | W. Brownfield & Sons | C | Jug |
| Dec 29 | 6 | Brown-Westhead, Moore & Co | Sh | Toilet jug |

## 1878 (D at right)

| Jan 3 | 4 | Minton, Hollins & Co | S | Tile designs |
|---|---|---|---|---|
| Jan 9 | 4 | Brownhills Pottery Co | T | Printed design |
| Jan 9 | 4 | Brownhills Pottery Co | T | Vase |
| Jan 9 | 4 | Brownhills Pottery Co | T | Jug |
| Jan 10 | 12 | J. Mortlock & Co★ | Ln | Fluted dish |
| Jan 14 | 1 | J. Maddock & Sons | B | Tureen form |
| Jan 14 | 2 | Cotton & Rigby | B | Teapot |
| Jan 14 | 3 | W. Adams | T | Dinnerwares |
| Jan 14 | 6 | Minton, Hollins & Co | S | Tile design |
| Jan 15 | 5 | J. Wedgwood & Sons | E | Tureen form |
| Jan 18 | 5 | Taylor, Tunnicliffe & Co | H | Rope guides |
| Jan 22 | 6 | J. Dimmock & Co | H | Printed pattern |
| Jan 24 | 6 | W. T. Copeland & Sons | S | Cupid wall pocket |
| Jan 25 | 9 | W. Brownfield & Sons | C | Spoon warmer |
| Jan 25 | 9 | W. Brownfield & Sons | C | Vase |
| Jan 28 | 11 | Brown-Westhead, Moore & Co | Sh | Dessertwares |
| Jan 30 | 3 | G. Jones & Sons | S | Jug |
| Jan 30 | 3 | G. Jones & Sons | S | Vase |
| Jan 30 | 15 | Brownhills Pottery Co | T | Jug |
| Jan 30 | 15 | Brownhills Pottery Co | T | Vase |
| Jan 31 | 1 | B. & S. Hancock | S | Swallows print |
| Feb 1 | 4 | G. Jones & Sons | S | Jardinere |
| Feb 1 | 11 | Minton, Hollins & Co | S | Tile designs |
| Feb 1 | 16 | Derby Crown Porcelain Co Ltd | D | Vases |

| Feb 1 | 16 | Derby Crown Porcelain Co Ltd | D | Figure centrepiece |
|---|---|---|---|---|
| Feb 5 | 5 | Campbell Brick & Tile Co | S | Tile design |
| Feb 9 | 6 | J. Dimmock & Co | H | Printed design |
| Feb 11 | 5 | Brown-Westhead, Moore & Co | Sh | Toiletwares |
| Feb 12 | 5 | Derby Crown Porcelain Co Ltd | D | Vases |
| Feb 12 | 5 | Derby Crown Porcelain Co Ltd | D | Wall pocket |
| Feb 20 | 6 | Minton, Hollins & Co | S | Tile design |
| Feb 20 | 7 | Worcester Royal Porcelain Co Ltd | W | Printed design |
| Feb 21 | 10 | W. E. Cartlidge | B | Teapot |
| Feb 22 | 8 | Campbell Brick & Tile Co | S | Tile design |
| Feb 28 | 3 | Dunn, Bennett & Co | H | Jug |
| Mar 5 | 2 | Grove & Stark | L | Oval tureen |
| Mar 6 | 5 | Minton, Hollins & Co | S | Tile design |
| Mar 7 | 4 | J. Edwards | F | Oval tureen |
| Mar 9 | 1 | Brownhills Pottery & Co | T | Tureen |
| Mar 9 | 1 | Brownhills Pottery & Co | T | Printed design |
| Mar 9 | 8 | Moore Brothers | L | Floral bowl |
| Mar 9 | 11 | Powell & Bishop | H | Toiletwares |
| Mar 11 | 1 | Taylor, Tunnicliffe & Co | H | Knob forms |
| Mar 13 | 1 | Mintons | S | Printed design |
| Mar 13 | 7 | J. & T. Bevington | H | Cupid centrepiece |
| Mar 13 | 10 | W. T. Copeland & Sons | S | Jug |
| Mar 15 | 10 | J. Rose & Co | Cpt | Teawares |
| Mar 23 | 8 | Derby Crown Porcelain Co Ltd | D | Centrepieces |
| Mar 25 | 9 | F. J. Emery | B | Jug |
| Mar 27 | 6 | G. W. Turner & Sons | T | Printed design |
| Mar 27 | 15 | Minton, Hollins & Co | S | Tile design |
| April 2 | 6 | Belfield & Co | Sc | Teapot |
| April 10 | 4 | Mintons | S | "Denmark" print |
| April 13 | 9 | D. McBirney | Bel | Printed design |
| April 15 | 11 | Nestle & Huntsman★ | Ln | Ornamental figures |
| April 17 | 4 | Mintons | S | Teapot |
| April 17 | 14 | Ridgway, Sparks & Ridgway | S | Printed designs |
| April 20 | 2 | T. Furnival & Sons | C | Dinnerwares |
| April 20 | 2 | T. Furnival & Sons | C | Teawares |
| April 20 | 6 | Worcester Royal Porcelain Co Ltd | W | Horn flower holder |
| April 24 | 2 | W. Brownfield & Sons | C | Strawberry tray |
| April 27 | 12 | D. McBirney & Co | Bel | Teawares |
| April 30 | 7 | J. Wedgwood & Sons | E | Sardine box |
| April 30 | 7 | J. Wedgwood & Sons | E | Oyster tray |
| May 3 | 2 | J. Wedgwood & Sons | E | Jug |
| May 3 | 9 | Robinson & Leadbeater | S | Match stand |
| May 8 | 8 | Nestle & Huntsman★ | Ln | Figures |
| May 8 | 8 | Nestle & Huntsman★ | Ln | Fan ornament |
| May 8 | 9 | Bates & Bennett | C | Printed designs |
| May 14 | 6 | Elsmore & Son | T | Printed design |
| May 17 | 12 | J. Dimmock & Co | H | Shell form box |
| May 20 | 9 | Derby Crown Porcelain Co Ltd | D | Flower vases |
| May 21 | 11 | Banks & Thorley | H | Jug |
| May 23 | 3 | J. Wedgwood & Sons | E | Sardine box |
| May 23 | 4 | Moore Brothers | L | Figure flower holder |
| May 24 | 2 | J. Wedgwood & Sons | E | Oyster tray |

| May 27 | 20 | Edwin J. D. Bodley | B | Fancy box |
|--------|----|--------------------|----|-----------|
| May 29 | 9 | Minton, Hollins & Co | S | Inlaid tile |
| Jun 1 | 5 | J. Mortlock & Co★ | Ln | Menu stand |
| Jun 4 | 9 | T. Furnival & Sons | C | Jug |
| Jun 5 | 14 | W. T. Copeland & Sons | S | Dish forms |
| Jun 7 | 1 | G. Jones & Sons | S | Printed designs |
| Jun 8 | 8 | W. Wood & Co | B | Circular dish |
| Jun 12 | 10 | Harvey Adams & Co | L | Moulded plate |
| Jun 13 | 2 | John Tams | L | Teapot |
| Jun 13 | 3 | D. McBirney & Co | Bel | Moulded plate |
| Jun 19 | 7 | Edward F. Bodley & Co | B | Toiletwares |
| Jun 21 | 8 | Allen & Green | F | Card holder |
| Jun 27 | 7 | J. Wedgwood & Sons | E | Butter churn |
| Jun 29 | 1 | Wood, Son & Co | C | Oval tureen |
| July 1 | 1 | Burgess & Leigh | B | Jug |
| July 3 | 2 | Mintons | S | Tile design |
| July 8 | 6 | J. Wedgwood & Sons | E | Jug |
| July 9 | 8 | Mintons | S | Tureen forms |
| July 9 | 8 | Mintons | S | Bowl |
| July 9 | 9 | J. Wedgwood & Sons | E | Dejeune set |
| July 9 | 10 | J. Dimmock & Co | H | Toiletwares |
| July 10 | 14 | Bates & Bennett | C | Printed design |
| July 11 | 1 | Soane & Smith★ | Ln | Toiletwares |
| July 11 | 11 | W. & J. A. Bailey | Sc | Teapot |
| July 12 | 4 | J. Wedgwood & Sons | E | Butter dish |
| July 12 | 13 | Samuel Lear | H | Jug |
| July 12 | 15 | Brown–Westhead, Moore & Co | Sh | Printed designs |
| July 15 | 1 | Pratt & Simpson | F | Ornamental designs |
| July 17 | 9 | W. Adams | T | Printed portrait |
| July 18 | 2 | Ambrose Bevington | H | Oval tureen |
| July 20 | 1 | James Bevington | H | Fish shape basket |
| July 20 | 6 | J. Meir & Son | T | Jug |
| July 20 | 11 | Edwin J. D. Bodley | B | Teawares |
| July 20 | 11 | Edwin J. D. Bodley | B | Dinnerwares |
| July 26 | 3 | J. Wedgwood & Sons | E | Match holder |
| July 30 | 2 | J. Wedgwood & Sons | E | Brandy set – Punch |
| July 30 | 6 | Powell, Bishop & Stonier | H | Royal Arms motif |
| July 30 | 12 | Edward Clarke | Lpt | Oval tureen |
| July 31 | 8 | Mintons | S | Teawares |
| July 31 | 13 | J. Edwards & Son | B | Oval tureen |
| Aug 6 | 3 | Moore Brothers | L | Flower holder |
| Aug 7 | 3 | T. Hughes | B | Printed design |
| Aug 9 | 10 | Derby Crown Porcelain Co Ltd | D | Centrepiece |
| Aug 9 | 12 | Craven Dunnill & Co Ltd | Shrop | Tile designs |
| Aug 16 | 9 | Campbell Brick & Tile Co | S | Tile design |
| Aug 23 | 1 | Moore Brothers | L | Flower holder, peas |
| Aug 23 | 7 | J. Dimmock & Co | H | Printed design |
| Sept 5 | 3 | Moore Brothers | L | Flower holder |
| Sept 9 | 5 | W. Brownfield & Sons | C | Candlelabra |
| Sept 9 | 5 | W. Brownfield & Sons | C | Cart flower holder |
| Sept 9 | 5 | W. Brownfield & Sons | C | Shell cachepot |
| Sept 10 | 2 | J. Wedgwood & Sons | E | Printed designs |

| | | | | |
|---|---|---|---|---|
| Sept 10 | 5 | T. Hughes | B | Printed design |
| Sept 12 | 6 | James Bevington | H | Kitten ornament |
| Sept 13 | 5 | G. L. Ashworth & Bros | H | Toiletwares |
| Sept 13 | 16 | Worcester Royal Porcelain Co Ltd | W | Printed borders |
| Sept 20 | 19 | R. Wotherspoon & Co | G | Preserving jar |
| Sept 24 | 3 | Thomas Bevington | H | Printed border |
| Sept 27 | 1 | G. Stubbs | W | Crested tiles |
| Sept 28 | 5 | Minton, Hollins & Co | S | Peacock basket |
| Sept 30 | 1 | Mintons | S | Tortoise teapot |
| Oct 1 | 10 | Fyfe & Robinson★ | Ln | Tile design |
| Oct 2 | 2 | Mintons | S | Fish teapot |
| Oct 3 | 8 | J. T. Hudden | L | Printed design |
| Oct 4 | 8 | F. & R. Pratt & Co | F | "Cyprus" print |
| Oct 5 | 13 | Worcester Royal Porcelain Co Ltd | W | Dr Wall design |
| Oct 8 | 6 | Moore Brothers | L | Bird handle |
| Oct 8 | 7 | Bates, Gildea & Walker | B | Jug |
| Oct 9 | 9 | J. Wedgwood & Sons | E | Strawberry service |
| Oct 11 | 8 | Minton, Hollins & Co | S | Tile design |
| Oct 14 | 8 | W. T. Copeland & Sons | S | Bird handles |
| Oct 23 | 1 | Brownhills Pottery Co | T | Jug |
| Oct 23 | 11 | Pinder, Bourne & Co | B | Teawares |
| Oct 23 | 11 | Pinder, Bourne & Co | B | Printed design |
| Oct 24 | 1 | T. Furnival & Son | C | Printed design |
| Oct 24 | 2 | J. Dimmock & Co | H | Toiletwares |
| Oct 24 | 13 | Worcester Royal Porcelain Co Ltd | W | Teawares |
| Oct 26 | 4 | W. Brownfield & Co | C | Cup shape |
| Oct 30 | 3 | Minton, Hollins & Co | S | Tile design |
| Nov 1 | 3 | J. Bevington | H | Basket |
| Nov 4 | 1 | Edge, Malkin & Co | B | Jug |
| Nov 5 | 11 | Henry Burgess | B | Tureen form |
| Nov 5 | 17 | Edwin J. D. Bodley | B | Jug |
| Nov 6 | 3 | Samuel Lear | H | Teapot |
| Nov 13 | 13 | J. Rose & Co | Cpt | Teawares |
| Nov 15 | 1 | Craven, Dunnill & Co Ltd | Shrop | Tile design |
| Nov 15 | 11 | F. & R. Pratt & Co | F | Marmalade pot |
| Nov 16 | 5 | J. Dimmock & Co | H | Printed design |
| Nov 23 | 2 | E. & C. Challinor | F | "Lorne" print |
| Nov 26 | 14 | T. & R. Boote | B | Printed design |
| Nov 27 | 9 | J. McIntyre & Co | B | Letter weight |
| Nov 29 | 14 | W. & E. Corn | B | Coffee pot |
| Dec 2 | 7 | Brown-Westhead, Moore & Co | Sh | Jug |
| Dec 3 | 9 | J. McIntyre & Co | B | Salt cellar |
| Dec 4 | 2 | W. Brownfield & Sons | C | Bowl, boat form |
| Dec 6 | 3 | Mintons | S | Printed design |
| Dec 7 | 2 | Anthony Shaw | B | Printed design |
| Dec 19 | 8 | Thomas Hughes | B | Printed design |
| Dec 27 | 13 | T. & R. Boote | B | Tile design |
| Dec 28 | 4 | J. Gaskell, Son & Co | B | Door knob |

**1879 (Y at right)**

| | | | | |
|---|---|---|---|---|
| Jan 7 | 7 | W. T. Copeland & Sons | S | Teapot |
| Jan 8 | 11 | Minton, Hollins & Co | S | Tile design |

| Jan 9 | 8 | W. Brownfield & Sons | C | Toiletwares |
|---|---|---|---|---|
| Jan 9 | 8 | W. Brownfield & Sons | C | Fish vase |
| Jan 14 | 5 | New Wharf Pottery & Co | B | Printed design |
| Jan 14 | 6 | Campbell Brick & Tile Co | S | Tile design |
| Jan 16 | 3 | B. & S. Hancock | S | Printed border |
| Jan 16 | 13 | F. & R. Pratt & Co | F | Jug |
| Jan 20 | 15 | Derby Crown Porcelain Co Ltd | D | Baskets – donkey |
| Jan 22 | 4 | Dunn, Bennett & Co | H | Jug |
| Jan 28 | 11 | W. T. Copeland & Sons | S | Printed design |
| Jan 29 | 2 | T. Furnival & Son | C | Jug |
| Jan 29 | 3 | T. Bevington | H | Basket – shell |
| Jan 29 | 15 | Edwin J. D. Bodley | B | Plate form |
| Feb 1 | 13 | Clementson Brothers | H | Jug |
| Feb 3 | 1 | J. Wedgwood & Sons | E | Jardinere |
| Feb 5 | 7 | Mintons | S | Figure ornaments |
| Feb 8 | 1 | Mintons | S | Pierced flower holder |
| Feb 10 | 5 | William Oppenheim* | Ln | Lamp base |
| Feb 14 | 4 | T. Furnival & Sons | C | Oval tureen |
| Feb 15 | 2 | Campbell Brick & Tile Co | S | Tile design |
| Feb 17 | 6 | D. McBirney | Bel | Flower vase |
| Feb 24 | 2 | W. P. Jervis | S | Tile design |
| Feb 24 | 3 | W. & T. Adams | T | Printed designs |
| Feb 25 | 4 | Mintons | S | Jug |
| Feb 28 | 1 | Elijah Chetwynd (modeller) | Sh | Oval tureen |
| Feb 28 | 7 | Clementson Brothers | H | Covered dish |
| Mar 1 | 1 | T. Furnival & Sons | C | Jug |
| Mar 4 | 4 | Grove & Stark | L | Jug |
| Mar 6 | 10 | Powell, Bishop & Stonier | H | Printed design |
| Mar 12 | 4 | Edge, Malkin & Co | B | Teapot |
| Mar 12 | 12 | W. T. Copeland & Sons | S | Printed design |
| Mar 13 | 1 | W. Davenport & Co | Lpt | Dinnerwares |
| Mar 13 | 1 | W. Davenport & Co | Lpt | Toiletwares |
| Mar 13 | 14 | Clementson Brothers | H | Jug |
| Mar 14 | 9 | Edward Clarke | Lpt | Oval tureen |
| Mar 17 | 2 | Powell, Bishop & Stonier | H | "Aster" print |
| Mar 18 | 1 | J. Wedgwood & Sons | E | Jug |
| Mar 19 | 2 | John Hawthorne | C | Oval tureen |
| Mar 25 | 10 | E. Quinter & Co | Paris | Figure centrepieces |
| Mar 26 | 17 | Worcester Royal Porcelain Co Ltd | W | Candlestick |
| Mar 26 | 17 | Worcester Royal Porcelain Co Ltd | W | Teawares |
| Mar 27 | 9 | Candy & Co | De | Ornamental brick |
| Mar 28 | 6 | Clementson Brothers | H | Jug |
| Mar 29 | 4 | Beck, Blair & Co | L | Printed design |
| April 3 | 9 | Brown-Westhead, Moore & Co | Sh | Jug |
| April 4 | 12 | Pinder, Bourne & Co | B | Printed design |
| April 9 | 5 | H. Alcock & Co | C | Oval tureen |
| April 10 | 12 | Brown-Westhead, Moore & Co | Sh | Jug |
| April 12 | 1 | Worcester Royal Porcelain Co Ltd | W | Flower holder |
| April 15 | 6 | Brown-Westhead, Moore & Co | Sh | Toiletwares |
| April 22 | 2 | Linder & Co | Bir | Printed design |
| April 23 | 8 | Brown-Westhead, Moore & Co | Sh | Toiletwares |
| April 24 | 3 | J. Wedgwood & Sons | E | Printed designs |

| | | | | |
|---|---|---|---|---|
| May 2 | 5 | Ambrose Bevington | H | Printed design |
| May 5 | 1 | T. Furnival & Sons | C | Printed design |
| May 5 | 1 | T. Furnival & Sons | C | Tureen form |
| May 5 | 6 | Bates, Gildea & Walker | B | Jug form |
| May 6 | 7 | S. Bridgwood & Son | L | Jug forms |
| May 6 | 7 | S. Bridgwood & Son | L | Cup stand |
| May 7 | 11 | Worcester Royal Porcelain Co Ltd | W | Floral print |
| May 9 | 15 | Worcester Royal Porcelain Co Ltd | W | Jug |
| May 13 | 4 | Pinder, Bourne & Co | B | Jug |
| May 13 | 4 | Pinder, Bourne & Co | B | Toiletwares |
| May 13 | 8 | Clementson Brothers | H | Printed design |
| May 14 | 9 | Brown-Westhead, Moore & Co | Sh | Printed design |
| May 14 | 13 | Edwin J. D. Bodley | B | Vase |
| May 14 | 13 | Edwin J. D. Bodley | B | Cup form |
| May 19 | 1 | W. Brownfield & Sons | C | Bottle vase |
| May 19 | 1 | W. Brownfield & Sons | C | Centrepiece |
| May 21 | 5 | Harvey Adams & Co | L | Cup form |
| May 23 | 2 | Sampson Bridgwood & Son | L | Jug |
| May 23 | 2 | Sampson Bridgwood & Son | L | Covered box |
| May 23 | 14 | Harvey Adams & Co | L | Teawares |
| May 29 | 2 | J. Tams | L | "Stork" print |
| May 29 | 12 | Pinder, Bourne & Co | B | Jug |
| May 30 | 3 | D. McBirney & Co | Bel | Wash basin |
| May 30 | 10 | J. Dimmock & Co | H | Printed pattern |
| May 30 | 12 | Grove & Stark | L | Printed bird pattern |
| May 31 | 4 | Minton, Hollins & Co | S | Tile design |
| Jun 10 | 4 | T. Furnival & Sons | C | Printed design |
| Jun 11 | 8 | T. Till & Sons | B | Jug |
| Jun 13 | 13 | Brown-Westhead, Moore & Co | Sh | Jug |
| Jun 18 | 4 | Grove & Stark | L | Jug |
| Jun 24 | 11 | J. Wedgwood & Sons | E | Oval tureen |
| Jun 25 | 1 | Clementson Brothers | H | Cup form |
| Jun 26 | 13 | Haviland & Co | Fr | Fluted stand |
| Jun 26 | 13 | Haviland & Co | Fr | Dish forms |
| Jun 27 | 11 | Shorter & Boulton | S | Jug |
| Jun 30 | 12 | Birks, Brothers & Seddon | C | Toiletwares |
| Jun 30 | 12 | Birks, Brothers & Seddon | C | Teapot |
| July 2 | 2 | J. Wedgwood & Sons | E | Printed design |
| July 7 | 2 | James F. Wileman | F | Printed design |
| July 8 | 1 | Mintons | S | Jardinere |
| July 8 | 16 | Brown-Westhead, Moore & Co | Sh | Printed design |
| July 9 | 12 | Brown-Westhead, Moore & Co | Sh | Jug |
| July 10 | 2 | T. Bevington | H | Shell basket |
| July 10 | 3 | Moore Brothers | L | Floral vase |
| July 16 | 4 | Ambrose Bevington & Co | H | Printed design |
| July 16 | 14 | Brown-Westhead, Moore & Co | Sh | Printed jug design |
| July 18 | 18 | Stuart & Smith | Sd | Floral design |
| July 25 | 4 | Mintons | S | Sauce tureen |
| July 26 | 6 | Minton, Hollins & Co | S | Tile design |
| July 28 | 6 | G. G. MacWilliams★ | Ln | Washbasin |
| July 31 | 2 | Mintons | S | Ornate vase |
| Aug 2 | 2 | H. M. Williamson & Sons | L | Printed design |

| Aug 5 | 12 | J. Mortlock & Co★ | Ln | Centrepieces |
|---|---|---|---|---|
| Aug 6 | 6 | Wardle & Co | H | Jardinere |
| Aug 13 | 2 | Grove & Stark | L | Bullfinch print |
| Aug 22 | 4 | D. McBirney | Bel | Printed border |
| Aug 27 | 13 | Bates, Gildea & Walker | B | Printed design |
| Sept 4 | 6 | Brown-Westhead, Moore & Co | Sh | Printed design |
| Sept 10 | 13 | Brown-Westhead, Moore & Co | Sh | Printed design |
| Sept 17 | 4 | W. Brownfield & Sons | C | Tureen forms |
| Sept 26 | 4 | Brown-Westhead, Moore & Co | Sh | Printed design |
| Sept 26 | 4 | J. T. Hudden | L | Printed design |
| Sept 29 | 3 | Edge, Malkin & Co | B | Jug |
| Sept 29 | 12 | W. T. Copeland & Sons | S | Dish |
| Oct 9 | 6 | Bates, Gildea & Walker | B | Jug |
| Oct 10 | 2 | Brown-Westhead, Moore & Co | Sh | Plate form |
| Oct 11 | 5 | Edwin J. D. Bodley | B | Teawares, bamboo |
| Oct 15 | 1 | Mintons | S | Jug |
| Oct 16 | 5 | Joseph Roth★ | Ln | Printed design |
| Oct 16 | 16 | Minton, Hollins & Co | S | Tile design |
| Oct 17 | 2 | G. L. Ashworth & Bros | H | Tureen form |
| Oct 18 | 3 | J. Wedgwood & Sons | E | Strawberry dish |
| Oct 23 | 12 | Pillivuyt & Co | Fr | Oval dish |
| Oct 24 | 4 | Campbell Brick & Tile Co | S | Tile designs |
| Oct 27 | 9 | Edward F. Bodley & Co | B | Jug |
| Oct 29 | 5 | Mintons | S | Printed design |
| Oct 29 | 7 | Clementson Brothers | H | Moulded edge |
| Oct 29 | 15 | F. D. Bradley | L | Figures box |
| Oct 30 | 4 | Mintons | S | Printed design |
| Oct 31 | 8 | G. A. Stubbs | Ln | Tiles |
| Nov 3 | 12 | Minton, Hollins & Co | S | Tile design |
| Nov 3 | 14 | Tundley, Rhodes & Procter | B | Printed design |
| Nov 6 | 2 | J. Wedgwood & Sons | E | Covered dish |
| Nov 6 | 3 | Moore Brothers | L | Cupid flower bowls |
| Nov 6 | 4 | Wilcox & Co | Lds | Pressed tiles |
| Nov 12 | 11 | Worcester Royal Porcelain Co Ltd | W | Coffee pot |
| Nov 15 | 12 | Charles Ford | H | Printed floral design |
| Nov 15 | 16 | W. T. Copeland & Sons | S | Tureen forms |
| Nov 15 | 16 | W. T. Copeland & Sons | S | Fluted dinnerwares |
| Nov 17 | 2 | Powell, Bishop & Stonier | H | Oval tureen |
| Nov 19 | 5 | Powell, Bishop & Stonier | H | Oval tureen |
| Nov 20 | 4 | Elsmore & Son | T | Printed designs |
| Nov 21 | 6 | Mintons | S | Jug |
| Nov 21 | 14 | Soane & Smith★ | Ln | Dahlia bowl |
| Nov 22 | 7 | Worcester Royal Porcelain Co Ltd | W | Shell wall pocket |
| Nov 28 | 5 | W. Brownfield & Sons | C | Menu tablet |
| Nov 28 | 6 | Ambrose Bevington | H | Printed floral design |
| Nov 29 | 3 | Mintons | S | Oyster plate |
| Nov 29 | 4 | Brown-Westhead, Moore & Co | Sh | Printed border |
| Dec 1 | 2 | J. Holdcroft | L | Teapot |
| Dec 2 | 4 | Brown-Westhead, Moore & Co | Sh | Tureen |
| Dec 2 | 4 | Brown-Westhead, Moore & Co | Sh | Plate form |
| Dec 2 | 5 | Elsmore & Son | T | Printed design |
| Dec 2 | 17 | J. Aynsley & Sons | L | Comport |

| Dec 6 | 2 | T. & R. Boote | B | Printed designs |
|---|---|---|---|---|
| Dec 10 | 9 | Clementson Brothers | H | Oval tureen |
| Dec 11 | 4 | Moore Brothers | L | Floral bowls |
| Dec 11 | 4 | Moore Brothers | L | Centrepiece |
| Dec 17 | 11 | Ridgways | S | Tureen form |
| Dec 19 | 1 | Clementson Brothers | H | Cup form |
| Dec 20 | 5 | J. Wedgwood & Sons | E | Covered box |
| Dec 22 | 2 | Mintons | S | Leaf dish |
| Dec 24 | 2 | Sherwin & Cotton | H | Tile design |

## 1880 (J at right)

| Jan 3 | 1 | Sherwin & Cotton | H | Tile design |
|---|---|---|---|---|
| Jan 7 | 3 | T. Bevington | H | Floral bowls |
| Jan 7 | 4 | T. & R. Boote | B | Printed design |
| Jan 7 | 5 | Soane & Smith★ | Ln | Toiletwares |
| Jan 7 | 8 | Minton, Hollins & Co | S | Tile design |
| Jan 8 | 9 | Old Hall Earthenware Co Ltd | H | Dinnerwares |
| Jan 9 | 3 | Sherwin & Cotton | H | Tile design |
| Jan 9 | 12 | T. George Allen | Ln | "London" print |
| Jan 13 | 1 | Brown-Westhead, Moore & Co | Sh | Printed design |
| Jan 14 | 11 | Worcester Royal Porcelain Co Ltd | W | Printed designs |
| Jan 16 | 8 | S. Fielding & Co | S | Jug – shell |
| Jan 16 | 14 | Brockwell & Son★ | Ln | Salad bowl |
| Jan 21 | 7 | Pinder, Bourne & Co | B | Printed design |
| Jan 21 | 7 | Pinder, Bourne & Co | B | Dish & jug |
| Jan 22 | 2 | Mintons | S | Plate form |
| Jan 22 | 8 | Minton, Hollins & Co | S | Tile designs |
| Jan 26 | 11 | W. Brownfield & Sons | C | Teapot |
| Jan 27 | 13 | Wardle & Co | H | Jug |
| Jan 28 | 3 | Brown-Westhead, Moore & Co | Sh | Jug |
| Jan 28 | 4 | J. Aynsley & Sons | L | Tray form |
| Jan 28 | 12 | Powell, Bishop & Stonier | H | "Hong Kong" print |
| Jan 29 | 9 | Edwin J. D. Bodley | B | Covered boxes |
| Jan 30 | 2 | Taylor, Tunnicliffe & Co | H | Tablet |
| Feb 3 | 11 | Powell, Bishop & Stonier | H | Spoon warmer |
| Feb 9 | 14 | Albert Meisel★ | NY | Oyster plate |
| Feb 9 | 18 | Whittingham, Ford & Riley | B | Printed figure design |
| Feb 10 | 4 | Mintons | S | Printed design |
| Feb 10 | 4 | Mintons | S | Tureen form |
| Feb 10 | 4 | Mintons | S | Tile design |
| Feb 11 | 10 | T. Bevington | H | Basket – child |
| Feb 12 | 4 | W.A. Adderley | L | Printed design |
| Feb 12 | 7 | W. Brownfield & Sons | C | Teawares |
| Feb 14 | 14 | Bates, Gildea & Walker | B | Jug |
| Feb 18 | 12 | Derby Crown Porcelain Co Ltd | D | Printed design |
| Feb 24 | 2 | Mintons | S | Cigar stand |
| Feb 24 | 11 | W. Harrop & Co | H | Printed design |
| Feb 25 | 18 | Clementson Brothers | H | Tureen |
| Feb 25 | 23 | Sherwin & Cotton | H | Tile design |
| Feb 26 | 6 | Minton, Hollins & Co | S | Tile designs |
| Feb 27 | 7 | Moore Brothers | L | Vase |
| Feb 27 | 7 | Moore Brothers | L | Figure vases |

| Mar 2 | 6 | J. Holdcroft | L | Shell bowl |
|---|---|---|---|---|
| Mar 4 | 8 | Soane & Smith★ | Ln | Fancy bowls |
| Mar 8 | 4 | T. Furnival & Sons | C | Floral print |
| Mar 8 | 10 | W. Harrop & Co | H | Jug |
| Mar 10 | 15 | E. Quinter & Co★ | Paris | Bowl – cupids |
| Mar 12 | 4 | W .A. Adderley | L | Jug |
| Mar 16 | 3 | J. F. Wileman & Co | F | Printed design |
| Mar 16 | 11 | Sherwin & Cotton | H | Tile design |
| Mar 16 | 12 | J. Macintyre & Co | B | Egg cup |
| Mar 16 | 12 | J. Macintyre & Co | B | Ash tray |
| Mar 17 | 6 | J. Wedgwood & Sons | E | Garden pot |
| Mar 18 | 3 | Moore Brothers | L | Floral bowls |
| Mar 18 | 3 | Moore Brothers | L | Centrepieces, figures |
| Mar 22 | 4 | Powell, Bishop & Stonier | H | Tureen |
| Mar 23 | 4 | Taylor, Tunnicliffe & Co | H | Menu slate |
| Mar 25 | 6 | Mintons | S | Butterfly box |
| Mar 30 | 4 | Sherwin & Cotton | H | Tile design |
| Mar 31 | 3 | T. Peake | T | Edging tile |
| April 12 | 6 | Bates, Gildea & Walker | B | Printed designs |
| April 15 | 11 | Ridgways | Sh | Printed design |
| April 19 | 11 | Worcester Royal Porcelain Co Ltd | W | Teawares |
| April 19 | 11 | Worcester Royal Porcelain Co Ltd | W | Jug |
| April 22 | 4 | Sherwin & Cotton | H | Tile designs |
| April 22 | 5 | W. H. Grindley & Co | T | Jug & decoration |
| April 26 | 1 | T. Furnival & Sons | C | Printed design |
| April 27 | 11 | Moore Brothers | L | Lily basket |
| April 27 | 11 | Moore Brothers | L | Double vase |
| April 27 | 11 | Moore Brothers | L | Figure centrepiece |
| April 27 | 13 | Worcester Royal Porcelain Co Ltd | W | Figure candle-snuffers |
| April 29 | 4 | Mintons | S | Menu card |
| April 29 | 4 | Mintons | S | Divisional dish |
| April 30 | 6 | T. Furnival & Sons | C | Jug |
| May 3 | 3 | W. Brownfield & Sons | C | Dessertwares |
| May 3 | 3 | W. Brownfield & Sons | C | Menu card |
| May 5 | 11 | E. Quinter★ | Paris | Figure ornaments |
| May 5 | 13 | S. Fielding & Co | S | Jug |
| May 10 | 6 | Powell, Bishop & Stonier | H | Printed design – roses |
| May 11 | 15 | Soane & Smith★ | Ln | Fish strainer |
| May 12 | 3 | G. Skey & Co Ltd | Tam | Bear flower-holder |
| May 13 | 8 | Mintons | S | Dish forms |
| May 13 | 15 | Minton, Hollins & Co | S | Tile design |
| May 14 | 26 | Bates, Gildea & Walker | B | Bowl |
| May 25 | 4 | W. Brownfield & Sons | C | Jug |
| May 26 | 6 | Mintons | S | Strawberry dishes |
| Jun 1 | 4 | Mintons | S | Printed design |
| Jun 2 | 3 | Sherwin & Cotton | H | Tile design |
| Jun 7 | 6 | J. Dimmock & Co | H | Printed design |
| Jun 8 | 1 | G. Jones & Sons | S | Jug, fish design |
| Jun 10 | 3 | Sherwin & Cotton | H | Tile design |
| Jun 10 | 4 | Edwin J. D. Bodley | B | Jug |
| Jun 10 | 12 | J. Dimmock & Co | H | Oval tureen |
| Jun 11 | 3 | J. Wedgwood & Sons | E | Jug |

| Jun 14 | 12 | Joseph Roth★ | Ln | Floral encrustation |
|---|---|---|---|---|
| Jun 15 | 4 | Buckley, Wood & Co | B | Jug |
| Jun 16 | 3 | Wedgwood & Co | T | "Beatrice" print |
| Jun 17 | 4 | Samuel Lear | H | Jug |
| Jun 17 | 15 | Ridgways | H | Printed floral design |
| Jun 17 | 26 | J. Macintyre & Co | B | Menu slab |
| Jun 17 | 20 | Crystal Porcelain Co Ltd | H | Jug |
| Jun 17 | 21 | J. Dimmock & Co | H | Oval tureen |
| Jun 19 | 11 | J. Wedgwood & Sons | E | Butter dish |
| Jun 19 | 15 | Joseph Roth★ | Ln | Floral bowl |
| Jun 22 | 1 | W. H. Grindley & Co | T | Printed designs |
| Jun 26 | 13 | Worcester Royal Porcelain Co Ltd | W | Figure centrepieces |
| July 7 | 4 | Sherwin & Cotton | H | Tile design |
| July 7 | 5 | Mintons | S | Centrepiece |
| July 7 | 15 | F. J. Emery | B | Jug |
| July 12 | 4 | Mintons | S | Jug, ribbon motif |
| July 13 | 12 | Thomas Barlow | L | Covered box |
| July 15 | 3 | Dunn, Bennett & Co | H | Jug |
| July 15 | 4 | Grove & Stark | L | Printed design |
| July 16 | 9 | Sherwin & Cotton | H | Tile design |
| July 16 | 10 | Moore Brothers | L | Cupid flower bowl |
| July 16 | 19 | S. Fielding & Co | S | Teapot |
| July 23 | 9 | S. & H. Levi★ | Ln | Egg stand |
| July 28 | 2 | Brownhills Pottery Co | T | Printed design |
| July 31 | 8 | Old Hall Earthenware Co Ltd | H | Printed design |
| Aug 4 | 3 | Pinder, Bourne & Co | B | Printed design |
| Aug 11 | 14 | Clementson Brothers | H | Printed design |
| Aug 14 | 12 | W. Davenport & Co | Lpt | Toiletwares |
| Aug 14 | 12 | W. Davenport & Co | Lpt | Basket dish |
| Aug 17 | 6 | Sherwin & Cotton | H | Tile design |
| Aug 18 | 3 | J. Wedgwood & Sons | E | Jug, Longfellow |
| Aug 18 | 14 | Dean & Morris | H | Wine funnel |
| Aug 18 | 14 | Dean & Morris | H | Pie preserver |
| Aug 21 | 2 | Sherwin & Cotton | H | Tile design |
| Aug 21 | 10 | W. A. Adderley | L | Printed design |
| Aug 23 | 5 | Jackson & Gosling | F | Printed design |
| Aug 23 | 6 | Brown–Westhead, Moore & Co | Sh | Printed design |
| Aug 24 | 10 | Edwin J. D. Bodley | B | Teawares, bamboo |
| Sept 3 | 3 | Brown–Westhead, Moore & Co | Sh | Toilet jug |
| Sept 4 | 7 | J. Beech & Son | L | Teawares |
| Sept 11 | 3 | W. Brownfield & Sons | C | Vase forms |
| Sept 14 | 6 | Mintons | S | Printed design |
| Sept 15 | 6 | G. L. Ashworth & Bros | H | Teapot |
| Sept 15 | 12 | Minton, Hollins & Co | S | Tile design |
| Sept 23 | 3 | Ambrose Wood★ | H | Tile design |
| Sept 25 | 6 | Minton, Hollins & Co | S | Tile designs |
| Sept 25 | 13 | J. A. Briart & Co★ | Ln | Stoneware bottle |
| Sept 27 | 5 | John Marshall & Co | Sc | Printed designs |
| Sept 29 | 3 | Brownhills Pottery Co | T | Toiletwares |
| Sept 30 | 4 | Worcester Royal Porcelain Co Ltd | W | Jug |
| Oct 1 | 3 | Wade & Colclough | B | Teapot – Gladstone |
| Oct 6 | 4 | J. Wedgwood & Sons | E | Jug |

| Oct 12 | 4 | Mintons | S | Jardinere |
| Oct 13 | 5 | J. Wedgwood & Sons | E | Jug |
| Oct 20 | 10 | Burgess & Leigh | B | Jug – Roman |
| Oct 21 | 3 | Worcester Royal Porcelain Co Ltd | W | Flower vases |
| Oct 22 | 4 | Edward F. Bodley & Son | B | Teapot |
| Oct 22 | 12 | J. Aynsley & Sons | L | Jug |
| Oct 26 | 13 | Minton, Hollins & Co | S | Tile designs |
| Oct 27 | 5 | Taylor, Tunnicliffe & Co | H | Menu slab |
| Oct 27 | 20 | John Tams | L | Jug |
| Oct 27 | 21 | G. Woolliscroft & Son | E | Fireplace surround |
| Oct 28 | 2 | Sherwin & Cotton | H | Tile design |
| Oct 30 | 6 | Jones & Hopkinson | H | Jug |
| Nov 2 | 2 | W. H. Grindley & Co | T | Jug |
| Nov 4 | 4 | W. & T. Adams | T | Printed, crab, design |
| Nov 4 | 15 | Minton, Hollins & Co | S | Tile designs |
| Nov 9 | 4 | J. Wedgwood & Sons | E | Ink pot |
| Nov 10 | 2 | Wilcock & Co | Lds | Drain designs |
| Nov 10 | 13 | Bednall & Heath | H | Jug |
| Nov 18 | 3 | Samuel Radford | L | Printed leaf border |
| Nov 18 | 14 | Mintons | S | Bottle & decoration |
| Nov 19 | 15 | Crown Derby Porcelain Co Ltd | D | Printed design |
| Nov 24 | 4 | Grove & Stark | L | "Yeddo" print |
| Nov 24 | 5 | Bates, Gildea & Walker | B | "Kioto" print |
| Dec 6 | 2 | Powell, Bishop & Stonier | H | Printed design |
| Dec 7 | 10 | Pinder, Bourne & Co | H | Dinnerwares |
| Dec 7 | 10 | Pinder, Bourne & Co | H | Toiletwares |
| Dec 7 | 10 | Pinder, Bourne & Co | H | Printed design, fruit |
| Dec 8 | 5 | Wittman & Roth★ | Ln | Fancy flower holders |
| Dec 15 | 15 | W. Brownfield & Sons | C | Vase forms |
| Dec 15 | 15 | W. Brownfield & Sons | C | Jardinere |
| Dec 15 | 15 | W. Brownfield & Sons | C | Menu holder |
| Dec 18 | 2 | Bates, Gildea & Walker | B | Printed design |
| Dec 24 | 8 | Brown-Westhead, Moore & Co | Sh | Printed design, leaf |
| Dec 29 | 7 | Doulton & Co | Ln | Mug designs |
| Dec 29 | 7 | Doulton & Co | Ln | Sporting jug |
| Dec 29 | 7 | Doulton & Co | Ln | Covered jar |
| Dec 31 | 1 | Old Hall Earthenware Co Ltd | H | Floral print |
| Dec 31 | 4 | Sherwin & Cotton | H | Tile designs |

**1881 (E at right)**

| Jan 5 | 7 | Joseph Roth★ | Ln | Floral motifs |
| Jan 6 | 2 | B. & S. Hancock | S | Printed design |
| Jan 6 | 8 | F. D. Bradley | L | Flower bowl |
| Jan 7 | 13 | Sherwin & Cotton | H | Tile design |
| Jan 12 | 5 | Sherwin & Cotton | H | Tile design |
| Jan 14 | 1 | C. F. Boseck & Co★ | Ln | Printed designs |
| Jan 14 | 10 | Worcester Royal Porcelain Co Ltd | W | Floral print |
| Jan 14 | 18 | Edwin J. D. Bodley | B | Teawares |
| Jan 15 | 4 | Holmes, Stonier & Hollinshead | H | Printed designs |
| Jan 20 | 3 | Mintons | S | Two dimensional dish |
| Jan 21 | 11 | W. & T. Adams | T | Eagle device |
| Jan 26 | 4 | Minton, Hollins & Co | S | Tile design |

| Jan 27 | 15 | Worcester Royal Porcelain Co Ltd | W | Teapot |
|--------|----|----------------------------------|---|--------|
| Jan 28 | 3 | G. Woolliscroft & Son | H | Tile design |
| Feb 8 | 5 | Grove & Stark | L | Printed design |
| Feb 8 | 6 | W. Brownfield & Sons | C | Toiletwares |
| Feb 8 | 6 | W. Brownfield & Sons | C | Teapot forms |
| Feb 11 | 10 | F. J. Emery | B | Jug |
| Feb 15 | 6 | W. A. Adderley | L | Printed design |
| Feb 16 | 3 | F. D. Bradley | L | Rose bowl |
| Feb 17 | 2 | Murray & Co | G | Teapot |
| Feb 18 | 3 | Samuel Radford | L | Printed design |
| Feb 21 | 4 | Taylor, Waine & Bates | L | National emblems |
| Feb 24 | 8 | W. Harrop & Co | H | Vase |
| Feb 25 | 14 | J. MacIntyre & Co | B | Menu holder |
| Feb 28 | 9 | Edwin J. D. Bodley | B | Teawares |
| Mar 3 | 5 | J. Dimmock & Co | H | Jug, swan |
| Mar 7 | 11 | J. Aynsley & Sons | L | Printed borders |
| Mar 8 | 3 | Grove & Stark | L | Jug |
| Mar 10 | 12 | Martin Gray★ | Ln | Oval tureen |
| Mar 14 | 1 | Edwin J. D. Bodley | B | Teawares |
| Mar 17 | 9 | Shorter & Boulton | S | Jug |
| Mar 19 | 4 | Mintons | S | Tile design |
| Mar 19 | 4 | Mintons | S | Printed design |
| Mar 23 | 4 | Mintons | S | Boy ornament |
| Mar 24 | 2 | T. S. Pinder | B | Printed design |
| Mar 24 | 3 | W. A. Adderley | L | Jug |
| Mar 29 | 6 | T. A. Simpson | H | Tile design |
| Mar 31 | 2 | J. T. Hudden | L | Printed design |
| April 7 | 2 | Sherwin & Cotton | H | Tile design |
| April 7 | 9 | Old Hall Earthenware Co Ltd | H | Printed design |
| April 8 | 2 | W. Harrop & Co | H | "Pekin" print |
| April 8 | 3 | Wedgwood & Co | T | "Louise" print |
| April 8 | 14 | Worcester Royal Porcelain Co Ltd | W | Boy with basket |
| April 9 | 5 | R. H. Plant & Co | L | Jug |
| April 11 | 1 | A. Bevington & Co | H | Oval tureen |
| April 12 | 4 | Mintons | S | Dish forms |
| April 12 | 4 | Mintons | S | Plate shape |
| April 14 | 10 | Mintons | S | Printed design |
| April 16 | 17 | J. Marshall & Co | G | Floral print |
| April 19 | 3 | Sherwin & Cotton | H | Tile design |
| April 19 | 5 | T. & R. Boote | B | Tile design |
| April 21 | 4 | Sherwin & Cotton | H | Tile design |
| April 21 | 5 | Edwin J. D. Bodley | B | Teawares, floral |
| April 21 | 5 | Edwin J. D. Bodley | B | Marmalade pot |
| April 23 | 7 | J. F. Wileman | F | "Swallow" print |
| April 28 | 12 | W. T. Copeland & Sons | S | Printed design |
| April 30 | 3 | Trubshaw, Hand & Co | L | Printed design |
| April 30 | 4 | J. Wedgwood & Sons | E | Carlyle print |
| May 3 | 4 | William Wood & Co | B | Menu holder or tablet |
| May 3 | 5 | Sherwin & Cotton | H | Tile design |
| May 4 | 2 | Sherwin & Cotton | H | Tile design |
| May 4 | 3 | W. Brownfield & Sons | C | Plate form |
| May 4 | 3 | W. Brownfield & Sons | C | Teawares |

| May 4 | 3 | W. Brownfield & Sons | C | Jug |
|---|---|---|---|---|
| May 5 | 2 | W. & T. Adams | T | Printed design |
| May 6 | 4 | R. H. Plant & Co | L | Jug |
| May 11 | 3 | J. Tams | L | "Violet" fruit |
| May 13 | 2 | Mintons | S | Plate form |
| May 16 | 2 | J. Wedgwood & Sons | E | Beaconsfield jug |
| May 17 | 8 | S. & H. Levi★ | Ln | Vase forms |
| May 17 | 9 | J. Mortlock & Co★ | Ln | Tureen form |
| May 17 | 9 | J. Mortlock & Co★ | Ln | Plate form |
| May 20 | 11 | W. A. Adderley | L | Teapot |
| May 21 | 3 | Powell, Bishop & Stonier | H | Teawares |
| May 24 | 5 | G. L. Ashworth & Bros | H | Toiletwares |
| May 24 | 6 | Mintons | S | Tile designs |
| May 24 | 7 | F. J. Emery | B | Measure-jug |
| May 25 | 3 | Powell, Bishop & Stonier | H | Teawares |
| May 25 | 9 | Worcester Royal Porcelain Co Ltd | W | National figures |
| May 25 | 10 | J. Wedgwood & Sons | E | Umbrella stands |
| May 26 | 7 | G. Woolliscroft & Son | H | Tile design |
| May 30 | 1 | T. Furnival & Sons | C | Printed design |
| May 30 | 2 | Decorative Art Tile Co | H | Tile design |
| Jun 1 | 3 | Mintons | S | Tile design |
| Jun 1 | 13 | J. Mortlock & Co★ (manufactured by Doulton & Co) | Ln | Stoneware jug |
| Jun 3 | 4 | S. P. Ledward | L | Printed design |
| Jun 4 | 3 | T. Furnival & Sons | C | Printed border |
| Jun 4 | 4 | Decorative Art Tile Co | H | Tile design |
| Jun 7 | 3 | Edward F. Bodley & Sons | B | Spittoon |
| Jun 7 | 4 | Decorative Art Tile Co | H | Tile designs |
| Jun 7 | 17 | Worcester Royal Porcelain Co Ltd | W | National figures |
| Jun 8 | 6 | Crystal Porcelain Co Ltd | H | Tile design |
| Jun 13 | 1 | Samuel Lear | H | Teapot |
| Jun 13 | 4 | S. P. Ledward | L | Printed design |
| Jun 16 | 8 | S. Fielding & Co | S | Fan jug |
| Jun 16 | 8 | S. Fielding & Co | S | Fan plate |
| Jun 18 | 1 | Jackson & Gosling | F | Floral print |
| Jun 21 | 13 | Birks, Brothers & Seddon | C | Teawares |
| Jun 21 | 13 | Birks, Brothers & Seddon | C | Toiletwares |
| Jun 21 | 13 | Birks, Brothers & Seddon | C | Tureen form |
| Jun 21 | 20 | Gildea & Walker | B | Printed pattern |
| July 2 | 1 | D. McBirney & Co | Bel | Moulded plate |
| July 2 | 5 | T. Furnival & Sons | C | Printed design |
| July 6 | 7 | J. Wedgwood & Sons | E | Tureen form |
| July 9 | 10 | Wardle & Co | H | Toiletwares |
| July 14 | 6 | Brown-Westhead, Moore & Co | Sh | Toiletwares |
| July 16 | 3 | Trubshaw, Hand & Co | L | Teawares – grape |
| July 25 | 2 | John H. Davis | H | Printed border |
| July 28 | 3 | D. McBirney & Co | Bel | Shell border |
| July 28 | 4 | A. Wood★ | H | Tile design |
| July 28 | 14 | Ridgways | H | Fern print |
| July 29 | 2 | Sherwin & Cotton | H | Tile design |
| July 29 | 3 | Whittman & Roth★ | Ln | Owl lamp |
| July 30 | 3 | Sampson Bridgwood & Son | L | Comport |

| July 30 | 4 | Sherwin & Cotton | H | Tile design |
|---|---|---|---|---|
| July 30 | 5 | Mintons | S | Garden seat |
| July 30 | 15 | W. T. Copeland & Sons | S | Tureen form |
| Aug 2 | 1 | Edwin J. D. Bodley | B | Printed design |
| Aug 5 | 12 | Pinder, Bourne & Co | B | Chandelier |
| Aug 10 | 13 | Old Hall Earthenware Co Ltd | H | Jug |
| Aug 20 | 11 | Worcester Royal Porcelain Co Ltd | W | John Bull |
| Aug 23 | 3 | Grove & Stark | L | "Nankin" print |
| Aug 24 | 11 | T. & R. Boote | B | Fireplace surround |
| Aug 26 | 16 | W. B. Simpson & Sons | Ln | Tile designs |
| Aug 27 | 3 | Samuel Lear | H | Jug |
| Aug 27 | 9 | Gildea & Walker | B | Printed design |
| Aug 27 | 9 | Gildea & Walker | B | Jug |
| Aug 29 | 7 | W. & T. Adams | T | Printed mark |
| Aug 30 | 7 | R. M. Brundige★ | NY | Lamp base |
| Sept 2 | 4 | Dale, Page & Goodwin | L | Printed design |
| Sept 3 | 11 | T. A. Simpson | H | Tile design |
| Sept 6 | 1 | Derby Crown Porcelain Co Ltd | D | Printed design |
| Sept 7 | 10 | Adams & Sleigh | B | Floral print |
| Sept 9 | 11 | Worcester Royal Porcelain Co Ltd | W | Printed design |
| Sept 10 | 12 | Joseph Roth★ | Ln | Floral encrustation |
| Sept 16 | 10 | G. Jones & Sons | S | Tureen |
| Sept 22 | 9 | S. Bold & M. Michelson★ | H | President Garfield |
| Sept 23 | 21 | Minton, Hollins & Co | S | Tile designs |
| Sept 27 | 9 | Pinder, Bourne & Co | B | Printed design |
| Sept 28 | 4 | Edwin J. D. Bodley | B | Tureen |
| Sept 28 | 13 | Gildea & Walker | B | Tureen |
| Sept 29 | 3 | G. Jones & Sons | S | Printed ivy design |
| Sept 30 | 3 | Davenports Ltd | Lpt | Toiletwares |
| Sept 30 | 15 | Mintons | S | Garden seat |
| Sept 30 | 15 | Mintons | S | Oyster plate & dishes |
| Oct 4 | 6 | W. Brownfield & Sons | C | Jug |
| Oct 6 | 5 | T. & R. Boote | B | Teapot |
| Oct 6 | 7 | Campbell Brick & Tile Co | S | Tile design |
| Oct 7 | 27 | Mintons | S | Jug |
| Oct 13 | 3 | Adderley & Lawson | L | Printed design |
| Oct 13 | 5 | T. & R. Boote | B | Oval tureen |
| Oct 20 | 1 | F. J. Emery | B | Parnell print |
| Oct 20 | 2 | Robinson & Chapman | L | Printed border |
| Oct 22 | 1 | Mintons | S | Tureen |
| Oct 25 | 14 | W. B. Simpson | Ln | Tile designs |
| Oct 26 | 8 | Mintons | S | Printed design |
| Oct 26 | 16 | Brown-Westhead, Moore & Co | Sh | Cuff-links |
| Oct 27 | 1 | Robinson & Chapman | L | Printed border |
| Oct 29 | 3 | T. & R. Boote | B | Tile design |
| Oct 29 | 4 | W. Brownfield & Sons | C | Printed design U.S.A. |
| Oct 29 | 11 | Wardle & Co | H | Jug |
| Oct 29 | 14 | Minton, Hollins & Co | S | Tile design |
| Nov 2 | 1 | Brown-Westhead, Moore & Co | Sh | Jug forms |
| Nov 3 | 12 | Worcester Royal Porcelain Co Ltd | W | Floral print |
| Nov 4 | 24 | Worcester Royal Porcelain Co Ltd | W | Teawares |
| Nov 8 | 1 | T. & R. Boote | B | Tile design |

| Nov 9 | 6 | Grove & Stark | L | Toiletwares |
|---|---|---|---|---|
| Nov 9 | 7 | Edwin J. D. Bodley | B | Jugs |
| Nov 9 | 7 | Edwin J. D. Bodley | B | Floral cup |
| Nov 10 | 2 | Brough & Blackhurst | L | Printed design |
| Nov 14 | 10 | W. B. Simpson & Sons | Ln | Tile designs |
| Nov 19 | 3 | Sampson Bridgwood & Son | L | Plate form |
| Nov 19 | 12 | Worcester Royal Porcelain Co Ltd | W | Tureen |
| Nov 21 | 1 | John Bevington | H | Ewer – swan |
| Nov 22 | 9 | John Tams | L | Oval tureen |
| Nov 22 | 17 | Ambrose Wood★ | H | Tile design |
| Nov 23 | 13 | Shorter & Boulton | S | Jug |
| Nov 25 | 1 | Adams & Sleigh | B | Jug |
| Nov 25 | 15 | Joseph Roth★ | Ln | Sunflower motif |
| Nov 26 | 1 | W. G. MacWilliam★ | Ln | Condiment |
| Nov 26 | 1 | W. G. MacWilliam★ | Ln | Floral border |
| Nov 29 | 6 | James Hill★ | Ln | Door furniture |
| Nov 29 | 10 | Worcester Royal Porcelain Co Ltd | W | Acorn condiment |
| Dec 2 | 16 | Joseph Roth★ | Ln | Rose motif |
| Dec 5 | 11 | J. Rose & Co | Cpt | Teawares |
| Dec 8 | 9 | Adderley & Lawson | L | Floral print |
| Dec 9 | 2 | Edwin J. D. Bodley | B | Menu tablet |
| Dec 9 | 12 | J. Defries & Sons★ | Ln | Floral prints |
| Dec 10 | 7 | Brown-Westhead, Moore & Co | Sh | Plate form |
| Dec 12 | 12 | John Fell | L | Butter dish |
| Dec 16 | 3 | Mintons | S | Printed border |
| Dec 20 | 9 | Bednall & Heath | H | Jug |
| Dec 21 | 3 | Frederick Grosvenor | G | Teapot |
| Dec 21 | 9 | Worcester Royal Porcelain Co Ltd | W | Teapot |
| Dec 24 | 5 | James Broadhurst | F | Printed design |

## 1882 (L at right)

| Jan 3 | 6 | Holmes, Plant & Maydew | B | Printed design |
|---|---|---|---|---|
| Jan 4 | 2 | W. T. Copeland & Sons | S | Toiletwares |
| Jan 4 | 7 | Joseph Roth★ | Ln | Floral reliefs |
| Jan 4 | 9 | F. & R. Pratt & Co | F | Teapot |
| Jan 7 | 2 | W. H. Grindley & Co | T | Printed design |
| Jan 7 | 11 | Ridgways | H | "Chintz" print |
| Jan 10 | 5 | Samuel Lear | H | Jug |
| Jan 11 | 1 | Minton, Hollins & Co | S | Tile designs |
| Jan 13 | 4 | Decorative Art Tile Co | H | Tile designs |
| Jan 18 | 10 | Robinson & Son | L | Printed design |
| Jan 24 | 1 | W. H. Micklethwaite & Co | Y | Printed design |
| Jan 26 | 5 | J. T. Hudden | L | Printed design |
| Jan 26 | 16 | S. Fielding & Co | S | Printed design |
| Jan 27 | 8 | Craven Dunnill & Co Ltd | J | Tile form |
| Jan 30 | 2 | Hollinshead & Kirkham | T | Printed design |
| Jan 30 | 3 | Grove & Stark | L | "Cora" print |
| Feb 1 | 1 | Edge, Malkin & Co | B | Jug |
| Feb 3 | 4 | Brown-Westhead, Moore & Co | Sh | Tureen forms |
| Feb 4 | 10 | Minton, Hollins & Co | S | Tile design |
| Feb 6 | 4 | Campbell Tile Co | S | Tile designs |
| Feb 7 | 2 | William Mills | H | Jug |

| Feb 8 | 7 | Wardle & Co | H | Jug |
|---|---|---|---|---|
| Feb 15 | 4 | Grove & Stark | L | Blossom print |
| Feb 16 | 6 | Mintons | S | Tile designs |
| Feb 18 | 5 | J. F. Wileman & Co | F | Bird print |
| Feb 20 | 6 | W. B. Simpson & Sons | Ln | Tile design |
| Feb 23 | 17 | Minton, Hollins & Co | S | Tile designs |
| Feb 24 | 3 | Taylor, Tunnicliffe & Co | H | Floral print |
| Mar 1 | 11 | Worcester Royal Porcelain Co Ltd | W | Printed border |
| Mar 1 | 12 | Minton Hollins & Co | S | Tile design |
| Mar 7 | 7 | Minton Hollins & Co | S | Tile designs |
| Mar 13 | 3 | J. T. Hudden | L | Floral print |
| Mar 15 | 3 | Powell, Bishop & Stonier | H | Jug |
| Mar 15 | 4 | Murray & Co | G | Teapot |
| Mar 20 | 5 | W. A. Adderley | L | Jug |
| Mar 23 | 2 | W. & T. Adams | T | Mark device |
| Mar 23 | 15 | T. A. Simpson | H | Teapot |
| Mar 27 | 3 | D. Chapman | L | Printed swan design |
| Mar 27 | 10 | Shorter & Boulton | S | Jug |
| Mar 28 | 12 | Ambrose Wood★ | H | Tile design |
| Mar 28 | 16 | A. Bevington & Co | H | Printed designs |
| Mar 28 | 16 | A. Bevington & Co | H | Cheese dish |
| Mar 29 | 9 | Oetzmann & Co★ | Ln | Printed design |
| Mar 30 | 13 | J. Rose & Co | Cpt | Floral dish form |
| Mar 30 | 17 | S. Fielding & Co | S | Jug |
| Mar 31 | 3 | A. Bevington & Co | H | Floral print |
| April 4 | 2 | W. Brownfield & Sons | C | Jug |
| April 4 | 2 | W. Brownfield & Sons | C | Basket flower holder |
| April 11 | 6 | G. Jones & Sons | S | Strawberry dish |
| April 11 | 7 | Minton, Hollins & Co | S | Tile designs |
| April 14 | 14 | Oetzmann & Co★ | Ln | Floral print |
| April 21 | 7 | Sampson Bridgwood & Son | L | Coffee pot |
| April 27 | 14 | New Wharf Pottery Co | B | Print for Greece |
| May 2 | 5 | G. L. Ashworth & Bros | H | Toiletwares |
| May 3 | 1 | Samuel Radford | L | Floral print |
| May 5 | 2 | Wood, Hines & Winkle | H | Jug |
| May 6 | 5 | Powell, Bishop & Stonier | H | London print |
| May 6 | 6 | Whittaker, Edge & Co | H | Jug forms |
| May 8 | 18 | Davenports Ltd | Lpt | Toiletwares |
| May 8 | 18 | Davenports Ltd | Lpt | Tureen |
| May 9 | 3 | Henry Alcock & Co | C | Tureen forms |
| May 9 | 4 | Whittaker, Edge & Co | H | Printed border |
| May 9 | 7 | W. Brownfield & Sons | C | Cup form |
| May 9 | 11 | Minton, Hollins & Co | S | Tile design |
| May 10 | 4 | John Edwards | F | Tureen |
| May 10 | 4 | John Edwards | F | Jug |
| May 10 | 14 | S. Fielding & Co | S | Jug |
| May 13 | 6 | G. Jones & Sons | S | Dish |
| May 17 | 2 | Edwin J. Bodley | B | Printed designs |
| May 24 | 4 | Minton, Hollins & Co | S | Tile design |
| May 24 | 21 | Doulton & Co | B | Coffee pot |
| May 25 | 11 | W. A. Adderley | L | Printed design |
| May 27 | 3 | Samuel Lear | H | Teapot |

| May 30 | 5 | W .H. Grindley & Co | T | Printed design |
|---|---|---|---|---|
| Jun 5 | 6 | Mintons | S | Tile design |
| Jun 5 | 7 | Wood, Hines & Winkle | H | Printed design |
| Jun 9 | 3 | Hall & Read | B | Teapot |
| Jun 9 | 4 | W. A. Adderley | L | Toiletwares |
| Jun 13 | 11 | A. Shaw & Son | B | Shakespeare print |
| Jun 13 | 14 | Wardle & Co | H | Jug forms |
| Jun 17 | 3 | A. Boyd & Son★ | Ln | Tile design |
| Jun 21 | 4 | William Lowe | L | Printed design |
| Jun 21 | 5 | Sampson Bridgwood & Son | L | Teawares |
| Jun 21 | 11 | Old Hall Earthenware Co Ltd | H | Brighton print |
| Jun 23 | 1 | J. Wedgwood & Sons | E | Tureen |
| Jun 23 | 1 | J. Wedgwood & Sons | E | Jug |
| Jun 23 | 5 | Burgess & Leigh | B | Printed design |
| Jun 28 | 2 | Derby Crown Porcelain Co Ltd | D | Printed design |
| Jun 29 | 11 | J. Defries & Sons★ | Ln | Teawares |
| July 1 | 8 | Taylor, Tunnicliffe & Co | H | Menu tablet |
| July 3 | 2 | Mintons | S | Tile design |
| July 3 | 3 | Edwin J. D. Bodley | B | Printed design |
| July 4 | 3 | Wright & Rigby | H | Jug |
| July 6 | 4 | W. Brownfield & Sons | C | Floral print |
| July 6 | 4 | W. Brownfield & Sons | C | Printed border |
| July 14 | 3 | G. Jones & Sons | S | Ornaments |
| July 14 | 10 | Wardle & Co | H | Teapot |
| July 14 | 10 | Wardle & Co | H | Jug |
| July 14 | 14 | Beech & Tellwright | C | Figure box |
| July 17 | 8 | Wood & Son | B | Tureen |
| July 18 | 13 | Shuffrey & Co★ | Ln | Tile design |
| July 19 | 7 | Wardle & Co | L | Floral jug |
| July 20 | 1 | John Edwards | F | Coffee pot & jug |
| July 20 | 1 | John Edwards | F | Tureen |
| July 22 | 8 | G. Jones & Son | S | Jug |
| July 25 | 3 | Frederick Grosvenor | G | Bird fountain |
| July 25 | 9 | Brownhills Pottery Co Ltd | T | "Hizen" print |
| July 25 | 9 | Brownhills Pottery Co Ltd | T | Water set |
| July 25 | 9 | Brownhills Pottery Co Ltd | T | Jug |
| July 26 | 4 | Adderley & Lawson | L | Floral print |
| July 28 | 3 | Hawley & Co | F | Teapot |
| July 31 | 2 | Sampson Bridgwood & Son | L | Teawares |
| July 31 | 9 | Mintons | S | Jardineres |
| Aug 5 | 4 | W. Brownfield & Sons | C | Dish – fish |
| Aug 5 | 4 | W. Brownfield & Sons | C | Printed design |
| Aug 10 | 5 | Wright & Rigby | H | Teapot Gen. Booth |
| Aug 11 | 10 | Oetzmann & Co★ | Ln | Printed designs |
| Aug 21 | 2 | John Tams | L | "Rangoon" print |
| Aug 21 | 8 | Adams & Bromley | H | Jug |
| Aug 25 | 2 | Mintons | S | Figure lamp base |
| Aug 26 | 4 | W. Wood & Co | B | Teapot |
| Aug 28 | 2 | Belfield & Co | Sc | Fluted jardinere |
| Aug 28 | 9 | Mintons | S | Toiletwares |
| Aug 29 | 12 | W. Brownfield & Sons | C | Flower tray |
| Aug 29 | 14 | Shuffrey & Co★ | Ln | Vase |

| Aug 30 | 14 | Worcester Royal Porcelain Co Ltd | W | Dish |
|--------|----|----|----|----|
| Aug 31 | 3 | A. Bevington & Co | H | Jug |
| Sept 6 | 2 | Hawley & Co | F | Jug |
| Sept 8 | 5 | Mintons | S | Tile design |
| Sept 8 | 5 | Mintons | S | Toiletwares |
| Sept 9 | 3 | Taylor, Tunnicliffe & Co | H | Lamp base |
| Sept 11 | 4 | Adams & Bromley | H | Jug |
| Sept 16 | 2 | Hulme & Massey | L | Printed designs |
| Sept 19 | 2 | W. H. Grindley & Co | T | Printed design |
| Sept 28 | 4 | Brown-Westhead, Moore & Co | Sh | Printed designs |
| Sept 28 | 22 | Bridgett & Bates | L | Leafage print |
| Sept 29 | 2 | Brownhills Pottery Co | T | Printed designs |
| Oct 6 | 2 | Mintons | S | Tile designs |
| Oct 9 | 3 | W. T. Copeland & Sons | S | Jug |
| Oct 9 | 4 | Dean, Capper & Dean | H | Teapot |
| Oct 11 | 3 | Sampson Bridgwood & Son | L | Toiletwares |
| Oct 11 | 4 | Wood & Son | B | Printed design |
| Oct 12 | 17 | T. Furnival & Sons | C | Jug |
| Oct 16 | 4 | Wood & Son | B | Floral print |
| Oct 19 | 4 | Lowe, Ratcliffe & Co | L | Printed design |
| Oct 31 | 2 | William Lowe | L | Beehive print |
| Nov 1 | 14 | Stonier, Hollinshead & Oliver | H | Jug |
| Nov 1 | 14 | Stonier, Hollinshead & Oliver | H | Savoy print |
| Nov 4 | 19 | Worcester Royal Porcelain Co Ltd | W | Printed design |
| Nov 8 | 2 | Mintons | S | Printed design |
| Nov 10 | 10 | Ridgways | H | Jasper jug |
| Nov 10 | 12 | Pratt & Simpson | F | Jug |
| Nov 10 | 12 | Pratt & Simpson | F | Printed designs |
| Nov 11 | 2 | Powell, Bishop & Stonier | H | Floral print |
| Nov 13 | 1 | Edge, Malkin & Co | B | Jug |
| Nov 13 | 2 | Sampson Bridgwood & Son | L | Printed design |
| Nov 14 | 3 | Edward Steel | H | Falstaff jug |
| Nov 14 | 3 | Edward Steel | H | Frog jug |
| Nov 15 | 7 | S. Fielding & Co | S | Jugs |
| Nov 16 | 3 | Taylor, Tunnicliffe & Co | H | Menu stand |
| Nov 21 | 4 | Joseph Holdcroft | L | Jug |
| Nov 21 | 8 | Gildea & Walker | B | Printed design |
| Nov 22 | 11 | S. Fielding & Co | S | Floral print |
| Nov 24 | 19 | Minton, Hollins & Co | S | Tile design |
| Nov 27 | 3 | Henry Alcock & Co | C | Jug |
| Nov 27 | 4 | Derby Crown Porcelain Co Ltd | D | Printed design |
| Nov 27 | 5 | James F. Wileman & Co | F | Blossom print |
| Dec 2 | 8 | Minton, Hollins & Co | S | Tile design |
| Dec 4 | 7 | A. Bevington & Co | H | Leafage print |
| Dec 6 | 2 | Brown-Westhead, Moore & Co | Sh | Tureen |
| Dec 6 | 2 | Brown-Westhead, Moore & Co | Sh | Octagonal plate |
| Dec 6 | 11 | G. Jackson & Son* | Ln | Relief plaques |
| Dec 9 | 5 | W. H. Micklethwaite & Co | Y | Tile design |
| Dec 13 | 4 | Mintons | S | Tile designs |
| Dec 13 | 4 | Mintons | S | Jug |
| Dec 13 | 5 | J. Wedgwood & Sons | E | Jug |
| Dec 14 | 6 | Samuel Lear | H | Jug |

| Dec 15 | 3 | Old Hall Earthenware Co Ltd | H | "Farm" print |
|---|---|---|---|---|
| Dec 18 | 9 | John Lockett & Co | L | Toilet pan |
| Dec 19 | 3 | Henry Kennedy | G | Figure print |
| Dec 21 | 4 | Edwin J. D. Bodley | B | Jug, tusk |
| Dec 21 | 5 | Wood, Hines & Winkle | H | Toast rack |
| Dec 22 | 2 | Grove & Stark | L | "Rubus" jug |
| Dec 22 | 14 | L. Hutschenreuther | Ger | Printed design |
| Dec 23 | 4 | James F. Wileman | F | Floral print |
| Dec 23 | 12 | New Wharf Pottery Co | B | Printed border |
| Dec 23 | 14 | Worcester Royal Porcelain Co Ltd | W | Figure group |
| Dec 23 | 14 | Worcester Royal Porcelain Co Ltd | W | Single figures |
| Dec 27 | 1 | New Wharf Pottery Co | B | Jug |

### 1883 (K at right)

| Jan 2 | 2 | Derby Crown Porcelain Co Ltd | D | Printed border |
|---|---|---|---|---|
| Jan 3 | 1 | William Hines | L | Printed design |
| Jan 3 | 14 | T. Furnival & Sons | C | Tureen |
| Jan 3 | 18 | J. Rose & Co | Cpt | Fluted teawares |
| Jan 4 | 5 | Brown-Westhead, Moore & Co | Sh | Printed design |
| Jan 8 | 5 | W. T. Copeland & Sons | S | Tureen |
| Jan 8 | 12 | Worcester Royal Porcelain Co Ltd | W | Flower holder |
| Jan 9 | 3 | Powell, Bishop & Stonier | H | Toiletwares |
| Jan 9 | 4 | Edward F. Bodley & Son | L | Printed design |
| Jan 9 | 5 | Hall & Read | H | "Tokio" print |
| Jan 9 | 5 | Hall & Read | H | Tureen forms |
| Jan 9 | 11 | Davenports Ltd | Lpt | Tureen form |
| Jan 10 | 17 | Gildea & Walker | B | Printed design |
| Jan 12 | 3 | Holmes, Plant & Madew | B | Printed design |
| Jan 13 | 6 | Moore & Co | L | Printed design |
| Jan 13 | 17 | T. & R. Boote | B | No entry |
| Jan 16 | 1 | Blair & Co | L | Printed design |
| Jan 17 | 3 | W. H. Grindley & Co | T | Printed design |
| Jan 17 | 11 | Alfred Clark* | Ln | Jug |
| Jan 22 | 1 | W. H. Micklethwaite & Co | Y | Tile design |
| Jan 23 | 8 | Edward F. Bodley & Son | L | Tureen |
| Jan 23 | 10 | W. T. Copeland & Sons | S | Toiletwares |
| Jan 24 | 1 | Sampson Bridgwood & Son | L | Tureen |
| Jan 24 | 2 | W. Brownfield & Sons | C | Tureen |
| Jan 25 | 3 | Brownhills Pottery Co | T | Trinket set |
| Jan 26 | 8 | William Lowe | L | Printed design |
| Jan 27 | 8 | G. W. Turner & Sons | T | Tureen |
| Jan 29 | 6 | W. Brownfield & Sons | C | Umbrella stand, bear |
| Jan 29 | 7 | W. H. Grindley & Co | T | Printed design |
| Jan 29 | 7 | W. H. Grindley & Co | T | Tureen |
| Jan 30 | 1 | Edward F. Bodley & Son | L | Tureen |
| Jan 30 | 12 | Wedgwood & Co | T | Printed design |
| Jan 31 | 14 | Minton Hollins & Co | S | Tile design |
| Feb 1 | 3 | Sampson Bridgwood & Son | L | Tureen |
| Feb 1 | 17 | Edwin J. D. Bodley | B | Cup form |
| Feb 2 | 4 | S. Hancock | S | Printed design |
| Feb 2 | 17 | Wedgwood & Co | T | Tureen |
| Feb 3 | 3 | Mintons | S | Tile design |

| Feb 5 | 2 | Joseph Holdcroft | L | Teapot |
|---|---|---|---|---|
| Feb 6 | 1 | Wood, Hines & Winkle | H | Toilet jug |
| Feb 7 | 4 | Hawley & Co | F | Jug |
| Feb 7 | 5 | Mountford & Thomas | H | Jug |
| Feb 9 | 9 | Edwin J. D. Bodley | B | Oyster plate |
| Feb 12 | 3 | Dunn, Bennett & Co | H | "Marlborough" print |
| Feb 13 | 11 | Baw & Dotter | Fr | Oval tureen |
| Feb 14 | 3 | W. H. Grindley & Co | T | Printed design |
| Feb 15 | 5 | J. H. Davis | H | "Chatsworth" print |
| Feb 16 | 11 | G. Jackson & Sons★ | Ln | Figure plaques |
| Feb 17 | 13 | G. W. Turner & Sons | T | Jug |
| Feb 17 | 13 | G. W. Turner & Sons | T | Printed design |
| Feb 19 | 1 | W. A. Adderley | L | Coffee pot |
| Feb 20 | 13 | Davenports Ltd | Lpt | Printed design |
| Feb 20 | 14 | G. Siebdrat★ | Ln | Toast rack, condiment |
| Feb 20 | 17 | Gildea & Walker | B | Printed design |
| Feb 21 | 3 | G. Jones & Sons | S | Leaf dish |
| Feb 22 | 6 | Hall & Read | H | Printed design |
| Feb 22 | 6 | Hall & Read | H | Tureen forms |
| Feb 22 | 6 | Hall & Read | H | Jug |
| Feb 22 | 20 | Worcester Royal Porcelain Co Ltd | W | Welled dish |
| Feb 22 | 21 | Old Hall Earthenware Co Ltd | H | Tureen |
| Feb 24 | 12 | J. Wedgwood & Sons | E | Toiletwares |
| Feb 24 | 13 | Worcester Royal Porcelain Co Ltd | W | Small vase |
| Feb 26 | 6 | Williamson & Sons | L | Blossom print |
| Feb 27 | 18 | W. B. Simpson & Sons | Ln | Tile design |
| Feb 28 | 3 | T. Till & Sons | B | Tureen |
| Mar 2 | 12 | G. Richardson & Son★ | Ln | Figure plaque |
| Mar 8 | 5 | M. Massey | H | Jug |
| Mar 8 | 20 | Edward F. Bodley & Son | Lpt | Jug |
| Mar 8 | 20 | Edward F. Bodley & Son | Lpt | Teaset on tray |
| Mar 14 | 3 | Derby Porcelain Co Ltd | D | Printed design |
| Mar 15 | 3 | T. Furnival & Sons | C | Printed design |
| Mar 16 | 6 | J. Broadhurst | F | Printed design |
| Mar 17 | 7 | Carron Company | Sc | Tile designs |
| Mar 17 | 8 | Mintons | S | "Wynn" tray |
| Mar 20 | 3 | Elizabeth Wood★ | H | Jug |
| Mar 20 | 4 | J. Wedgwood & Sons | E | Jug |
| Mar 24 | 3 | Sampson Bridgwood & Sons | L | Teapot |
| Mar 30 | 1 | Mintons | S | Tile design |
| Mar 30 | 9 | Minton, Hollins & Co | S | Tile design |
| April 2 | 3 | T. & E. L. Poulson | Y | "Raikes" print |
| April 3 | 3 | Emelius Warburton★ | L | Jug |
| April 6 | 14 | G. & J. Hobson | B | Baking dish |
| April 10 | 1 | Banks & Thorley | H | Jug |
| April 18 | 13 | W.B. Simpson & Sons | Ln | Tile designs |
| April 19 | 3 | R.H. Plant & Co | L | Floral print |
| April 21 | 1 | James F. Wileman & Co | F | Printed design |
| April 23 | 8 | W. B. Simpson & Sons | Ln | Tile design |
| April 24 | 7 | G. L. Ashworth & Bros | H | Tureen |
| April 25 | 14 | Pratt & Simpson | F | Tureen |
| April 27 | 17 | C. Littler & Co | H | Dinnerwares |

| April 27 | 18 | J.H. Davis | H | Tureen |
|---|---|---|---|---|
| April 27 | 19 | Powell, Bishop & Stonier | H | Floral print |
| April 2 | 4 | Brown-Westhead, Moore & Co | Sh | Jug forms |
| May 5 | 4 | Whittaker, Edge & Co | H | Tureen |
| May 7 | 8 | S. Fielding & Co | S | Jug – "Avon" |
| May 8 | 6 | T. G. & F. Booth | T | Tureen |
| May 8 | 6 | T. G. & F. Booth | T | Printed design |
| May 11 | 5 | R. H. Plant & Co | L | Fruit print |
| May 16 | 12 | T. A. Simpson | S | Tile design |
| May 16 | 13 | Ambrose Wood★ | H | Printed designs |
| May 22 | 11 | Powell, Bishop & Stonier | H | Teapot |
| May 23 | 7 | T. G. & F. Booth | T | Centrepiece |
| May 23 | 7 | T. G. & F. Booth | T | Covered box |
| May 23 | 8 | Elizabeth Wood★ | H | Jug |
| May 24 | 3 | Brownhills Pottery & Co | T | Printed design |
| May 25 | 4 | W. A. Adderley | L | Tureen |
| May 28 | 2 | O. G. Blunden | Sussex | Cooking vessels |
| May 29 | 14 | W. B. Simpson & Sons | Ln | Tile designs |
| May 31 | 7 | Wardle & Co | H | Jug |
| Jun 2 | 9 | Minton, Hollins & Co | S | Tile designs |
| Jun 4 | 8 | Clementson Brothers | H | Tureen |
| Jun 4 | 8 | Clementson Brothers | H | Printed designs |
| Jun 8 | 2 | H. Alcock & Co | C | Tureen |
| Jun 9 | 2 | Sampson Bridgwood & Son | L | Tureen |
| Jun 9 | 6 | Mintons | S | Floral print |
| Jun 11 | 2 | Grove & Stark | L | Tureen |
| Jun 11 | 8 | J. Mathews | WsM | Flower pot |
| Jun 11 | 9 | J. Mathews | WsM | Slug trap |
| Jun 13 | 3 | Belfield & Co | Sc | Teapot |
| Jun 13 | 7 | Pratt & Simpson | F | Printed design |
| Jun 14 | 2 | Grove & Stark | L | Printed designs |
| Jun 18 | 11 | J. Tams | L | Jug |
| Jun 18 | 12 | W. Brownfield & Sons | C | Tureens |
| Jun 18 | 12 | W. Brownfield & Sons | C | Jugs |
| Jun 18 | 12 | W. Brownfield & Sons | C | Cruet |
| Jun 20 | 3 | T. & R. Boote | B | Teapot |
| Jun 20 | 4 | Mintons | S | Printed design |
| Jun 20 | 16 | W. & E. Corn | B | Tureen |
| Jun 21 | 22 | Wardle & Co | H | Jug |
| Jun 23 | 4 | J. Wedgwood & Sons | E | Flower pot |
| Jun 25 | 5 | Ford & Riley | B | "Florence" print |
| Jun 25 | 10 | W. Brownfield & Sons | C | Figure candlesticks |
| July 2 | 4 | Edge, Malkin & Co | B | Tureen |
| July 2 | 4 | Edge, Malkin & Co | B | Printed design |
| July 3 | 3 | J. Aynsley & Sons | L | Teawares |
| July 3 | 4 | Moore Brothers | L | Leaf dishes, plates |
| July 4 | 4 | Wittmann & Roth★ | Ln | Lamp bases |
| July 4 | 7 | W. Brownfield & Sons | C | Ice tray |
| July 5 | 6 | Grove & Stark | L | Tureen |
| July 5 | 19 | T. Furnival & Sons | C | Jug |
| July 5 | 21 | Owen, Raby & Co | Lpt | Tureen |
| July 6 | 2 | Blackhurst & Bourne | B | Printed design |

| July 10 | 9 | Ambrose Wood★ | H | Tile design |
|---|---|---|---|---|
| July 10 | 10 | J. Macintyre & Co | B | Inkwells |
| July 11 | 1 | J. Wedgwood & Sons | E | Lobster salad bowl |
| July 19 | 4 | Davenports Ltd | Lpt | Jug |
| July 19 | 21 | G. Jones & Sons | S | Jug |
| July 19 | 21 | G. Jones & Sons | S | Printed design |
| July 20 | 11 | Hollinshead & Kirkham | T | Tureen |
| July 21 | 3 | Bridgett & Bates | L | Floral design |
| July 23 | 3 | J. Wedgwood & Sons | E | Printed design |
| July 26 | 1 | W. A. Adderley | L | Jug |
| July 27 | 4 | Brown-Westhead, Moore & Co | Sh | Printed design |
| July 27 | 13 | W. Bennett | H | Printed design – birds |
| July 30 | 10 | W. Brownfield & Sons | C | Lamp base |
| July 31 | 3 | T. & R. Boote | B | Tile design |
| Aug 1 | 3 | Wagstaff & Brunt | L | Printed design |
| Aug 1 | 4 | G. Jones & Sons | S | Coffee pot |
| Aug 1 | 4 | G. Jones & Sons | S | Jug |
| Aug 1 | 9 | Brown-Westhead, Moore & Co | Sh | Printed design |
| Aug 2 | 3 | Davenports Ltd | Lpt | Toiletwares |
| Aug 3 | 17 | Edward F. Bodley | B | Jug |
| Aug 8 | 9 | J. & E. Ridgway | H | "Variety" print |
| Aug 9 | 15 | Haviland & Co | Fr | Tureen forms |
| Aug 17 | 5 | Edwin J. D. Bodley | B | Jug |
| Aug 20 | 8 | Worcester Royal Porcelain Co Ltd | W | Double dish |
| Aug 22 | 1 | Brownhills Pottery Co | T | "Kioto" print |
| Aug 22 | 1 | Brownhills Pottery Co | T | Tureen |
| Aug 23 | 2 | Grove & Cope | H | Garden seat |
| Aug 23 | 2 | Grove & Cope | H | Basket |
| Aug 24 | 12 | Mountford & Thomas | H | Jug |
| Aug 25 | 11 | W. Brownfield & Sons | C | Jug |
| Aug 29 | 3 | J. Aynsley & Sons | L | Cup form |
| Aug 31 | 6 | W. & E. Corn | B | Tureen |
| Aug 31 | 7 | J. F. Wileman & Co | F | Printed design |
| Sept 1 | 10 | S. Fielding & Co | S | Thistle print |
| Sept 5 | 3 | W. Brownfield & Sons | C | Toast racks |
| Sept 7 | 4 | Derby Crown Porcelain Co Ltd | D | "Arab Star" print |
| Sept 7 | 16 | Haines, Batchelor & Co★ | Ln | Burmese print |
| Sept 7 | 19 | Powell, Bishop & Stonier | H | Tureen |
| Sept 11 | 4 | J. Wedgwood & Sons | E | Jug |
| Sept 13 | 17 | H. Aynsley & Co | L | Printed designs |
| Sept 14 | 1 | W. & T. Adams | T | Printed design |
| Sept 14 | 2 | Mintons | S | Tile designs |
| Sept 17 | 14 | Derby Crown Porcelain Co Ltd | D | Floral print |
| Sept 20 | 12 | Hall & Read | H | Toiletwares |
| Sept 20 | 12 | Hall & Read | H | Printed designs |
| Sept 20 | 13 | Derby Crown Porcelain Co Ltd | D | "Pembroke" print |
| Sept 21 | 4 | Brown-Westhead, Moore & Co | S | "Florette" print |
| Sept 24 | 9 | Jones & Hopkinson | H | Jug |
| Sept 25 | 4 | Grove & Stark | L | "Rosebud" print |
| Sept 25 | 5 | Sampson Bridgwood & Son | L | Comport |
| Sept 25 | 5 | Sampson Bridgwood & Son | L | Covered box |
| Sept 27 | 21 | Meigh & Forester | L | Printed design, fish |

| Sept 28 | 4 | Blair & Co | L | Printed design |
|---------|-----|------------|---|----------------|
| Sept 28 | 5 | Edwin J. D. Bodley | B | Printed design |
| Sept 29 | 4 | Sampson Bridgwood & Son | L | Footed bowl |
| Oct 2 | 15 | Mellor, Taylor & Co | B | Tureen |
| Oct 2 | 22 | Meigh & Forester | L | Printed design |
| Oct 2 | 22 | Meigh & Forester | L | Shell cruet |
| Oct 4 | 4 | Sampson Bridgwood & Sons | L | Teapot |
| Oct 4 | 5 | Whittaker, Edge & Co | H | Printed design |
| Oct 4 | 24 | Worcester Royal Porcelain Co Ltd | W | Fish dish-plate |
| Oct 6 | 2 | W. H. Grindley & Co | T | Printed design |
| Oct 8 | 1 | Hollinson & Goodall | L | Jug |
| Oct 8 | 2 | T. G. & F. Booth | T | Tile designs |
| Oct 8 | 3 | Hall & Read | H | Printed designs |
| Oct 9 | 9 | A. Bevington & Co | H | Cruet |
| Oct 9 | 9 | A. Bevington & Co | H | Covered dish |
| Oct 9 | 9 | A. Bevington & Co | H | Egg cup stand |
| Oct 11 | 2 | Wittmann & Roth★ | Ln | Bird ornament |
| Oct 12 | 13 | Bridgett & Bates | L | Floral print |
| Oct 13 | 3 | Wood & Son | B | Tureen |
| Oct 13 | 11 | W. Brownfield & Sons | C | Teapot |
| Oct 13 | 11 | W. Brownfield & Sons | C | Jug |
| Oct 17 | 5 | New Wharf Pottery Co | B | Tureen |
| Oct 17 | 6 | Hall & Read | H | Floral print |
| Oct 17 | 6 | Hall & Read | H | Tureen |
| Oct 20 | 3 | W. A. Adderley | L | Stratford prints |
| Oct 20 | 4 | W. Brownfield & Sons | C | Oyster trays |
| Oct 20 | 4 | W. Brownfield & Sons | C | Candlelabra |
| Oct 23 | 8 | J. Dimmock & Co | H | Jug |
| Oct 24 | 11 | Minton, Hollins & Co | S | Tile designs |
| Oct 25 | 17 | Taylor, Tunnicliffe & Co | H | Menu card |
| Oct 25 | 17 | Taylor, Tunnicliffe & Co | H | Ash tray |
| Oct 26 | 7 | Jones & Hopkinson | H | Jug |
| Oct 27 | 1 | Brownhills Pottery Co | T | Printed design |
| Oct 30 | 2 | J. Marshall & Co | Sc | Jug – dog pattern |
| Oct 30 | 3 | New Wharf Pottery Co | B | Printed design |
| Oct 30 | 7 | Joseph Robinson | B | Printed design |
| Nov 1 | 1 | A. Bevington & Co | H | Jug |
| Nov 1 | 25 | Wood, Hines & Winkle | H | Jug |
| Nov 1 | 26 | S. Fielding & Co | S | Jug – thistle |
| Nov 1 | 27 | Davenports Ltd | Lpt | Jug |
| Nov 2 | 19 | Worcester Royal Porcelain Co Ltd | W | Vase forms |
| Nov 5 | 13 | Henry Alcock & Co | C | Printed design |
| Nov 6 | 3 | E. & C. Challinor | F | Tureen |
| Nov 7 | 2 | W. & E. Corn | B | Tureen |
| Nov 10 | 9 | Taylor, Tunnicliffe & Co | H | Lamp base – swan |
| Nov 10 | 10 | W. Brownfield & Sons | C | Plate form |
| Nov 13 | 10 | T. G. & F. Booth | T | "Sandringham" print |
| Nov 14 | 3 | Stonier, Hollinshead & Oliver | H | Tureen |
| Nov 15 | 17 | T. Furnival & Sons | C | Bowl form |
| Nov 17 | 2 | Derby Crown Porcelain Co Ltd | D | "Chandos" print |
| Nov 21 | 3 | F. J. Emery | B | Teapot |
| Nov 22 | 3 | S. Fielding & Co | S | "Lattice" print |

| Nov 23 | 7 | Minton, Hollins & Co | S | Tile design |
|---|---|---|---|---|
| Nov 24 | 3 | Powell, Bishop & Stonier | H | Floral print |
| Nov 26 | 2 | W. A. Adderley | L | Jug |
| Nov 26 | 3 | Sampson Bridgwood & Son | L | Pierced dish |
| Nov 28 | 12 | Worcester Royal Porcelain Co Ltd | W | Pair candlelabra |
| Nov 28 | 12 | Worcester Royal Porcelain Co Ltd | W | Four basket figures |
| Dec 1 | 3 | Worcester Royal Porcelain Co Ltd | W | Printed border |
| Dec 3 | 10 | James Wilson | L | Printed, rope, design |
| Dec 5 | 2 | Malkin, Edge & Co | B | Tile design |
| Dec 5 | 3 | Derby Crown Porcelain Co Ltd | D | Gladstone design |
| Dec 8 | 8 | James F. Wileman & Co | F | Cup form |
| Dec 14 | 4 | Brownhills Pottery Co | T | Nations print |
| Dec 15 | 13 | T. G. & F. Booth | T | Antique teapot form |
| Dec 15 | 14 | Hollinson & Goodall | L | Jug |
| Dec 29 | 4 | Powell, Bishop & Stonier | H | Oval tureen |

The 1842–83 registration system ended at this point. There had been well over 5,000 basic shapes or designs registered. Any one of these could be produced in different sizes, adorned with different patterns or appear on various objects. Of these registrations some 85 per cent related to Staffordshire firms, a fact that underlines the importance of the Staffordshire Potteries as the centre of the world ceramic industry.

## REGISTRATION NUMBERS 1884–1999

In January 1884 a new system of simple numbering of designs, patents and trade marks commenced, giving a five-year coverage. The first ceramic design was number 130, a printed design issued by J. Dimmock & Co., of Hanley. This numbering system continued in sequence until 1990 when it was rebased to 2,000,000. These post-1883 registered numbers are found prefixed $R^d$ $N^o$ (or similar abbreviations). They should not be confused with earlier entry numbers, or with patent numbers or with numbered trade marks. (A design registration is quite different from a patented novel process or object. Objects bearing patent references, whilst normally indicating the earliest possible date of introduction, do not link with registered design records. British patents can be researched at the Patent Office.) Whilst one cannot list all these entries – there were 19,753 in 1884 alone – I do publish the approximate number reached by January of each year. This enables one to at least discover the year of registration and therefore the earliest possible date of manufacture. It should be noted, however, that some manufacturers extended their official coverage by registering one object, say a relief-moulded jug, but then used that design or elements of it on other articles, using the original registration mark!

This table shows the approximate number reached by January of each year.

| | | | | | |
|---|---|---|---|---|---|
| 1 | = | 1884 | 224720 | = | 1894 |
| 19754 | = | 1885 | 246975 | = | 1895 |
| 40480 | = | 1886 | 268392 | = | 1896 |
| 64520 | = | 1887 | 291241 | = | 1897 |
| 90483 | = | 1888 | 311658 | = | 1898 |
| 116648 | = | 1889 | 331707 | = | 1899 |
| 141273 | = | 1890 | 351202 | = | 1900 |
| 163767 | = | 1891 | 368154 | = | 1901 |
| 185713 | = | 1892 | 385180 | = | 1902 |
| 205240 | = | 1893 | 403200 | = | 1903 |

| | | | | | |
|---|---|---|---|---|---|
| 424400 | = | 1904 | 876067 | = | 1955 |
| 447800 | = | 1905 | 879282 | = | 1956 |
| 471860 | = | 1906 | 882949 | = | 1957 |
| 493900 | = | 1907 | 887079 | = | 1958 |
| 518640 | = | 1908 | 891665 | = | 1959 |
| 535170 | = | 1909 | 895000 | = | 1960 |
| 552000 | = | 1910 | 899914 | = | 1961 |
| 574817 | = | 1911 | 904638 | = | 1962 |
| 594195 | = | 1912 | 909364 | = | 1963 |
| 612431 | = | 1913 | 914536 | = | 1964 |
| 630190 | = | 1914 | 919607 | = | 1965 |
| 644935 | = | 1915 | 924510 | = | 1966 |
| 653521 | = | 1916 | 929335 | = | 1967 |
| 658988 | = | 1917 | 934515 | = | 1968 |
| 662872 | = | 1918 | 939875 | = | 1969 |
| 666128 | = | 1919 | 944932 | = | 1970 |
| 673750 | = | 1920 | 950046 | = | 1971 |
| 680147 | = | 1921 | 955342 | = | 1972 |
| 687144 | = | 1922 | 960708 | = | 1973 |
| 694999 | = | 1923 | 965185 | = | 1974 |
| 702671 | = | 1924 | 969249 | = | 1975 |
| 710165 | = | 1925 | 973838 | = | 1976 |
| 718057 | = | 1926 | 978426 | = | 1977 |
| 726330 | = | 1927 | 982815 | = | 1978 |
| 734370 | = | 1928 | 987910 | = | 1979 |
| 742725 | = | 1929 | 993012 | = | 1980 |
| 751160 | = | 1930 | 998302 | = | 1981 |
| 760583 | = | 1931 | 1004456 | = | 1982 |
| 769670 | = | 1932 | 1010583 | = | 1983 |
| 779292 | = | 1933 | 1017131 | = | 1984 |
| 789019 | = | 1934 | 1024174 | = | 1985 |
| 799097 | = | 1935 | 1031358 | = | 1986 |
| 808794 | = | 1936 | 1039055 | = | 1987 |
| 817293 | = | 1937 | 1047479 | = | 1988 |
| 825231 | = | 1938 | 1056078 | = | 1989 |
| 832610 | = | 1939 | 2003720 | = | 1990 |
| 837520 | = | 1940 | 2012047 | = | 1991 |
| 838590 | = | 1941 | 2019933 | = | 1992 |
| 839230 | = | 1942 | 2028115 | = | 1993 |
| 839980 | = | 1943 | 2036116 | = | 1994 |
| 841040 | = | 1944 | 2044227 | = | 1995 |
| 842670 | = | 1945 | 2053121 | = | 1996 |
| 845550 | = | 1946 | 2062149 | = | 1997 |
| 849730 | = | 1947 | 2071420 | = | 1998 |
| 853260 | = | 1948 | 2080158 | = | 1999 |
| 856999 | = | 1949 | | | |
| 860854 | = | 1950 | | | |
| 863970 | = | 1951 | | | |
| 866280 | = | 1952 | | | |
| 869300 | = | 1953 | | | |
| 872531 | = | 1954 | | | |

# Collectors' Clubs, Societies and Groups

It is natural and healthy that groups of collectors and others sharing like hobbies should get together to share interests, carry out research, hold meetings, publish magazines or journals and in general help to further the study and understanding of their chosen field of collecting.

I list here the various clubs and societies that relate to different aspects of British ceramics. I am unable to give the addresses of the various secretaries or other officials as these change and out-of-date information can be embarrassing. However, leading museums may well be able to supply details. Some magazines such as the *Antique Diary* (P.O. Box 30, Twyford, RG10 8DQ) also publish details of such clubs. If you wish to write to any source for information do remember to enclose a stamped and self-addressed envelope. Public libraries should have details of any local collectors' clubs, of which several exist.

National organizations such as NADFAS (National Association of Decorative and Fine Art Societies) hold monthly lecture meetings to broaden your understanding of the arts in general. The specialist speakers may include from time to time ceramic subjects. Details of your nearest local society may be obtained from their head office, 8 Guilford Street, London, WC1N 1DT (S.A.E. please).

The most senior of the societies devoted to the study of British ceramics is the English Ceramic Circle formed in May 1931, from the English Porcelain Circle which was formed in February 1927 by a group of private collectors 'seeking to increase the knowledge of early English porcelain by communications and discussions at meetings'. Various well-researched members' papers have been published in the society's *Transactions* which are available on subscription. The ECC is based in London and its interests tend to be confined to pre-1820 ceramics.

The club with the widest interests and the largest, international, membership is undoubtedly the (mis-named) Northern Ceramic Society. Their lecture meetings are usually held in the northern part of the country but reports, research papers and other information are circulated by regular *Newsletters* and a *Journal*. The NCS also holds educational exhibitions and seminars. Details regarding the Northern Ceramic Society can be obtained from the Ceramics Department at The Potteries Museum, Hanley, Stoke-on-Trent, ST1 3DW. Membership is open (by subscription) to all, not only to northern collectors.

More specialist groups include the following. Each of these may be expected to hold meetings and to publish or at least circulate details of their deliberations and research to their members.

Aynsley Collectors' Society

Belleek Collectors' Group (UK)
Beswick Collectors Club

Carlton Ware Collectors' Club
Clarice Cliff Collectors' Club
Cornish Ware Collectors' Club

Derby Porcelain International Society

Friends of Blue (mainly blue-printed earthenwares)

Goss Collectors' Club

Honiton Pottery Collectors' Society
Hornsea Pottery Collectors' & Research Club

Langley Collectors' Society

Mason Collectors' Club
(The Potteries Museum, Stoke-on-Trent)
Moorcroft Collectors' Club
Moore Brothers Club
Morley College Ceramic Circle (London)

Paragon International Collectors' Club
Pilkington Royal Lancastrian Pottery Society
Pinxton Porcelain Society

Royal Doulton Collectors' Club
(Minton House, London Road, Stoke-on-Trent, ST4 7QD)

Scottish Pottery Society
Shelley Group
SylvaC Collectors' Circle

Tiles & Architectural Ceramics Society
Torquay Pottery Collectors' Society

Wade Collectors' Club
Wedgwood Society
Worcester, Friends of
XYZ Study Group

Some societies and individuals also hold annual Seminars or specialist meetings, with helpful slide-illustrated lectures. These are listed for the late 1990s. Corrections or details of other Seminar-type meetings of interest to collectors of British pottery and porcelain would be welcomed by the author (for address see Godden Seminars, page 249).

Academy of Antiques & Fine Arts
P.O. Box 18, Lydney, GL15 4YJ

Bridgnorth Seminars
M. Berthoud, 64 St Mary's Street, Bridgnorth, WV16 4DR

Godden Seminars
G. Godden, 3 The Square, Findon, W. Sussex, BN14 0TE

International Ceramics Fair & Seminar (London, in June)
B. Haughton, 31 Old Burlington Street, London, W1X 1LB

Keele University August Seminar
Dr C. Wakeling, Keele University, Staffs, ST5 5BG

Mercury Antiques evening meetings
Mrs L. Richards, 1 Ladbroke Road, London, W11 3PA

Morley College Ceramic Circle Seminar (London)
Mrs J. Boff, Clarebrook, Clasemont Road, Claygate, Esher, Surrey, KT10 0PL

Sevenoaks Ceramic Seminar
G. Fisk, Hawthorn Cottage, 43 Garth Road, Sevenoaks, Kent, TN13 1RX

Stow-on-the-Wold Ceramic House Parties
G. Godden, 3 The Square, Findon, W. Sussex, BN14 0TE

# Selected Bibliography

Several specialist reference books have already been mentioned under the relevant factories in the main section of this book. The following general books listed by date of publication give good background and often detailed information on the subjects suggested by their various titles. All these books should be available in a good reference library even if some are not currently in print and available for purchase.

*The Ceramic Art of Great Britain.* L. Jewitt (1878; revised 1883; further revised with additional material and illustrations by G. A. Godden, Barrie & Jenkins, 1972).

*A History and Description of English Porcelain.* W. Burton (Cassell, 1902).

*English Earthenware and Stoneware.* W. Burton (Cassell, 1904).

*Staffordshire Pots and Potters.* G. W. & F. A. Rhead (Hutchinson, 1906).

*The A.B.C. of English Saltglaze Stoneware.* J. F. Blacker (Stanley Paul, 1922).

*Guide to Collectors of Pottery and Porcelain.* F. Litchfield (Truslove & Hanson, 1925).

*Old English Porcelain.* W. B. Honey (Faber & Faber, 1928, new edition, 1977).

*English Pottery and Porcelain.* W. B. Honey (A. & C. Black, 1933, 5th edition, 1962).

*English Pottery Figures 1660–1860.* R. G. Haggar (Phoenix House, 1947).

*English Country Pottery.* R. G. Haggar (Phoenix House, 1950).

*Nineteenth Century English Pottery and Porcelain.* G. Bemrose (Faber & Faber, 1952).

*The Concise Encyclopaedia of English Pottery and Porcelain.* R. G. Haggar and W. Mankowitz (Deutsch, 1957).

*Victorian Porcelain.* G. Godden (H. Jenkins, 1961).

*Victorian Pottery.* H. Wakefield (H. Jenkins, 1962).

*English Blue and White Porcelain of the 18th Century.* B. Watney (Faber & Faber, 1963, revised 1973).

*Encyclopaedia of British Pottery and Porcelain Marks.* G. Godden (Barrie & Jenkins, 1964, revised 1991).

*An Illustrated Encyclopaedia of British Pottery and Porcelain.* G. Godden (Barrie & Jenkins, 1966).

*British Pottery and Porcelain: For Pleasure and Investment.* H. Sandon (J. Gifford, 1969).

*Staffordshire Blue.* W. L. Little (Batsford, 1969).

*Caughley & Worcester Porcelains 1775–1800.* G. A. Godden (Antique Collectors' Club, 1969; new edition, 1981).

*Coalport & Coalbrookdale Porcelains.* G. A. Godden (Antique Collectors' Club, 1970, new edition, 1981).

*Staffordshire Portrait Figures.* P. D. G. Pugh (Antique Collectors' Club, 1971, revised edition, 1987).

*British Porcelain*. G. A. Godden (Barrie & Jenkins, 1974).

*British Pottery*. G. A. Godden (Barrie & Jenkins, 1974).

*Yorkshire Pots and Potteries*. H. Lawrence (David & Charles, 1974).

*Godden's Guide to English Porcelain*. G. A. Godden (Granada, 1978).

*Derby Porcelain*. J. Twitchett (Barrie & Jenkins, 1980).

*18th Century English Porcelain Figures 1745–1795*. P. Bradshaw (Antique Collectors' Club, 1981).

*The Dictionary of Blue and White Printed Pottery 1780–1880*. A. Coysh & R. Henrywood (Antique Collectors' Club, 1982).

*English Brown Stoneware 1670–1900*. A. Oswald, R. Hildyard & R. Hughes (Faber & Faber, 1982).

*Chamberlain-Worcester Porcelain 1788–1852*. G. A. Godden (Barrie & Jenkins, 1982).

*An Anthology of British Cups*. M. Berthoud (Micawber, 1982).

*Staffordshire Porcelain*, edited by G. A. Godden (Granada, 1983).

*Eighteenth-Century English Porcelain*. G. A. Godden (Granada, 1985).

*Art Deco Tableware*. J. Spours (Ward Lock, 1988).

*Encyclopaedia of British Porcelain Manufacturers*. G. A. Godden (Barrie & Jenkins, 1988).

*English Decorative Ceramics Art Nouveau to Art Deco*. J. Barlett (Kevin Francis, 1989).

*Majolica. British, Continental and American Wares 1851–1915*. V. Bergesen (Barrie & Jenkins, 1989).

*Phillips Guide to English Porcelain*. J. Sandon (Merehurst Press, 1989).

*British Studio Ceramics in the 20th Century*. P. Rice & C. Gowing (Barrie & Jenkins, 1989).

*The Concise Guide to British Pottery and Porcelain*. G. A. Godden (Barrie & Jenkins, 1990).

*Encyclopaedia of British Art Pottery, 1870–1920*. V. Bergesen (Barrie & Jenkins, 1991).

*English Earthenware Figures 1740–1840*. P. Halfpenny (Antique Collectors' Club, 1991).

*Collecting Lustreware*. G. Godden & M. Gibson (Barrie & Jenkins, 1991).

*Collector's History of British Porcelain*. J. & M. Cushion (Antique Collectors' Club, 1992).

*Printed English Pottery 1760–1820*. D. Drakard (Jonathan Horne, 1992).

*British Teapots & Tea Drinking 1700–1850*. R. Emmerson (HMSO 1992).

*Antique Porcelain* (Starting to Collect Series). J. Sandon (Antique Collectors' Club, 1997).

*True Blue. Transfer Printed Earthenware*, edited by G. Blake Roberts (Friends of Blue, 1998).

*English Dry-Bodied Stoneware. Wedgwood and Contemporary Manufacturers 1774 to 1830*. D. Edwards & R. Hampson (Antique Collectors' Club, 1998).

*Godden's Guide to Ironstone, Stone and Granite Wares*. G. Godden (Antique Collectors Club, 1999).

# *Index*

It is obviously unnecessary to duplicate here the alphabetical entries in the Mark Section, pp. 40–150, nor the multitude of initials and names found in British ceramic markings in the subsequent two sections, pp. 151–245. The following index is, however, helpful in listing the potters' names, trade-names, types of ware, and other information in this book that is not covered in the main section's headings. For example, the entry 'Denby' refers to a trade-name of J. Bourne & Son on p. 50.

OTHER WORKS BY GEOFFREY A. GODDEN, FRSA
PUBLISHED BY BARRIE & JENKINS

# Encyclopaedia
# British Pottery and
# Porcelain Marks

This authoritative work lists well over four thousand British
ceramic marks. The main section is alphabetical in order of
potters, with address, date of establishment, working period, types
of wares, a brief history, the location of typical specimens and
specialised reference books. Then follow reproductions of the
marks used by each potter, in chronological order, with
their period.

'The most efficient, comprehensive and well-arranged collection
of English ceramic marks yet published.' *Connoisseur*

'Of a scale and comprehensiveness not previously existing ...
admirable in layout, legibility of type-faces and reproduction of
illustrations.' *Antique Collector*

'The result of years of brilliant, joyful and laborious study.'
*Observer*

ISBN 0 257 65782 7

# Encyclopaedia of
# British Porcelain Manufacturers

Gathered together in accessible form in this major reference work is information on all porcelain manufacturers working in the British Isles from the 1740s up to the 1980s, a total of over 2,000. The book corrects many hitherto accepted errors of dating, and documents many firms which have never hitherto been listed in any ceramics book. It is profusely illustrated with photographs and reproductions of marks, and will be indispensable for collectors, dealers, museum curators and all those interested in British ceramics and their identification and dating.

ISBN 0712 62100 8

# The Concise Guide to British
# Pottery and Porcelain

Here are the basic facts about the principal British pottery and porcelain manufacturers, attractively illustrated in colour and black and white, and presented in inexpensive paperback as a companion to the present volume. Entries are arranged alphabetically, and are devoted to the various potteries and the main types of collectable items. Aids to recognition and warnings of pitfalls are also given, and there are useful lists of important dates, notable collections and a bibliography.

ISBN 0712 63600 5